D0849647

Supply Chain Financial Management

Best Practices, Tools, and Applications for Improved Performance

Robert J. Trent

J.ROSS PUBLISHING

Copyright © 2016 by J. Ross Publishing

ISBN-13: 978-1-60427-116-4

Printed and bound in the U.S.A. Printed on acid-free paper.

10 9 8 7 6 5 4 3 2 1

Library of Congress Cataloging-in-Publication Data

Trent, Robert J., author.
  Supply chain financial management : best practices, tools, and applications
for improved performance / by Robert J. Trent.
      pages cm
    Includes index.
    ISBN 978-1-60427-116-4 (hardcover : alk. paper)
  1. Business logistics—Management. 2. Business logistics—Cost effectiveness.
  I. Title.
    HD38.5.T743 2015
    658.7—dc23
                        2015024816

Direct all inquiries to J. Ross Publishing, Inc., 300 S. Pine Island Rd., Suite 305,
Plantation, FL 33324.

Phone: (954) 727-9333
Fax: (561) 892-0700
Web: www.jrosspub.com

DEDICATION

To my wife Jan; my daughter Ellen, her husband Ryan, and their son Colin; and my son Jack, his wife Natalie, and their kids Sophia, Jackson, and Allison. There is nothing better than family!

TABLE OF CONTENTS

PREFACE

Improved communications, increased international trade, accessible transportation, and expanded cross-cultural ties have all made the world a smaller place. Conversely, these same factors have combined to make the world of supply chain management a bigger place.

Most observers would agree that supply chain management (SCM) is still an evolving discipline. If we trace the evolution of SCM, we will find an early emphasis on the downstream portion of the supply chain, usually in a domestic setting. This early emphasis involved primarily a focus on transportation and distribution channels. Suppliers and the upstream part of the supply chain were simply not part of the equation.

As international competition intensified during the 1980s, and as companies began to source and sell all over the world, the domain of SCM expanded. Intense global competition and an end-to-end (supplier to customer) focus forced managers to expand their horizons—figuratively and literally. SCM was no longer about managing only downstream activities.

Intense global competition not only brought about a need to manage the entire supply chain, it also brought about a relentless need to reduce costs. The role of supply chain managers expanded further to include that of a cost manager. Supply chain managers, through no choice of their own, were forced to expand the set of tools and techniques they relied on, to attack costs wherever they resided. This forced supply managers to be analytic and creative.

Increased worldwide sourcing and selling inevitably introduced increased complexity to supply chains. Increased complexity, combined with commodity, financial, climate, and political instability, elevated just about everyone's awareness of risk. Supply chain managers are now assuming another role—they are becoming risk managers. It is safe to say that the worlds of SCM and risk management will increasingly overlap. And, in ten years or so, it is safe to predict that risk management will be a firmly embedded part of SCM, just as cost management is now a firmly embedded part of SCM.

Somewhere along the way something else began to change. It became clear that working with other parties in the supply chain offered new and exciting opportunities to expand the value pie. This awakening highlighted the importance of cooperative and even collaborative supply chain relationships, something that took the typical supply chain professional out of his or her comfort zone. In addition to their roles as cost and risk managers, supply chain managers were now being thrust into the role of relationship managers.

We are entering yet another phase of supply chain evolution. It is now time for supply chain managers to step up and become financial managers. After all, everything that happens within a supply chain ends up on the balance sheet, the income statement, and/or the cash flow statement. Shouldn't we know how we affect those statements? And shouldn't we tap into the tools and techniques that finance professionals spent decades refining? For SCM to continue maturing as a discipline, supply chain professionals must act like financial managers and begin to speak the one true language of business. That language is finance.

This book is what would happen if SCM and finance got together and produced offspring. The result would be a decidedly mixed gene pool of supply chain and financial topics. And, this book is decidedly a mixed pool of best practices, concepts, tools, and approaches from diverse, yet interconnected worlds.

OBJECTIVES OF THE BOOK

The primary objective of this book is to help readers grow as organizational leaders by taking them out of their comfort zone. As the domain of SCM expands, so too must your knowledge and skill set. If you are coming from the supply chain world, this means becoming more adept at using financial techniques and language to support the attainment of your supply chain objectives. If you reside in the finance world, becoming more familiar with supply chain practices will allow you to better understand how a major portion of your business operates.

Herminia Ibarra, an organizational researcher, argues that throughout her research she has observed that career advances almost always require us to move well outside our comfort zone. By viewing ourselves as works in progress and evolving our professional identities, we can develop a personal style that feels right for us and suits our organizational needs. For supply chain professionals, this means changing the way we have traditionally viewed our discipline and how we go about our work.

Moving past our comfort zone is harder than it sounds. Ibarra notes that if we are unsure of ourselves or our ability to measure up in a new setting, we will likely retreat to familiar behaviors and styles and go back to doing what we know. The intent of this book is to give us the confidence to move forward into new areas without retreating back to our comfort zone.

Beyond the broader objective of becoming a better leader by moving out of a well-established comfort zone, more specific objectives underlie this book. These objectives include:

- Appreciate the language of finance, including key terms, concepts, tools, techniques, and applications
- Understand how to use financial tools and techniques to support better supply chain decision making, better cost management, and better risk management to achieve better performance
- Understand how supply chain initiatives affect corporate performance indicators
- Develop professional capabilities through the application of new knowledge
- Impress colleagues with a grasp of not only supply chain best practices, but also financial practices

STRUCTURE OF THE BOOK

Let's consider the title of this book—*Supply Chain Financial Management: Best Practices, Tools, and Applications for Improved Performance*—to better understand how the book is organized. This book has five distinct sections that take us to different parts of the supply chain. Each section includes three chapters that flow within a specific sequence. The first chapter focuses primarily, but not exclusively on the best practices characterizing that subject area. These practices are the result of years of research and experience with hundreds of firms. The second chapter presents relevant financial concepts, tools, techniques, and approaches that support that section's topic. The section on supplier evaluation and selection, for example, features the use of financial data to predict supplier financial distress. The section on worldwide sourcing features total cost models. The third chapter challenges the reader with exercises and cases to apply the concepts and tools presented in that section.

The first chapter of this book sets the stage for combining supply chain and financial management. Specifically, it positions our thinking regarding what the world of finance offers the supply chain professional. The remainder of the book is organized into five sections:

Section I (Chapters 2-4): Evaluating and Selecting Suppliers

The evaluation and selection of suppliers is one of the most important business processes that firms practice today. Select the wrong supplier and be prepared to experience long and painful consequences. Section I presents a set of best practices that characterize firms that are at the top of their supplier selection game. The financially related topics in this section include ratio analysis; using financial data to predict supplier bankruptcy; using qualitative factors to predict supplier distress; and using financial data to estimate supplier capacity.

Section II (Chapters 5-7): Managing and Developing Supplier Capabilities

Selecting a supplier, which represents the end of one process, is also the start of something special. That something is the commencement of the buyer-seller relationship, a relationship that could span many years. This section shifts our thinking from supplier evaluation and selection to supplier management and development. The financially related topics presented here include financial investment techniques applied to supplier management and development projects. These techniques include simple payback; net present value models; and internal rate of return calculations.

Section III (Chapters 8-10): Managing Costs across the Supply Chain

The need to manage costs is relentless and severe—and, this need will not go away in our lifetime. This section presents a fundamental understanding of costs, combined with a comprehensive set of cost management practices. The financially related topics in this section include learning curve models; theoretical best pricing; configured sourcing networks; using external price indexes to manage costs; target pricing; employee and supplier suggestion programs; value analysis workshops; cost-driven pricing contracts; and cooperative cost management.

Section IV (Chapters 11-13): Worldwide Sourcing

For a variety of reasons worldwide sourcing has grown dramatically over the last 25 years. Besides addressing a set of worldwide sourcing best practices, this section discusses what it takes to operate at the highest global levels. The financially related topics in this section include the development of total cost models and the calculation of inventory carrying charges.

Section V (Chapters 14-16): Managing Inventory

The effective management of working capital is on the minds of most executives. This section emphasizes the control and management of inventory, which is a major component of working capital. The financially related topics in this section include calculating the costs associated with extended payment terms; the cost of forgoing a trade discount; calculating work-in-process turns; *what-if* analysis using the Strategic Profit Model; EOQ modeling; reorder point systems; and the cash conversion cycle.

GET READY FOR A NEW YOU

After reading this book you will be stunned, hopefully in a good way, with your new insights, knowledge, and skills. And, you will be anxious, not only to think about these insights, you will be anxious to apply them in ways that will impress executives, colleagues, friends, your spouse and kids, even the family pet. Here is just a sample of where you will bring the *wow* factor:

- **Know more about your supplier than the supplier knows.** Through your financial analytical skills, you will learn more about a supplier than you ever thought possible.
- ***R* you ready to run with the big dogs?** Amaze your colleagues as you model how your supply chain initiatives will affect (and have affected) corporate indicators that begin with the letter *R*. These *return on* indicators are the same ones that excite the CEO and the Board of Directors.
- **Expenses are bad, investments are good!** Get out of the mindset that expenses are a given. Learn to frame certain expenses as investments and watch a magical transformation take place.
- **Let's manage working capital (the right way).** The way that many companies manage working capital will damage supplier relationships for years. You will be more enlightened regarding how to manage working capital—the right way.
- **Sitting around costs money.** Be one of the few people in your company that actually knows what that inventory sitting idly in a corner really costs.

- **Sometimes it's okay to go with a higher price.** Be that special person who can make the financial case that a higher price option might actually be the lower total cost option.

To sum it all up, some things are meant to be together, like peanut butter and jelly, beer and pizza, and SCM and finance. The inevitable merger between SCM and finance has started. Don't be left behind.

ABOUT THE AUTHOR

Robert J. Trent, Ph.D., is the supply chain management program director at Lehigh University. He holds a B.S. degree in materials logistics management from Michigan State University, an M.B.A. degree from Wayne State University, and a Ph.D. in purchasing/operations management from Michigan State University.

Prior to his return to academia, Bob worked for the Chrysler Corporation. His industrial experience includes assignments in production scheduling, packaging engineering with responsibility for new part packaging set-up and the management of nonproductive materials, distribution planning, and operations management. He also worked on numerous special industry projects. Bob stays active with industry through research projects, consulting, and training services. He has consulted with or provided training services to dozens of government agencies and corporations and worked directly with numerous companies on research visits.

Bob has authored or coauthored seven books and close to 50 articles appearing in a variety of business publications. He has also coauthored eight major research studies that were published by *CAPS Research* and has made presentations at dozens of conferences and seminars.

He and his family reside in Lopatcong Township, New Jersey. He can be reached at rjt2@lehigh.edu.

At J. Ross Publishing we are committed to providing today's professional with practical, hands-on tools that enhance the learning experience and give readers an opportunity to apply what they have learned. That is why we offer free ancillary materials available for download on this book and all participating Web Added Value™ publications. These online resources may include interactive versions of material that appears in the book or supplemental templates, worksheets, models, plans, case studies, proposals, spreadsheets and assessment tools, among other things. Whenever you see the WAV™ symbol in any of our publications, it means bonus materials accompany the book and are available from the Web Added Value Download Resource Center at www.jrosspub.com.

Downloads for *Supply Chain Financial Management: Best Practices, Tools, and Applications for Improved Performance* consist of slide presentations on:

- Financial investment evaluation techniques, including projected future cash flows, pay-back period, net present value, and internal rate of return
- Financial statements, financial ratios, financial analysis using performance metrics, and the preeminent bankruptcy prediction tool, known as the Altman Z-Score
- How to create an end-to-end lean supply chain with a thorough treatment of lean management and myths, lean supply, lean transportation, lean operations, and lean distribution, as well as lean measurements and tools
- Total cost of ownership (TCO) and associated topics, including reasons for total cost systems, a continuum of measurement models, three types of total cost models and their applicability, TCO cost elements, and challenges with total cost systems
- Managing costs, including important cost management concepts, a set of cost management best practices, and the illustration of a set of price and cost analytic techniques
- Managing inventory investment effectively, including a set of inventory management best practices, the Three-V Model of inventory management, and ways to better manage the investment of inventory

- Managing supply chain complexity, including a definition of the concept of complexity, types of complexity, a discussion of why complexity is (generally) bad, a review of why supply chains and organizations become complex, and approaches for reducing unwanted complexity
- Supplier development best practices and processes, including a definition of supplier development and an explanation of why it is a competitive necessity, a set of supplier development best practices, the triage approach for segmenting supplier development candidates, and an illustration of the growth of various supplier development activities
- Supplier selection best practices and processes, including a model of the supply management process and how supplier selection fits into that model, a set of supplier selection best practices, a discussion of the steps that make up the supplier selection process, and a detailed explanation of the concept of supply base rationalization and how it supports the supplier selection process
- Quantitative inventory control and management techniques, including the calculation of inventory carrying charges, economic order quantity, cash conversion cycle, return on assets with the DuPont Model, the cost of foregoing a trade discount, and a return on assets excel template

Supplemental resources for training and course instruction are also available

UNDERSTANDING SUPPLY CHAIN FINANCIAL MANAGEMENT

Imagine the following scenario, which is based on a true story. After years of trying to convince your colleagues about the value of supply chain management, the day finally arrives when you are invited to make a presentation to your company's executive committee, including the CEO. And, if all goes well, an invitation to present to the Board of Directors could be on the horizon. This will be your shining moment as you demonstrate, at the highest levels, the accomplishments and importance of supply chain management. Life is going to be good.

While your presentation went well, it was not received with the enthusiasm that you had expected. In fact, despite your best efforts to excite the group about the value of your company's supply chain efforts, you felt your session came across *flat*. How could this group not appreciate the significance of improved inventory turns, reduced purchase costs, new longer-term supply contracts, improved forecast accuracy, and a streamlined material releasing system? What is wrong with these people?

Just as men are from Mars and women are from Venus (or so the saying goes), corporate executives and supply chain professionals are also from different planets. The make-up of executive committees and boards of directors includes people who are largely not from the supply chain world. Talking about faster inventory turns probably invokes some mental image of material spinning around in some god-forsaken facility that few in this group have ever visited. To put it bluntly, you entered the lair of a group whose obsession is strategy, corporate-level indicators, and financial results. You, on the other hand, brought to them a world that is more about tactical operations, nonfinancial indicators, and activities instead of accomplishments. Can anyone spell *disconnect*? Would it not have been better to speak their language?

This chapter begins our journey through the world of supply chain financial management. We first define the terms *finance* and *supply chain management*, then present a set of reasons supporting the integration of supply chain management and finance, and identify what finance has to offer supply chain professionals. A discussion of financial statements and financial indicators will help build the knowledge base that underlies this book. The chapter concludes with a case that illustrates the benefits of taking a financial perspective when pursuing supply chain improvements.

WHAT IS FINANCE? WHAT IS SUPPLY CHAIN MANAGEMENT?

Let's define two major concepts that populate this book—*finance* and *supply chain management*. So, what is finance? We can think of finance in terms of a noun and a verb. When we think of finance as a noun, we are referring to a formal entity within the organizational structure—just as marketing, purchasing, and engineering are formal entities. As a functional entity, the finance group or department has the right to perform activities that are central to running any organization. A corporate finance group (a noun) is concerned with activities such as pursuing sound investments, obtaining low-cost credit, allocating funds to pay for liabilities, managing tax obligations, and banking (the verbs).

As a body of knowledge, finance deals with the allocation of assets and liabilities over time—under conditions of certainty and uncertainty. Some refer to finance as the science of money management. Finance also applies various economic theories.[1] One thing that we know for certain is that the body of knowledge that populates finance is well-developed and has evolved over many years.

Supply chain management (SCM) is much less mature, compared with finance. SCM is concerned with the two-way management of some important flows—funds, information, materials, and services. One way to view SCM is in terms of a broad domain with many activities under that domain's *umbrella*. These domain activities include purchasing and materials management; demand and supply planning, including forecasting; transportation; distribution; material handling; receiving; some parts of operations and new product development; and inventory management. Without question SCM is still maturing, particularly in terms of financial management and risk management.

Much of what finance concerns itself with is not directly relevant to what we cover in this book. Conversely, finance has developed a host of tools, techniques, and concepts that supply chain professionals can draw upon to enhance their personal expertise, support more effective decision making, and present results in a way that corporate executives understand. Along the way you might even gain the respect and admiration of some important people in your company, which should bode well for your future advancement.

WHY INTEGRATE SUPPLY CHAIN AND FINANCE?

We are going to start this section by making a bold statement—the language of business is finance. If this is the case, and many would argue this to be true, it makes sense to have a working knowledge of that language. One of the main reasons for integrating SCM and finance is to become comfortable with speaking a language that is spoken at the upper echelons of governments, nonprofit organizations, and corporations.

Think about when news services report business results. We typically do not hear that a company increased its inventory turns last quarter. And, if we do hear that inventory turns increased, it is usually as a footnote or a corollary to explain something that was financially related. What we hear about are changes to gross margins, cash flow, and net income; stock buy-backs or sales; and the return on invested capital or assets. Occasionally we hear about market share, which usually excites the marketing people (except when it drops).

Rarely does the focus of these news reports have anything to do with supply chain indicators, even though, as we will see, the supply chain group affects more financial levers than any other group. The time has come to start thinking like a financial manager, not just a cost, supply, and risk manager. Frankly, executive leaders are not going to learn to speak the language of SCM. As you think about your professional development, learn to speak a foreign language called finance.

Supply chain financial management represents a maturing of the supply chain discipline. Compared with other business disciplines, SCM is relatively young. And, that means it is still evolving. Three areas appear to define the next level of maturation for SCM—the use of big data and data analytics, global risk management, and supply chain financial management. This book is about financial management for the supply chain professional, although finance professionals may appreciate a better understanding of supply chain practices.

Why else should we integrate SCM and finance? Without question, finance is characterized by a sophisticated body of knowledge populated by a diverse set of tools, techniques, and concepts. Some of what resides within that body can be employed directly by supply chain professionals to support better analyses, decision making, and risk management. Throughout this book we are going to borrow selectively from finance (and then use ruthlessly) those tools and techniques.

WHAT FINANCE BRINGS TO THE SUPPLY CHAIN TABLE

Finance is a mature discipline that offers a robust and accepted set of concepts, tools, and techniques. The word *robust* means that financial concepts, tools, and techniques are applicable across a range of settings. While some of the financial topics presented in this book were not intended to be applied to supply chains, later chapters will demonstrate how to use these techniques in ways Mother Nature never intended.

Besides a robust body of knowledge, what else does finance offer? Finance is perhaps the only corporate entity with the validity to bless the cost savings that supply chain professionals claim they are achieving. This has been an ongoing struggle for most supply chain groups. It is not uncommon for a chief procurement officer (CPO) to claim that her procurement group saved $100 gazillion last year. Upon hearing this, the CEO suspiciously asks how that money mysteriously *disappeared*? After all, gazillions of dollars did not make it to the bottom line. The CPO then responds that different operating units siphoned off the money before it reached the bottom line, like a river being diverted before it reaches its final destination. The savings never stood a chance! When this scenario occurs, and it occurs more often than we realize, it becomes evident why the CPO not only appreciates what finance has to offer—but, that the CPO *needs* what finance has to offer.

Finance can also help determine how supply chain initiatives affect corporate performance indicators, although by the end of this book, the reader will also be able to make these determinations. If we better manage inventory and increase inventory turns, how does that affect return on assets (ROA)? If procurement negotiates a major contract that lowers costs of goods sold, how does this affect various financial indicators, including net income? Linking changes (i.e., causes) to specific outcomes (i.e., effects) is something that finance professionals understand well. It is also something we are going to understand.

As we progress through the book, the reader will be exposed to many financial approaches, making reliance on finance personnel less of an issue. Examples include using supplier financial data to predict supplier bankruptcy, using financial investment techniques to evaluate the viability of supply chain projects, gauging the impact of inventory management approaches on working capital, and interpreting the impact of supply chain initiatives on key corporate performance indicators. It is time to transfer some of that finance magic over to the supply chain group.

The bottom line is that the finance community is skillful at managing financial and corporate risk activities. Never doubt that finance people are some of the smarter people in the corporate world (which at times has gotten us into some serious trouble). Unfortunately, finance support is not always available or the finance group may show minimal interest in supporting supply chain activities. The Hackett Group reported that since 2004, the median number of full-time finance department employees has declined by 40% to 71 people for every $1 billion of revenue—down from 119.[2] There are just some things we are going to have to learn to do for ourselves.

As we progress through this book, keep in mind that certain topics will remain the responsibility of finance. In particular, four areas should remain firmly entrenched in the finance camp. This includes currency and commodity hedging, the calculation of reported corporate performance indicators, the calculation of the inventory carrying cost rate, and the calculation of the corporate hurdle rate. Each of these important topics requires finance support and input.

Some Finance Shortfalls

While, over the years, finance has developed a comprehensive set of tools and techniques, without question there are areas where finance does not offer as much to the supply chain professional. In other words, there are shortcomings regarding the availability or applicability of financial tools and techniques.

Supply chain professionals will have to take the lead when developing certain techniques because these techniques have not been the historical focus of finance or accounting groups. In particular, total cost of ownership (TCO) models, except for capital expenditure models, have never been stressed by the financial community, even though these models rely extensively on financial information. Many of the cost categories embedded in total cost systems have no corresponding financial or accounting category that allows easy data retrieval. TCO modeling is an area where finance and accounting professionals could learn a thing or two from supply chain professionals. Chapter 12 covers TCO systems in depth.

Another shortfall involves calculating the true cost of switching from one supplier to another—or what we call supplier switching costs. Supplier switching costs are not something the finance and accounting community usually think about, even though these costs are often significant. Ideally, an account would exist where all related costs associated with supplier switching is easily accessible. With the emergence of information technology (IT) systems that allow users to sift through huge amounts of data, the ability to identify supplier switching costs may become routine. At this time supplier switching costs remain elusive.

Finance and managerial accounting will also not be much help when trying to quantify transaction costs. This is due partly to the fact that transactions occur just about everywhere and across all parts of the supply chain. We see an extensive amount of transactions in the commercial exchanges of goods, services, and funds—transactions involving the exchange of electronic data and information; transactions where material moves internally from one part of a process to another during production; financial transactions of all kinds; and transactions associated with just about any kind of change.

It is not that finance and accounting systems do not address transactions. The problem is they often do not address the kinds of transactions that are of interest to supply chain professionals. Finance and managerial accounting systems came of age well before SCM evolved as a business discipline. As a result, supply chain transactions are often buried in overhead accounts. What is the transaction cost, for example, of issuing purchase orders, paying invoices with electronic funds transfers, changing forecasts or material due dates, or issuing material releases to suppliers? Transaction costs are like the elusive quarks that populate the universe. They are everywhere, yet they are nowhere to be found.

A divergence also exists regarding how the supply chain and finance community view expenses and investments. Let's use supplier development as an example. Finance and accounting systems almost always look at the resources put toward developing a supplier's capabilities as an expense item. Not surprisingly, we know that expenses are not viewed internally as favorably as investments. Most financial managers strive to cut expenses while maximizing the returns from investments. Shifting our perception from an expense to an investment opens up a new world of possibilities. Chapter 6 will show how to use investment techniques to support that shift.

Another area where finance falls short from a supply chain perspective relates to managing working capital. Finance and supply chain professionals view working capital and its management quite differently. And, as we progress through the book, these differences will be meaningful. Technically speaking, finance defines working capital as the difference between current assets and current liabilities, which relies on information taken from the balance sheet. Furthermore, finance professionals stress the management of receivables and payables when managing working capital.

Supply chain managers have (or should have) a different perspective of working capital and its management. Besides defining working capital from an operational perspective, supply chain professionals generally focus on managing the inventory portion of the working capital equation. These differences will become clearer when we reach the chapters on managing inventory as an investment.

The fields of finance and managerial accounting have much to offer supply chain professionals. But, let's not lose sight of the fact that finance and managerial accounting are mature disciplines that have grown up over the last 125 years—well before SCM was even a glimmer in someone's eye. To think that every supply chain requirement will have a corresponding financial technique or approach to support it is naïve. At times, we will have to adapt financial approaches to fit our needs—at other times, we will have to invent our own approaches to fill any voids. It is perfectly acceptable for supply chain managers to be creative regarding how they approach their analytical needs.

UNDERSTANDING FINANCIAL STATEMENTS

Everything we do within a supply chain ends up somewhere on a financial statement. Since that is the case, we have to make sure we have a working knowledge of three important financial documents—the balance sheet, the income statement, and the cash flow statement. So much of what we talk about in this book relates to items that appear on these statements. The purpose of this section is not to make the reader an expert at reading and interpreting all the nuances of financial statements. The intent is to develop a working knowledge of these statements that is just enough to make you dangerous.

Balance Sheet

The balance sheet is a financial statement that summarizes a company's assets, liabilities, and shareholders' equity (also called stockholders' equity or net worth). The balance sheet is also called a *statement of financial position* or a *statement of financial condition*.[3] It represents a company's financial position for a specific date. From a financial perspective, companies have been known to manipulate their asset base, particularly inventories, when the balance sheet *snapshot* is taken. This allows a company to look better on some important financial indicators, particularly ROA.

Table 1.1 presents an actual balance sheet. You might notice that a balance sheet is divided into two major parts: assets and liabilities plus shareholders' equity. This statement is called a balance sheet because the two major parts of the statement balance out, which means they are equal. Why are they equal? A company has to pay for all of its assets either by borrowing money and/or raising money from shareholders. In equation form, a balance sheet is:

Total Assets = Total Liabilities + Shareholders' Equity

Table 1.1   Balance sheet statement—TRW

	Dec 31, Current Year	Dec 31, Previous Year	Dec 31, Two Years Ago
			Figures are in thousands.
Assets			
Current Assets			
Cash and Cash Equivalents	1,729,000	1,223,000	1,241,000
Short-term Investments	—	—	—
Net Receivables	2,702,000	2,365,000	2,415,000
Inventory	1,019,000	975,000	845,000
Other Current Assets	178,000	165,000	126,000
Total Current Assets	5,628,000	4,728,000	4,627,000
Long-term Investments	—	—	—
Property, Plant, and Equipment	2,718,000	2,385,000	2,137,000
Goodwill	1,760,000	1,756,000	1,753,000
Intangible Assets	292,000	293,000	298,000
Accumulated Amortization	—	—	—
Other Assets	1,538,000	1,315,000	1,360,000
Deferred Long-term Asset Charges	316,000	380,000	87,000
Total Assets	12,252,000	10,857,000	10,262,000
Liabilities			
Current Liabilities			
Accounts Payable	2,909,000	2,713,000	2,658,000
Short/Current Long-term Debt	641,000	93,000	104,000
Other Current Liabilities	1,205,000	1,075,000	1,078,000
Total Current Liabilities	4,755,000	3,881,000	3,840,000
Long-term Debt	1,473,000	1,369,000	1,428,000
Other Liabilities	1,483,000	1,715,000	1,682,000
Deferred Long-term Liability Charges	145,000	123,000	173,000
Minority Interest	202,000	191,000	199,000
Negative Goodwill	—	—	—
Total Liabilities	8,058,000	7,279,000	7,322,000
Stockholders' Equity			
Common Stock	1,000	1,000	1,000
Retained Earnings	2,858,000	2,408,000	1,668,000
Treasury Stock	—	—	—
Capital Surplus	1,715,000	1,635,000	1,602,000
Other Stockholder Equity	(380,000)	(466,000)	(331,000)
Total Stockholder Equity	4,194,000	3,578,000	2,940,000
Total Liabilities and Stockholder Equity	12,252,000	1,529,000	889,000

Adapted from public domain information retrieved at finance.yahoo.com.

Total Assets

The asset portion of the balance sheet is divided into two distinct parts—current assets and noncurrent assets. A current asset is one that can or will be converted into cash within a year. The primary categories of current assets include cash and cash equivalents (such as marketable securities), receivables, and inventories. For a manufacturing firm, inventories include a company's raw materials, work-in-process, and finished goods. For a retailer, inventory typically consists of goods purchased for resale from manufacturers or distributors. The issue of treating inventories as current assets from a supply chain perspective is addressed at various points in this book.

Noncurrent assets have three defining features—they cannot be turned readily into cash, they are not expected to be converted into cash within the next year, or they have a lifespan of more than a year. Plant and equipment often represents a large portion of noncurrent assets, particularly for capital intensive companies. Most of the assets in this category are subject to depreciation, which means the asset is subject to lost value due to age, wear and tear, and obsolescence. Depreciation is treated by accountants as a noncash expense. It is the economic cost of an asset over its life. Noncurrent assets also include intangible assets such as goodwill, patents, or copyrights.

Total Liabilities

Liabilities represent financial obligations owed by a company. Similar to assets, liabilities are also presented in terms of current and long-term. Current liabilities are those liabilities that must be paid within a year. This includes primarily accounts payables, short-term notes, and the current portion of any long-term debt. Long-term liabilities include debt and other non-debt financial obligations that are not due within one year from the date of the balance sheet.

Shareholders' Equity

Mathematically, the total value of shareholders' equity is the equivalent of total assets minus total liabilities. Breaking down shareholders' equity further: shareholders' equity comes from two main sources—the first source is the original investment in the company as well as any subsequent investments; the second source includes the retained earnings that a company has accumulated over time through its operations. Oftentimes, the retained earnings portion comprises a major portion of shareholders' equity, particularly for older firms. Technically, retained earnings are the net earnings that are not paid as dividends.[4] Instead, these are earnings retained by the company for reinvestment or to pay debt, hence the designation *retained earnings*. In formula form, a current period's retained earnings equals ([Beginning Retained Earnings + Net Income] – Dividends).

What parts of the balance sheet are of interest to supply chain professionals? Supply chain professionals affect, more than any other group, the inventory portion of current assets. Supply professionals also affect the value of longer-term assets through the negotiated contracts for capital expenditures. The supply group also plays an important role with outsourcing, which is essentially a transfer of a company's asset requirements (and associated liabilities) to a third party. This affects the longer-term assets portion of the balance sheet.

Income Statement

Unlike the balance sheet, an income statement measures a company's financial performance over a specific time period, such as a quarter or year. At its most basic level, the income statement considers a company's revenues (often called sales or net sales) and subtracts expenses to arrive at a net income (or loss) figure. The top line of the statement represents revenue, while everything following that line is presented in a logical sequence of expenses. Table 1.2 presents a sample income statement.

Two basic formats characterize an income statement.[5] The *single-step* format includes only two measures of profitability: pretax income and net income. A multi-step format includes four measures of profitability: gross income or profit, operating income, pretax income, and net income. For our purposes we favor the multi-step format. The following describes the four profitability measures included in the multi-step format.

Gross income (also called gross profit) equals revenues minus cost of goods sold. As a side note, gross income/revenue equals the often reported gross margin percentage. This is an especially important part of the income statement for supply chain managers. In manufacturing, cost of goods sold is equal to the combined total of direct material, direct labor, and factory overhead costs that are incurred when producing a product. While it sometimes appears separately, depreciation expense is also part of cost of goods sold.

We know that materials comprise a large portion of the costs of goods sold at most manufacturers, particularly as firms rely on greater amounts of value-add from suppliers through outsourcing contracts. In retail the cost of goods sold represents the cost of merchandise. For service providers, cost of goods sold equals the cost of providing the service. And, when the figure is called *cost of revenue*, it also includes the cost of delivering a product or service.

Operating income represents a firm's income from its operations. It is also called *earnings before interest and taxes* (EBIT). This is an important figure when calculating certain financial ratios and the Z-Score bankruptcy predictor, something that Chapter 3 addresses. Operating income equals gross profit less selling, general, and administrative expenses (SG&A). Moving down to the next level,

Table 1.2 Income statement—Apple

			Figures are in thousands.
Period Ending	Sep 27, Current Year	Sep 28, Previous Year	Sep 29, Two Years Ago
Total Revenue	**182,795,000**	**170,910,000**	**156,508,000**
Cost of Revenue	112,258,000	106,606,000	87,846,000
Gross Profit	**70,537,000**	**64,304,000**	**68,662,000**
Operating Expenses			
Research Development	6,041,000	4,475,000	3,381,000
Selling, General, and Administrative Expenses	11,993,000	10,830,000	10,040,000
Operating Income or Loss	**52,503,000**	**48,999,000**	**55,241,000**
Income from Continuing Operations			
Total Other Income/Expenses Net	980,000	1,156,000	522,000
Earnings before Interest and Taxes	53,483,000	50,155,000	55,763,000
Interest Expense	—	—	—
Income before Tax	53,483,000	50,155,000	55,763,000
Income Tax Expense	13,973,000	13,118,000	14,030,000
Net Income from Continuing Ops	39,510,000	37,037,000	41,733,000
Net Income	**39,510,000**	**37,037,000**	**41,733,000**

Adapted from public domain information retrieved at finance.yahoo.com.

pretax income adds in any interest income earned by a company and then subtracts out interest expenses. As a formula, pretax income = (operating income + interest revenue) – interest expense. Finally, net income is what we call *the bottom line* on the income statement. It represents all sources of revenue minus all expenses. As we move down the income statement, it equals pretax income minus any taxes paid during the income statement period.

Cash Flow Statement

A cash flow statement identifies the cash that flows in and out of a company for a particular period. It identifies where a company makes its money and where it spends its money. Cash flow statements consider the amount, timing, and predictability of cash inflows and outflows. These statements are especially useful for budgeting and business planning.[6] If the cash flow statement were a movie, it would be known by the famous line, "Show me the money!"

Interestingly, many finance professionals believe the cash flow statement is more useful than the income statement as an indicator of a company's true financial well-being. The reason for this is most companies use what is called an accrual method of accounting. With this method a quarterly income statement, for example, may not reflect actual changes in a company's cash position. A company may book revenue from a new customer contract even though the total revenue from that contract is not realized until a later date. Boeing, for example, books as revenue the sale of an aircraft at the time of the order even though it will be a considerable period before payment is received from an airline or leasing company.

Table 1.3 presents a sample cash flow statement. As the statement shows, the accounting data are organized into three main areas—operating activities, investing activities, and financing activities. The bottom of the statement includes any miscellaneous adjustments that do not fall cleanly into one of the main sections. In this case, there is an adjustment due to exchange rate changes. Nonparenthetical items represent net cash inflows while items with a parenthesis represent net cash outflows.

In this example Xerox realized an improvement of $518 million in available cash from the previous year. This compares with a cash flow decrease of $309 million two years earlier. How was the $518 million figure computed?

	Total cash flow from operating activities:	$2,375
+	Total cash flow from investing activities:	($452)
+	Total cash flow from financing activities:	($1,402)
+	Exchange rate changes	($3)
=	**Change in cash and cash equivalent**	**$518**

UNDERSTANDING CORPORATE PERFORMANCE INDICATORS

A desired goal of supply chain professionals should be to routinely articulate the affect that supply chain initiatives have on corporate level indicators. Rest assured that a performance indicator that starts with the word *return* is almost always a key corporate indicator. We will examine three such indicators—ROA, return on investment (ROI), and return on invested capital (ROIC).

Return on Assets

ROA, which is a ratio we usually present as a percentage, shows earnings that are generated from invested capital (assets). ROA provides an idea of how efficient assets are utilized to generate earnings. In a later chapter we will calculate ROA in the context of something called the DuPont model.

The basic formula for ROA is net income/total assets. If, for example, a company earns $1 million and has assets of $10 million, its ROA is 10%. The ROA

Table 1.3 Cash flow statement—Xerox

Period Ending	Dec 31, Current Year	Dec 31, Previous Year	Dec 31, Two Years Ago
		Figures are in thousands.	
Operating Activities, Cash Flows Provided by or Used in			
Net Income	1,159,000	1,195,000	1,295,000
Depreciation	1,358,000	1,301,000	1,251,000
Adjustments to Net Income	(17,000)	(64,000)	(188,000)
Changes in Accounts Receivables	573,000	641,000	174,000
Changes in Liabilities	(76,000)	91,000	149,000
Changes in Inventories	(38,000)	—	(124,000)
Changes in Other Operating Activities	(604,000)	(612,000)	(629,000)
Total Cash Flow from Operating Activities	**2,375,000**	**2,580,000**	**1,961,000**
Investing Activities, Cash Flows Provided by or Used in			
Capital Expenditures	(346,000)	(388,000)	(338,000)
Investments	—	—	—
Other Cash Flows from Investing Activities	(106,000)	(373,000)	(337,000)
Total Cash Flows from Investing Activities	**(452,000)**	**(761,000)**	**(675,000)**
Financing Activities, Cash Flows Provided by or Used in			
Dividends Paid	(352,000)	(324,000)	(287,000)
Sale Purchase of Stock	(629,000)	(1,050,000)	(684,000)
Net Borrowings	(434,000)	(108,000)	49,000
Other Cash Flows from Financing Activities	(3,000)	—	(670,000)
Total Cash Flows from Financing Activities	**(1,402,000)**	**(1,472,000)**	**(1,586,000)**
Effect of Exchange Rate Changes	(3,000)	(3,000)	(9,000)
Change in Cash and Cash Equivalents	**518,000**	**344,000**	**(309,000)**

Adapted from public domain information retrieved at finance.yahoo.com.

formula appears in a variety of formats, which is true for a number of financial indicators. Some companies may use average assets over a time period for the denominator while others use the asset figure derived from the balance sheet. Others rely on a return on net asset (RONA) formulation, which uses fixed assets plus net working capital rather than total assets in the denominator. Still others replace net income in the numerator with EBIT. Regardless of the specific formula used, ROA is a high-level indicator that considers income over assets.

Supply chain professionals affect ROA most directly through their inventory management activities. Recall from Table 1.1, that inventory is treated as an asset (i.e., the denominator of the ROA formula) on the balance sheet. Effective inventory management by supply chain professionals also affects the numerator of the ROA equation. More effective inventory management will lead to lower inventory carrying costs. And, when the net result of better inventory management is cost reductions, then income should increase. Chapter 15 will show how to model the impact of inventory changes on the ROA formula.

Return on Investment

ROI attempts to measure the profitability of an investment and, as such, there is no one *right* calculation.[7] ROI is often used to calculate the return from specific investments, and the term investment might be used loosely. A marketing executive might be interested in the financial return from a marketing campaign (i.e., the investment) while an investor wants to know the return from a particular stock. When it is used in these contexts, the ROI is a relatively straightforward calculation: ROI = (gain from investment − cost of investment)/(cost of investment).

Many sources interchange the definition of ROI and the basic definition just provided for ROA, particularly when looking at returns at the corporate level. This can be confusing. Keep in mind that the calculation for ROI and its definition can be modified to suit a particular situation. This flexibility has a downside since ROI calculations can be easily manipulated to suit a particular purpose.[8]

Even though ROI is widely used, and most people would say ROI as their first choice if asked to name a measure that starts with the word *return*, we will not use this indicator directly in our analysis. When examining returns at the corporate level, we will use ROA (which, as mentioned, also can refer to ROI when looking at the company as a whole). When considering a particular investment, we will use simple payback, net present value, or internal rate of return (IRR).

Why won't we use ROI when considering the merits of a particular investment? One problem with ROI is it is historical—it looks back at what happened. When considering the return potential of capital projects, we often need to look forward at what we expect will happen. Chapter 6 will review a set of forward-looking techniques in detail. You will not want to skip that chapter.

Return on Invested Capital

ROIC is one of the most important financial indicators in use today. ROIC is also referred to as *return on capital* or *return on total capital*. It is a calculation that assesses a company's efficiency (i.e., its return percentage) at allocating the capital under its control to profitable investments. The ROIC measure gives a sense of how well a company is using its money to generate returns.[9] Like ROA, a search of respected financial sources reveals different perspectives regarding how to calculate ROIC. Several examples of ROIC formulas include:[10]

ROIC = (net income – dividends)/(debt + equity), or

ROIC = (net income – dividends)/total capital, or

ROIC = (net income after taxes)/(total assets – excess cash – non-interest-bearing liabilities)

We will not employ ROIC directly in any of our financial calculations or *what if* scenario exercises in this book. This does not mean that ROIC is not worth understanding or that we should not appreciate how supply chain activities affect the ROIC calculation. In fact, the opposite is true. ROIC is considered by many to be the granddaddy of corporate financial performance. Understanding how the return rate is derived, and appreciating how to affect the components of ROIC is important. Rest assured, if you can articulate how SCM affects these corporate indicators, you might just be ready to run with the big dogs.

Several other important corporate indicators not addressed here include return on capital employed (ROCE) and return on equity (ROE). Both are indirectly related to what we are trying to do (i.e., show a direct link between supply chain performance and the indicator).

TAKING A FINANCIAL VIEW OF THE SUPPLY CHAIN AT STEEL CORP

A number of years ago, executive managers at Steel Corp directed its operating units to concentrate on RONA as their key financial performance indicator. As a corporation, all units were expected to achieve at least a 20% RONA. The challenge was issued—the game was on.

This directive also applied to the subsidiaries of Steel Corp, which includes six railroads, a trucking company, and an intermodal carrier. Each subsidiary operates as a separate business entity, and the parent company measures the financial performance of each unit. This case focuses on actions taken by the six railroads to achieve the mandated RONA target. It shows the benefits of applying a financial perspective when pursuing functional improvements. It also demonstrates the value of rallying around a superordinate measure, which is defined as a measure of a higher (i.e., corporate) condition. Perhaps the most important characteristic of a superordinate measure is that no single group can achieve the measure on its own. The most relevant financial metrics tend to also be superordinate measures.

The Background

The emphasis on net asset return began when executive management challenged the company's operating units to develop ways to meet or exceed the established RONA target. The corporate decision to improve RONA forced different groups to search for ways to increase earnings while simultaneously reducing assets and other current liabilities. The centralized purchasing group that represented the railroads made a decision to focus extensively on the denominator of the RONA equation. This group concluded it had to develop creative ways to manage purchased inventory. Locomotives, railroad cars, and the material required to maintain railroad tracks comprise the main components of inventory.

Other functional groups were each responsible for specific parts of the RONA equation. Managers from the various departments met monthly to discuss progress against their financial return targets. Managers took this process seriously because the parent corporation frequently evaluated whether it should even own railroads. Each group developed, in coordination with other groups, ways to improve the RONA metric.

Systems Contracting with Consignment Inventory

The purchasing group's approach to increasing RONA involved the development of systems contracts featuring consignment inventory. Inventory consignment involves deferring payment for an item until a user physically takes an item from a railroad yard or warehouse and receives or *posts* the material into the railroad's inventory. The primary purpose of consignment inventory was to reduce the average amount of inventory that each railroad maintained financially.

The purchasing group initially developed 30 or so corporate-wide systems contracts with six suppliers. Each contract covers approximately 25 items, with renewal or renegotiation occurring every three years. The contracts are subject to review earlier than three years if suppliers fail to meet performance expectations. While contract items primarily involve higher value items, the railroads also apply systems contracting to lower unit value items (less than $500) that have higher volume requirements.

Although each railroad operates as a separate entity, a centralized purchasing department is responsible for working directly with users at each railroad to develop and negotiate these contracts. Specifically, purchasing identifies potential items for systems contracts; aggregates the requirements at each railroad for these items; identifies and analyzes potential systems contract suppliers; coordinates the calculation of annual demand estimates; and represents each railroad during negotiations. Each year, purchasing works with field managers to identify new items to add to existing systems contracts, identify items for new contracts, and develop estimates of annual demand at each railroad.

Users at each railroad participate during the development of annual purchase requirements. Since local managers have the best idea concerning planned maintenance projects and expected usage, they are responsible for developing local demand forecasts. Before each negotiation, the different railroads receive an e-mail with a sample *boiler plate* systems contract attached. Each railroad has an opportunity to identify the contractual options they prefer, and users can expand the contract by listing any items they would like to see addressed in the final agreement. A supplier will have a contract addendum for each railroad it services.

Determining when inventory is used and issuing payment are vital parts of systems contracting, and this timing has major financial implications. As a railroad employee removes an item, the local railroad posts the item as a receipt into a computerized inventory control system. The railroads forward usage reports to purchasing, which consolidates the usage into a single report. The report is then forwarded to suppliers for billing purposes. Each supplier sends a single invoice for the total usage, not separate invoices to each unit. This streamlines the accounts payable and receivable process.

Show Me the Money

Ironically, while the parent company has not achieved its own RONA target, the railroads eventually achieved net asset returns of over 50%! The railroads view their asset return achievements as evidence of their contribution to the parent company. Greatly exceeding the RONA target quieted the rumblings about why the parent company owned railroads.

Systems contracting featuring consignment inventory has resulted in other direct benefits. Perhaps foremost, purchasing is achieving its primary goal of reducing inventory investment as average inventory on a financial basis decreased by almost 40% over a three-year period. And, the railroads expect further reductions as they expand their use of systems contracts. The railroads also avoided or deferred price increases due to fixed pricing in the three-year agreements. Systems contracts have also allowed for some staff downsizing since suppliers assumed responsibilities for delivering and placing physical inventory in storage. Finally, acquisition costs are lower because users submit annual orders for the items covered by the systems contracts.

Lessons Learned

The most important part of any case involves the lessons it provides. At first glance, RONA appears to be just another corporate indicator. What's the lesson here? In reality, a superordinate measure like RONA cannot be achieved unless functional groups coordinate their efforts. The presence of superordinate measures demands that different groups work together or risk failing individually. A second lesson is that our finance friends have provided us with a fair number of superordinate measures. Do not underestimate the value of knowing how to map your group's contribution to these measures. (Chapter 16 will provide a tool for identifying how improvements affect specific parts of the ROA formula.) When someone asks, "What have you done lately?" you will be able to show, in no uncertain terms, the linkage between activity and accomplishment. The ability to show that linkage never gets old.

CONCLUDING THOUGHTS

Combining the worlds of supply chain and finance is going to take many of us out of our comfort zone. That is to be expected as we apply new concepts, tools, and techniques in some exciting ways. But, as we expand our base of knowledge, a confidence should emerge—perhaps even a swagger that tells the world you are bringing your *A* game to the table.

Let's not lose sight of what we are trying to accomplish as we apply financial thinking to SCM. For SCM to mature as a discipline, we must appreciate the language of finance, including its terms, concepts, tools, and techniques. We must also understand how to apply financial tools and techniques to support better decision making and risk management. And, we must demonstrate the value that supply chain managers create by showing how supply chain initiatives affect a company's most important financial indicators. Finally, we must continue to develop as professionals through the application of new knowledge.

REFERENCES

1. http://en.wikipedia.org/wiki/Finance.
2. Vipal Monga, "The New Bookkeeper is a Robot," *The Wall Street Journal*, May 5, 2015, p. B1.
3. http://www.investopedia.com/terms/b/balancesheet.asp.
4. http://www.investopedia.com/terms/r/retainedearnings.asp.
5. Loth, Richard, "Understanding the Income Statement," www.investopedia.com/articles/04/022504.asp.
6. www.businessdictionary.com/definition/cash-flow-statement.html.
7. www.investopedia.com/terms/r/returnoninvestment.asp.
8. www.investopedia.com/terms/r/returnoninvestment.asp.
9. www.investopedia.com/terms/r/returnoninvestmentcapital.asp.

10. www.investorwords.com/4317/ROIC.html and http://www.investing answers.com/financial-dictionary/ratio-analysis/return-invested -capital-roic-1188.

2

BEST PRACTICES IN EVALUATING AND SELECTING SUPPLIERS

Few could logically argue that the inputs received from suppliers do not affect the ability to satisfy or even exceed the exacting requirements of internal and external customers. Creating a world-class supply chain requires careful attention to the inputs and relationships that originate far upstream in a supply chain. It is difficult to conceptualize a scenario where a leading firm would ever ignore the direct relationship between the effectiveness of its supplier selection process and the effectiveness of its value chain.

A strategic focus on core capabilities and competencies, which often results in the outsourcing of noncore but still essential requirements, makes supplier evaluation and selection a critical process today. When external suppliers begin to receive over half of a buying firm's total revenue (as payment for purchased goods and services), the logic behind developing a world-class selection process becomes clear from a cost and financial perspective. Furthermore, a continuing reliance on suppliers to act as systems integrators within an original equipment manufacturer's (OEM's) supply chain magnifies the importance of suppliers.

The following discusses a set of best practices that define excellence in supplier evaluation and selection. Like all the best practices presented throughout this book, these are the result of extensive primary research with hundreds of firms across numerous industries. While this chapter focuses on supplier evaluation and selection best practices, the following two chapters will show how to apply an in-depth financial perspective when evaluating potential suppliers during the selection process.

SUPPLIER EVALUATION AND SELECTION BEST PRACTICES

Supplier evaluation and selection is the process of evaluating a set of potential suppliers against a set of predetermined criteria or requirements with the objective of entering into a formal business arrangement. Something that is important to recognize is that not all organizations will have the same sense of urgency or criticality as it relates to the supplier selection process—or even the importance of the supply management process. Table 2.1 presents a set of factors that can be viewed along a continuum. These factors affect how rigorously a company should stress its supplier selection process within the broader context of strategic supply management. Some companies, such as those in banking or insurance, will likely not perceive the importance of supplier selection the same way as companies, for example, in the aerospace or automotive industries.

A major factor that affects the importance of supplier selection is the amount of a company's revenue that suppliers receive. Recall from Chapter 1 that on a company's income statement is an important line item that resides just under the revenue line, which is the top line of the income statement. This line item, called costs of goods sold or cost of sales, includes the sum of direct materials, direct labor, and factory overhead required to make a product. In retailing, it includes the purchase price of merchandise. It is not unusual in some industries for suppliers

Table 2.1   Factors affecting the importance of suppliers and the supply management process

Less Importance		Greater Importance
Competition is stable	↔	Competition is dynamic and rapidly changing
New product development cycle times are stable	↔	New product development cycle times are shortening rapidly
Industry features slow technological change	↔	Industry features rapid technological change
Customer improvement expectations are low	↔	Customer improvement expectations are high
Competitors are primarily domestic	↔	Competitors are primarily global
Suppliers are primarily domestic	↔	Suppliers are primarily global
Purchases make up a small portion of revenues	↔	Purchases make up an extensive portion of revenues
Suppliers minimally impact your ability to compete	↔	Suppliers extensively impact your ability to compete
Most production requirements are controlled internally	↔	System or finished goods outsourcing is extensive

Adapted from Robert J. Trent, *Strategic Supply Management*, J. Ross Publishing, 2008.

to receive 80 percent or more of the amount that appears in the cost of goods sold account. We must also consider how suppliers affect a firm's capital asset and inventory accounts. Supplier fingerprints are all over their customer's balance sheet and income statement.

The following is a set of supplier evaluation and selection best practices. This listing can serve as a guide when performing a self-audit for assessing your firm's selection practices. The following provides some key points about each practice.

Executive Managers Believe That Supplier Evaluation and Selection Is One of the Most Important Business Processes

Few would argue that supplier evaluation and selection represents important work. Executive managers at leading firms understand that the way they evaluate and select their suppliers can be a source of competitive advantage, particularly since many suppliers are being asked by their customers to take on new responsibilities. As a result they support it accordingly.

For critical and high-value goods and services, best-practice firms routinely evaluate firsthand a supplier's financial stability, capacity, logistics capability, labor relations, logistical networks, design capability, supply management practices, process capability, environmental compliance, willingness to work with the buyer, design capability, ability to act as a systems integrator, and technology innovation. The selection process can also allow a buying company to use its first-tier suppliers to gain insights into its second- and even third-tier suppliers.

Companies that are effective at selecting suppliers almost always have a higher-level executive and steering committee that is responsible for overseeing the selection process. Convincing evidence exists that shows the connection between a higher-level supply executive and a company's supplier evaluation, selection, and management capabilities. It is not the formal supply position, per se, that is important. Rather, what is critical is the opportunity for visibility, resources, and access to executive leaders that comes with having a position in the corporate hierarchy that is on par with other functional executives. It is hard to imagine the development of a world-class supply base becoming a reality without executive champions to make it happen.

Cross-functional Teams Are Responsible for Important Selection Decisions

Similar to product development, important selection and commodity management decisions are now made extensively by cross-functional teams that report directly to corporate executives. The use of selection teams composed of members from purchasing, operations, finance, and engineering reflects the organizational rather than functional nature of supply management decisions. These teams are often referred to as commodity or category teams.

A word of caution is in order here. Anyone who maintains that the use of teams guarantees better supply chain results is somewhat delusional. We know that high-performing teams have the potential to deliver benefits that far outweigh their cost. Conversely, we also know that poorly designed and managed teams can waste the time and energy of members, enforce lower performance norms, create destructive conflict, and make poor decisions. Teams can also exploit, stress, and frustrate members—sometimes all at the same time.[1]

We also know that structural barriers may exist that can limit the effectiveness of teams. Three noteworthy barriers include (1) an extensive reliance on part-time teams that create conflict with a team member's regular job responsibilities, (2) measurement systems that fail to recognize or reward team-based contribution and performance, and (3) a national culture, at least in the U.S., that is inherently individualistic rather than group-oriented.

Something we know for certain is that organizations that consider a range of issues when planning to use teams increase the likelihood of team success. What does planning effectively mean? It means performing the following—each of which has been shown to affect team success:

- Assigning appropriate (i.e., challenging) assignments to the team
- Selecting qualified members and leaders
- Determining member training requirements
- Identifying resource support requirements
- Determining team authority levels
- Establishing team performance goals
- Determining how to measure and reward participation and performance
- Developing a team charter to legitimize the team

The point here is that the use of teams to manage supply chain commodities is a best practice that requires some serious up-front work. If supply chain leaders ignore the issues and factors that affect team success, more often than not they will wonder why the reality of using teams does not match the expectations surrounding their use.

International Purchasing Offices Support the Selection Process

Supplier selection takes on added risk when international suppliers are part of the equation. Most managers understand they have limited ability to manage activities that occur thousands of miles away. At some point, companies conclude that traveling from the home market to evaluate a supplier is not ideal. And, making selection decisions without ever visiting a supplier is an invitation for trouble.

An important element of international purchasing that does not receive nearly enough attention is the use of international purchasing offices (IPOs).[2] Best-practice companies recognize the importance of having local resources available to represent their interests abroad, including during supplier evaluation. To that end, many firms have established IPOs that are responsible for identifying and evaluating suppliers (along with other important duties).

Overwhelming agreement exists regarding the importance of IPOs. One study found that over 85 percent of companies that maintain IPOs say these offices are extremely important to their international success, while 10 percent say IPOs are moderately important. About half of all companies that maintain at least one foreign buying office say their IPOs are more than meeting or exceeding expectations, while one-third indicate their IPOs are meeting expectations.[3]

A positive relationship exists between the number of IPOs that a company relies on and the percentage of total purchases that are obtained worldwide. As worldwide purchases increase as a percent of total purchases, the likelihood of having more than one IPO increases. And, the use of IPOs should increase as supply organizations continue to search the globe for buying opportunities. Using IPOs to support supplier selection is clearly a best supply chain practice.

The kinds of services that an IPO provides are varied, although research reveals there is agreement about a common set of responsibilities. At least 70 percent or more of companies with at least one IPO say these offices are responsible for identifying suppliers and evaluating their capabilities; negotiating and executing contracts with suppliers; resolving quality and delivery problems directly with suppliers; developing supplier capabilities; measuring supplier performance; evaluating product and service designs and samples; facilitating import and export activities; and performing logistical coordination when shipping material. IPOs assume some important responsibilities.

A Well-defined Evaluation and Selection Process Is Developed and Communicated across the Organization

Supplier selection incorporates many supply chain topics, including strategy segmentation and development, measurement, longer-term contracting, and negotiation. Each selection decision has some level of uniqueness, meaning there is no single way to evaluate and select suppliers. and no two selection decisions are exactly alike. However, all selection decisions should follow a logical process from recognizing that a selection need exists to reaching agreement with the selected supplier.

Ideally, a supplier selection process is developed at a central or centrally coordinated level rather than relying on each buying unit to develop its own process. Minimal value is gained by repeatedly *reinventing the wheel*, which is true for every organizational process. Unfortunately, no cost accounting system is available that captures the resources that are wasted when process development is sub-optimized or duplicated. Following a company-wide process also helps avoid a phenomenon called the *pockets of excellence* model—where one part of an organization demonstrates excellence while other parts of the organization fall short. The following presents the type of multi-step process that buying units should follow when evaluating and selecting suppliers:

- **Step 1: Recognize a supplier selection need exists**
- **Step 2: Identify supply requirements**—by involving internal and sometimes even external customers to arrive at a correct set of attributes, and eventually their weights, that will be used during a formal supplier assessment
- **Step 3: Determine the appropriate supply strategy**—by considering issues such as the use of single or multiple supply sources; the use of foreign suppliers; the use of a shorter-term or longer-term contract; the type of relationship that best fits the supply requirement; the use of regional or global agreements; and any corporate policies affecting the selection decision
- **Step 4: Identify potential suppliers**
- **Step 5: Reduce suppliers in the selection pool**—including through the use of supplier financial analyses
- **Step 6: Conduct a formal evaluation**—often through the use of site visits to directly evaluate supplier capabilities
- **Step 7: Select supplier(s) and reach agreement**—often through negotiation

The end of Step 7 is only the beginning of what is likely to be an extended buyer-seller relationship. After Step 7 the focus shifts from evaluating and selecting suppliers to managing and developing suppliers.

Company-wide Templates and Tools Are Available to Support the Selection Process

Since most selection decisions are long lasting with high switching costs, those responsible for making a selection decision will benefit from a host of tools and techniques that share a common objective—they are designed to help make the decision-making process more effective and efficient. Furthermore, it makes sense to standardize a set of support tools so that each decision-making unit or individual is not (a) sub-optimizing its decision or (2) duplicating effort as they continuously reinvent the wheel (i.e., the supporting tools and templates). These tools and templates should be easily accessible through a company's Intranet.

Perhaps the most important tool or template used during supplier evaluation is a weighted-point supplier assessment. A weighted-point assessment tool is used when evaluating and scoring suppliers across a set of predetermined performance categories. A cross-functional team, for example, may score a supplier's capacity, management capabilities, labor relations manufacturing process capability and quality, delivery performance, supplier management capabilities, lean capabilities, flexibility, or any other relevant category. The assessment tool should also incorporate any key objectives that a buyer seeks from the supplier relationship. A buyer may expect, for example, a potential supplier to take on product design responsibilities. The weighted-point assessment tool would logically include an assessment of a supplier's design capabilities.

No industry-standard weighted-point assessment format exists. Regardless of the final assessment format used, the steps to develop a weighted-point assessment should include:

1. Identify key supplier evaluation categories, such as total cost, management capability, quality, etc.
2. Weight each evaluation category (the sum of the category weights must equal 100%)
3. Identify and weight subcategories within the categories identified in Step 2
4. Identify individual assessment items and define the scoring system for each item
5. Evaluate and score the supplier directly across each category (many assessments provide a total supplier score out of 100)
6. Calculate a supplier's assessment score
7. Review evaluation results and make a selection decision

Effective assessment tools share certain features or characteristics, regardless of how the final format appears. First, the assessment tool must be straightforward and easy to calculate. Complexity is not an assessment tool's friend. Second, the assessment must also be reliable with scored measures that are well understood by the evaluators. Third, the assessment should be comprehensive, meaning that it includes all the important categories or criteria relevant to the selection decision. A fourth characteristic is that the assessment uses a quantitative scoring system that ensures objectivity. Finally, we like to see a system that is flexible. An example of flexibility involves users being able to populate the assessment with categories and weights that may differ from selection to selection.

Besides a weighted-point assessment tool, other tools are available that support decision making during supplier evaluation and selection. Fortunately, these tools are inexpensive to develop, easy to use, and usually quite effective:

- **List reduction approaches:** This approach subjects a large list of ideas or options to a preestablished set of criteria with the objective of reducing a larger set of choices to a smaller set
- **Paired comparisons:** These are used to select a preference by comparing every combination of possible decisions or choices with the objective of quickly determining if a group has agreement about a particular option
- **Balance sheet assessment:** This requires the identification of the pros and cons of a variety of options
- **Criteria rating forms:** Forms used to evaluate options head-to-head against various preestablished criteria
- **Weighted voting tools:** These are used to quantify the position or preference of group members by allowing weighted votes to be assigned to preferred positions

Various supplier selection techniques rely on mathematical models. These include mixed integer nonlinear programming models to solve multiple sourcing problems; stochastic integer programming approaches for simultaneous selection of suppliers based on loss functions and capability indices; a comparison of suppliers using data envelopment analysis; linear programming that considers tangible and intangible factors in selecting the best suppliers with optimum order quantities identified; and multi-criteria supplier selection using fuzzy logic and an analytic hierarchy process.

Supply Chain Personnel Anticipate Rather than React to Internal Customer Supplier Selection Needs

Across many parts of the supply chain we are trying to shift from being reactive to being anticipatory, including during supplier evaluation and selection. Anticipating supply chain needs can go a long way toward reducing the cycle time associated with the selection process. The central question becomes how to anticipate supplier selection requirements.

Early involvement of procurement personnel on product development teams affords perhaps the best opportunity to understand product requirements as they evolve. At a leading computer manufacturer, procurement personnel begin to prequalify potential suppliers—even before engineers finalize product requirements. Procurement personnel can do this because they are present when requirements are still in the concept phase. Early involvement on capital expenditure projects also supports a more anticipatory approach to supplier selection.

Another opportunity to anticipate requirements is during the development of strategies by groups that procurement supports. This is the approach practiced at a New Jersey company that assigns sourcing managers to marketing strategy teams to support the development of marketing-related contracts. Examples of areas where marketing groups require commercial support include printing services, conventions, meetings, promotional displays and tradeshows, marketing research services, and advertising and promotion. Sourcing involvement, for example, resulted in a reduction of worldwide printing suppliers from over 500 to 5.

Sourcing professionals add value to the marketing strategy development process by verifying that every unit within the corporation is charged the same and best rate from suppliers; reserving the right to audit advertising *job jackets* and costs; working to gain most favored customer status with media suppliers; controlling the process of buying advertising and media support; maintaining confidentiality through control of the process; working to retain the company's ownership of intellectual property; and assuming a major part of the strategy development process (contracting) that marketing simply does not want.

An organizational design mechanism that specifically promotes early insight into internal customer requirements is something called a co-location model. Besides gaining first-hand insight into internal customer requirements, research reveals that physically co-locating supply personnel should lead to a host of positive outcomes. These include increased interaction with other functional groups, enhanced role clarity and understanding, development of positive internal relationships and trust, faster decision making and problem solving, and enhanced creative thinking from working together physically. Any group that relies on suppliers is an internal customer of procurement. Figure 2.1 presents the co-location model.

Financial Analysis Takes Place to Evaluate the Financial Health of Potential Suppliers

Potential suppliers should be subjected, usually early in the selection process, to an assessment of their financial health. This should include an analysis of financial ratios and the calculation of bankruptcy predictor scores. Perhaps the best known tool for assessing supplier financial health (but certainly not the only tool) is the Z-Score. Developed by Dr. Edward Altman of New York University, the Z-Score combines a series of weighted ratios for public and private firms to predict financial health.

The Z-Score has several features that make this a financial tool that every supply organization should employ. The first is its simplicity. Only four ratios

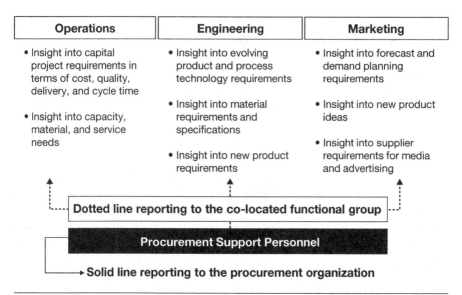

Operations	Engineering	Marketing
• Insight into capital project requirements in terms of cost, quality, delivery, and cycle time • Insight into capacity, material, and service needs	• Insight into evolving product and process technology requirements • Insight into material requirements and specifications • Insight into new product requirements	• Insight into forecast and demand planning requirements • Insight into new product ideas • Insight into supplier requirements for media and advertising

Dotted line reporting to the co-located functional group

Procurement Support Personnel

Solid line reporting to the procurement organization

Figure 2.1   Anticipating internal requirements through co-location

are needed to calculate the Z-Score for private firms—five are needed for public firms. Next, the Z-Score provides a single score that can be used during the preliminary evaluation of potential suppliers. A clear best practice is the use of financial assessment tools employed before selecting a supplier. Of course, a supplier's financial health should also be routinely monitored after supplier selection to prevent future surprises. The next chapter focuses extensively on the financial side of supplier evaluation and selection, including illustrations of how to calculate financial ratios and interpret a supplier's Z-Score.

Supply Strategy Segmentation Supports the Selection Process

Leading supply organizations know that not all selection decisions are created equally, or warrant comparable time and effort. These companies segment their selection decisions based on the attributes of their sourcing requirements. The way they subsequently manage their suppliers and relationships will also differ from requirement to requirement.

Figure 2.2 presents a strategy development tool called the portfolio matrix. The use of this tool forces supply organizations to segment their requirements and to recognize that a single supply strategy or selection approach does not fit all needs. This tool considers both the value and importance of a supply requirement as well as the number of qualified suppliers that comprise a marketplace.

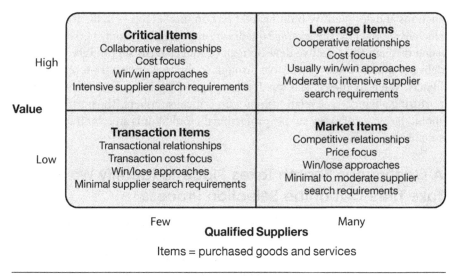

	Critical Items	**Leverage Items**
High	Collaborative relationships Cost focus Win/win approaches Intensive supplier search requirements	Cooperative relationships Cost focus Usually win/win approaches Moderate to intensive supplier search requirements
Value		
Low	**Transaction Items** Transactional relationships Transaction cost focus Win/lose approaches Minimal supplier search requirements	**Market Items** Competitive relationships Price focus Win/lose approaches Minimal to moderate supplier search requirements

Few   Many
Qualified Suppliers
Items = purchased goods and services

Figure 2.2   Segmenting supplier search requirements

Perhaps the most important reason for using the portfolio matrix is the guidance it prescribes. Segmentation helps identify what type of negotiating strategy to apply (win/win vs. win/lose), whether to pursue price versus cost analytic approaches, and how the procurement organization can best create value. The tool also helps define the intensity of the search. Clearly, items and services in the lower half of the matrix are less critical and require less intensive assessment compared with items in the upper half. Segmentation also helps prescribe the appropriate sourcing approaches and performance measures to employ. Supply market segmentation, something that leading companies routinely practice, should be an integral component of the supplier selection process.

The matrix also helps us understand the type of relationship to pursue with suppliers (transactional, competitive, cooperative, or collaborative). An important point is that a strong understanding of relationships is an essential part of supplier selection. Simply stated, not all supplier relationships are equally important. Knowing when, where, and how to apply an appropriate relationship is an area where supply professionals bring value to their organization. This topic should be front and center at the onset of the selection process.

The portfolio model also provides guidance regarding how procurement personnel create value through the strategy development and supplier selection process. In the transaction quadrant (lower left), value is derived from the creation of low-dollar purchase systems that remove transaction costs and allow internal customers to order as required. In the market quadrant (lower right), the focus is on the use of buying and contracting approaches, such as reverse Internet auctions and competitive bidding, that rely on market forces to identify the most efficient supplier. In the leverage quadrant (upper right), supply personnel create value through the selective development of longer-term supply agreements that deliver value that was unavailable through traditional or shorter-term contracts. Finally, value in the critical quadrant (upper left) comes from identifying and nurturing alliance-type relationships with critical suppliers. The portfolio matrix should be a part of every supply professional's toolkit. It is an essential part of the supplier selection process.

A Continuous Search Takes Place to Identify Ways to Take Time Out of the Selection Process

While not always the case, evaluation and selection decisions often support new product development. Given that development times for new products and services are declining, sometimes at a dramatic rate, it seems logical that the cycle time for any supporting processes must also decline. To put this in perspective, the time required to develop a new car or truck in the U.S. auto industry during the mid-1980s—something we call concept-to-customer (C-to-C) cycle time— was around 60 months. Now the C-to-C cycle time is 12 to 18 months. Best practice firms understand that any product development support processes, including supplier evaluation and selection, must also shorten dramatically. Other very good reasons exist for shortening the selection process even for requirements that are not part of product development.

Many creative ways exist to accelerate supplier evaluation and selection without sacrificing effectiveness. Some of the ways to reduce selection time include:

- Provide users with electronic systems to forward requirements to procurement
- Prequalify suppliers in anticipation of future needs
- Supply management personnel work concurrently with product design teams to identify purchase requirements early on
- Develop commodity and part numbering schemes and place purchase requirements into categories
- Identify selection requirements and supply strategies using a portfolio matrix approach
- Develop a preferred supplier list
- Use internal and external databases to identify potential sources quickly
- Send requests for information to maintain information about potential suppliers
- Perform supplier financial analyses using third-party data
- Prequalify or reject suppliers using electronic request for quotes and proposals

- Use international purchasing offices to evaluate foreign suppliers
- Join consortiums that collect supplier data
- Develop company-wide assessment templates and tools
- Develop preapproved contract language
- Use *cut and paste* contract clauses during negotiation
- Conduct electronic negotiations with suppliers
- Use target pricing, which preestablishes allowable costs, thereby reducing the need to engage in supplier negotiation

Gone are the days when supply managers had the luxury of spending months to evaluate, select, and negotiate agreements with suppliers. Selection decisions often have to occur in weeks, perhaps even days. When performed properly, reducing the selection cycle time should improve the effectiveness of selection decisions as a streamlined selection process requires supply managers to reduce time (and costs) and eliminate waste.

The Supplier Selection Process Is Aligned with Corporate Strategy and Functional Groups

Supplier evaluation and selection is not practiced in isolation from corporate strategy or other functional groups. Supply professionals should never forget they are part of a support activity, which means they have internal customers. If engineering requires a supplier that is on the cutting edge of a certain type of technology, then the selection team needs to factor this into its search. Or, engineering may require a supplier that is capable of taking on product design responsibilities. If the operations group requires a supplier that can produce and deliver on a just-in-time basis, then that requirement must become a key evaluation criterion. If a corporate strategy calls for a supply chain that is highly responsive to uncertainty and change, then suppliers must be responsive and flexible. And if a stated corporate objective is to be environmentally sensitive, selection teams will want to work with suppliers that have strong environmental records. Leading supply organizations understand the need to link their selection process with the needs of corporate and internal customers.

The Supplier Selection Process Supports Quality Management Objectives

The principles that are part of quality management (including Six Sigma) make up one of the most robust and powerful sets of organizational precepts ever developed. Unfortunately, being able to recite these principles is far different than living by them. This is particularly true for those responsible for selecting suppliers.

Even though external suppliers often provide over half the inputs required within a supply chain, a commitment to total quality is often lacking. If supplier quality is so important, why are so many buyers still measured by their ability to obtain a lower *price* rather than their contribution to total *value*? Why are so many critical supplier selection decisions made without ever analyzing first-hand a supplier's production processes or analyzing a supplier's financial health?

A well-crafted supplier selection process supports some important quality management principles. In particular, this includes the principles of practicing quality at the source, objective decision making, emphasizing the prevention rather than the detection of defects, and focusing on processes rather than output.

Let's consider the last principle just mentioned—focusing on processes rather than output. Historically, many selection decisions have been based on an evaluation of samples provided by a supplier. Think about some of the questions we can ask about product samples:

- What is the capability of the process that will be used during production?
- Were the samples hand-picked from a larger batch?
- Did the supplier produce the samples using the same equipment, personnel, materials, and technology that will be used during regular production?
- Did the supplier even make the samples?

Samples also provide no insight into a supplier's financial health, management capabilities, supply chain management skills, delivery capabilities, manufacturing costs, design capabilities, and customer service, to name but a few. It is far better to focus directly on the *supplier and the process* that produces output rather than simply the output.

The challenge becomes how to embed quality principles directly into the selection process. Some ways to accomplish this include:

- Develop ways, such as early involvement on product development teams, to identify internal customer requirements
- Communicate customer requirements directly to suppliers through well-crafted requests for proposals
- Use formal contracting approaches to formally define internal customer requirements
- Perform supplier financial health assessments early on, to prevent later surprises
- Perform preselection supplier site visits
- Develop a consistent source selection process used across all buying centers
- Demand evidence of supplier process capability—minimize reliance on samples

- Develop total cost of ownership systems to calculate supplier costs
- Develop fact-based supplier assessment systems for evaluating prospective suppliers
- Require ISO 9000 supplier certification

The Selection Process Routinely Demonstrates Results

This best practice is important because we often mistake activity for accomplishment. The truth is most supply chain tasks and initiatives are simply activities that we think are worthwhile. And, it is natural to feel good when pursuing activities that the prevailing wisdom says are good.

Activities mean nothing unless they lead to a set of desired outcomes. What benefits are we receiving from a selected supplier that justifies the intensity of the search? What does a longer-term contract provide that a traditional contract does not? What benefits have resulted because of an emphasis on strong supplier relationships? Did a supplier development project deliver a positive return? What are commodity teams doing to justify their expense? What values were created from face-to-face supplier performance review meetings? In short, what did these activities *accomplish*?

The reality is that most firms cannot easily translate or articulate the benefits they receive from their supply chain activities. This shortcoming is one of the primary motivations for writing this book. It is time to translate activities into accomplishment, and that means taking a financial perspective wherever possible. Best practice firms regularly articulate the financial benefits they receive from their supply chain efforts.

Supplier Selection and Supply Base Rationalization Objectives Are Aligned

Before elaborating on this practice, it is necessary to clarify some terms. A major part of building a world-class supply base involves determining the right mix and number of suppliers to maintain for each purchase item, category, or commodity. Talking about the right mix and number leads us to a term called rationalization. Another term we often hear used is optimization. To *optimize* is to make something as perfect, effective, or functional as possible. To a purist the concept of optimization implies a mathematically derived solution given a set of conditions or constraints (think linear programming, for example). Supply base optimization is a process that seeks to create a supply base that is as perfect, effective, or functional as possible, while rationalization seeks to determine the right mix and number of suppliers to maintain for each purchase item, category, or commodity. Some supplier selection decisions simply cannot be modeled, or at least modeled accurately from a mathematical perspective. The complexity is simply too great. In practice, many people interchange the terms rationalization and optimization.

Why is this topic presented with a discussion of best practices? During supply strategy development, supplier selection and rationalization targets go hand in hand. These are not topics that best practice firms perform independently. They are part of a coherent strategy development process that considers many different topics, including selection issues and rationalization targets.

A misconception is that supply base rationalization or optimization means reducing the size of the supply base in terms of total suppliers. At times, a firm may need to add suppliers to support greater volumes or to support geographic expansion. This could result in a net addition of suppliers or shipping locations for a particular commodity. Or, the decision may be made to eliminate lower-performing suppliers and to replace them with higher-performing ones. Either of these conditions may initiate a supplier selection search.

Like any process, supply base rationalization (or optimization) requires certain factors to be successful. And, as usual, number one on the chart is having the time to pursue any rationalization objectives. This process usually requires a detailed analysis that is not normally part of the supply management process. The complexity of supply base rationalization also mandates that we draw upon a variety of cross-functional skills. Many companies will assign this responsibility to their commodity teams. If a team is considering evaluating suppliers that are not currently part of the supply base, then all the resources that support supplier selection, including site visits and a defined selection process, will also be important here. The rationalization process also requires an extensive amount of data to support objective decision making.

Supply base rationalization will always be ongoing. The need to *tweak* the number of suppliers that a buying organization maintains will always be present. At some point, firms will want to replace good suppliers with even better suppliers— even if this means initiating a new supplier search. Furthermore, shifting demand patterns, changing supplier ownership, the introduction of new products, global expansion, and mergers and acquisitions all have a continuous impact on the size of the supply base and the need for supplier evaluation and selection. The supply base is a constantly evolving and dynamic entity.

CONCLUDING THOUGHTS

While not equally true at all organizations, supplier evaluation and selection is a major component of supply chain success. Along with cost, quality, and delivery performance, the selection process affects some important capabilities of a buying company—including its ability to be responsive, flexible, and fast. And, we have known for some time that buying customers are relying more and more on their suppliers as major sources of technology and innovation.

Few organizational leaders would reasonably argue that the inputs received from upstream suppliers do not affect the success of the entire value chain. We know that producers are afforded minimal forgiveness when they fail to meet or exceed the needs of their end customers. Developing a world-class supply base, with supplier evaluation and selection as the foundation, recognizes that exceeding customer requirements means paying attention to the inputs and relationships that originate far upstream in the supply chain. Understanding a set of best practices that define supplier evaluation and selection is not a convenience; it is a strategic necessity.

REFERENCES

1. J.R. Hackman, "The Design of Work Teams," chap. 20 in *Handbook of Organizational Behavior*, Prentice Hall, Englewood Cliffs, NJ, 1987, 315-342.
2. Some companies simply call IPOs foreign or international buying offices, international procurement centers, or international procurement organizations. No industry standard exists regarding what to call these offices.
3. Robert M. Monczka, Robert J. Trent, and Kenneth J. Petersen, *Effective Global Sourcing and Supply for Superior Results*, CAPS Research, Tempe Arizona, 2006, 59.

3

EVALUATING AND SELECTING SUPPLIERS—THE FINANCIAL PERSPECTIVE

From the last chapter we know that a best practice characterizing supplier evaluation and selection is the assessment of supplier financial health. In particular, the use of financial ratios and the calculation of bankruptcy predictors should be a regular part of the selection process. Failure to perform these analyses increases the risk of getting caught off-guard when an unfortunate reality sets in that a supplier is not financially strong.

This chapter explores why supplier financial analysis should become an embedded part of the supplier selection process. Next, the use of ratios to perform financial assessments is presented. The third section explains supplier bankruptcy predictors followed by a set of qualitative indicators that may indicate supplier distress. The chapter concludes with a technique that uses financial data to estimate supplier capacity.

WHY PERFORM SUPPLIER FINANCIAL ANALYSIS?

A supplier financial analysis is performed primarily for two reasons—to manage business risk and to eliminate marginal suppliers from the evaluation process. For our purposes we are concerned with financial assessments during the evaluation and assessment process. Many firms require suppliers to attain a certain level of financial stability before they receive further consideration, such as a site visit.

As an aside, financial assessments should also occur for incumbent suppliers, perhaps every three to six months. Evaluating a supplier's ongoing financial health is a risk management technique that all supply managers should practice. Current suppliers that are under financial duress should be placed on a *watch list* that requires more frequent reviews, perhaps weekly. Do we really want to rely on suppliers that will be insolvent at some indeterminate time that we cannot predict? Getting caught off-guard when a supplier closes its doors or struggles under bankruptcy protection is not the best way to manage a supply chain.

Perhaps the most powerful reason for conducting a supplier financial assessment stems from the reluctance of suppliers to tell you they are financially troubled. Have you ever bought a used car where the existing owner went out of his way to tell you everything that is wrong with the vehicle? When you interview a job candidate, do you inform that candidate about all the little nuances that make your company such an *interesting* place to work? On your first date with your eventual spouse did you make sure he or she was well aware of all your flaws and idiosyncrasies? The answer to these three questions is likely to be no, no, and no.

A supplier that tells a potential buyer about its financial problems may accelerate its own demise. Potential buyers will shy away from the supplier while existing buyers will begin to qualify new sources. While our parents told us that honesty is the best policy, it is a policy that is sometimes buried deep in the back of a supplier's playbook. It is not that the supplier's personnel are inherently bad or dishonest. They are simply practicing self-preservation.

Exceptions to relying on financially distressed suppliers certainly exist. A supplier's financial problems may be temporary, or the supplier may be developing a new technology that is vital to the buyer. This would make the supplier a candidate for supplier development, a topic that Chapter 5 covers. The supplier may also be the only source available, placing the buyer in a position where risk management becomes critical. Also, a supplier, while still under some duress, may be trending financially in the right direction, making a snapshot of the supplier's financial condition misleading. Eliminating marginal suppliers from consideration is not always the best course of action.

Apple's Rude Awakening

It is probably every supply manager's worst nightmare—you wake up one morning to find, to your complete surprise, that a critical supplier has ceased operations. Its doors are shut; no deliveries are planned; and the supplier is not returning phone calls. How could this happen? Why did this happen? This scenario was one that Apple experienced firsthand. And if it could happen to Apple, it could happen to you.

In 2013, working with GT Advanced Technologies, Apple announced it would invest $700 million to build the world's largest plant to produce artificial sapphires, a material that would be a substitute for hardened glass. Unfortunately, the supplier that Apple chose, besides needing massive financial support, never made sapphire glass in any significant quantities. It did make the equipment for growing synthetic sapphire. As the supplier soon realized, making the equipment is far different than growing the product in mass quantities. As production problems grew, Apple became reluctant to extend its last payment to the supplier. GT responded by filing for bankruptcy protection. Its shares immediately dropped 93%, essentially wiping out any value in the company. While we may never know if Apple could have done more to anticipate this dramatic turn of events, this case does illustrate the importance of monitoring a supplier's financial health. We perform supplier financial analyses to avoid, as much as possible, unwanted surprises.

FINANCIAL RATIO ANALYSIS

A common approach when evaluating a company's financial situation involves ratio analysis. Ratios, also called financial performance metrics, simply represent one number divided by another to arrive at a value that is then compared to an industry benchmark, an internal target, historical performance, or to other companies, usually in the same industry. Literally hundreds of financial ratios exist. Toss some financial data into a numerator, toss some financial data into a dominator, and *poof*—a ratio appears. The first test of a ratio should be that it tells us something of importance rather than being the result of numbers thrown into a formula.

The reasons for evaluating financial ratios are straightforward. We use supplier financial ratios to manage risk by providing insights that line-item data from financial statements cannot provide. Ratios take financial data and turn it into value-added information that is then interpreted. Furthermore, ratio analysis, when performed on a regular basis, can highlight trends. Ratios can also be used to determine the relative financial strength of a supplier compared with other suppliers in an industry. Perhaps most importantly, various tools use financial ratios to predict the potential of supplier bankruptcy. The most common bankruptcy predictor, the Z-Score, appears later in the chapter.

Ratios are used at different times. Within the context of supply chain risk management, financial ratios should be calculated when evaluating potential suppliers, especially when a purchase requirement involves a significant amount of dollars or when buying items that are critical to your business or product. Very importantly, ratio analysis should occur when planning to select a supplier where switching options are difficult once a company starts using that supplier. In other words, supplier switching costs are high, such as when entering into longer-term contractual agreements. Finally, ratio analysis is warranted when conducting regular risk scans of your supply base.

There are other reasons for rejecting a supplier early on in the evaluation process besides concerns about financial health. This includes, but is certainly not limited to, a history of poor performance, lack of available capacity, pending litigation involving the supplier, a supplier that is a direct competitor, the supplier has environmental or other workplace infractions, the supplier demonstrates relative indifference about doing business with the buyer, the supplier has questionable ethics, and unfamiliarity with the buyer's industry.

Financial Ratio Categories

Even though hundreds of ratios exist, most fall into one of six categories. It is important to note that not everyone agrees on these categories. Some sources present a different mix of categories, sometimes omitting the market and growth categories presented here and adding ratio categories with names such as solvency, financial efficiency, cash flow, and investment valuation ratios. Interestingly, a search of financial resources reveals that while some overlap exists regarding financial ratio categories, complete overlap is rare. Regardless of the categories used, each ratio category should answer a specific question or satisfy a specific objective unique to that category.

Here we present six ratio categories. The following describes each category:

- **Liquidity ratios:** Liquidity ratios help identify if a firm (i.e., the supplier) is capable of meeting its short-term financial obligations. Generally speaking, the higher the value of the ratio, the larger the margin of safety for covering short-term debts. These ratios do not consider long-term debt coverage.
- **Leverage ratios:** This category includes any ratio used to evaluate a company's methods of financing or to measure its ability to meet financial obligations. There are several different ratios, but the main factors considered in these ratios include debt, equity, assets, and interest expenses.[1]
- **Activity ratios:** Activity ratios help us understand how effectively a firm is managing its assets. These ratios are of particular interest when considering a supplier's supply chain capabilities.
- **Profitability ratios:** This is a popular and widely used group of ratios that are almost always included in any categorization scheme of financial ratios. Ratios in this group indicate how well a firm is performing in terms of its ability to generate a profit.
- **Market ratios:** This is a set of ratios that indicate how well a supplier is performing compared with market indicators, such as price/earnings and shareholder return. The measures in this category evaluate the current market price of a share of common stock versus an indicator of the company's ability to generate profits or assets held by the company.[2]

- **Growth ratios:** Growth ratios provide insight into the rate of growth over time that is occurring at a firm for various categories, such as sales or net income. These ratios are often compared from one period to another period and require data from multiple periods for their calculation, which is not true of the other ratio categories. Taken at a specific point in time, growth ratios will not provide much insight.

Obtaining Financial Data

A key to successful financial ratio analysis is obtaining reliable and timely data, something that is easier said than done. One challenge is that almost all companies use suppliers that are not publicly owned, meaning the shareholders are private owners. Private companies are under no obligation to make financial documents available, which is not the case for publicly traded companies.

A second challenge is that gaining the right data about public companies can be problematic. Large companies, in particular, will almost always have multiple operating units that are aggregated in the financial statements. Breaking out specific results can be next to impossible.

A third challenge involves the use of international suppliers. The quality of financial data might be questionable in certain parts of the world. This is particularly true when we think about China. The *two sets of books* method, which is unthinkable (and illegal) in developed countries is not so far-fetched in other countries. The author once held a supply chain finance workshop in China. As the instructor reviewed ratio analysis and bankruptcy predictors, several participants refused to participate in the exercises. When asked why, they responded that suppliers in China never let buyers see the real numbers, so, why bother with the exercises? While this example is anecdotal, it was a revealing insight into the mindset and culture.

In practice, companies should establish an information technology (IT) repository that houses supplier information collected from multiple sources. This repository should allow access at any point during the supplier evaluation and supplier management process. What are some types of supplier financial information that could be available? A partial listing includes:

- Company-published financial statements
- 10-K and 10-Q reports as required by the Securities and Exchange Commission
- Dun & Bradstreet reports
- Credit reports and bank references
- Third-party supplier ratings provided by an independent firm, such as Moody's
- Trade and business journal information

- Press reports and other news releases gleaned from external sources
- Supplier provided data

This last item is particularly important. One advantage of working with suppliers over an extended period is the opportunity to build trust through cooperative relationships. And, one of the primary characteristics of a cooperative relationship is the sharing of data and information. As relationships and trust evolve, a supplier should be more willing to share information with the buyer—including insights into financial and operating issues that may have been hidden for fear of what the customer might do with that information.

Applying the Ratios

The best way to illustrate the use of ratios is through an example. Assume NASA wants to enter into a long-term agreement with a supplier (Orbital Sciences Corporation) to develop, build, and launch unmanned rockets to supply the International Space Station.[3] Clearly, NASA should be interested in an array of topics, particularly this company's technical prowess, financial integrity, and other risk considerations, such as the company's reliance on Russian engines to power its rockets. At the onset we hope that NASA will evaluate the financial integrity of any potential supplier. What good is a company that will not be financially viable in a year, thereby subjecting the space program to an unusual amount of risk?

Tables 3.1 and 3.2 contain financial data retrieved from public domain sources for Orbital Sciences Corporation, a potential rocket launch supplier to NASA. Please note that to simplify the statement, line items that may appear on financial statements, such as negative goodwill, are deleted here if the company has nothing to report for that item. Also, we are not using the cash flow statement, although it does contain information that is required when calculating certain ratios. For example, return on invested capital (ROIC) requires dividend data, which is found on the cash flow statement. The cash flow statement also provides capital expenditure data.

We will use two years of financial data to calculate and interpret a set of financial ratios, instead of the three years presented in the statements. Chapter 4 will provide the reader with the opportunity to perform a three-year supplier financial analysis.

Table 3.3 presents the results of a financial ratio analysis for Orbital Sciences using four common categories of ratios. By no means does this table represent a comprehensive set of ratios. As mentioned, literally hundreds of ratios exist across multiple categories. Presenting more ratios than what appears in Table 3.3 provides minimal value for what we are trying to do here.

Whenever a ratio assessment is performed, be sure to interpret the conclusions derived from the analysis. What can we conclude here? We can conclude that over this multiyear period Orbital Sciences has remained financially stable

Table 3.1 Orbital Sciences balance sheet

Period Ending	All numbers are in thousands		
	Dec 31, Current Year	Dec 31, Previous Year	Dec 31, Two Years Ago
Assets			
Current Assets			
Cash and Cash Equivalents	265,837	232,324	259,219
Net Receivables	613,672	537,438	384,880
Inventory	61,675	61,251	64,335
Other Current Assets	9,889	17,810	46,965
Total Current Assets	**951,073**	**848,823**	**755,399**
Long-term Investments	—	—	8,500
Property, Plant, and Equipment	246,060	251,360	259,972
Goodwill	71,260	75,261	75,261
Other Assets	16,368	36,010	28,937
Deferred Long-term Asset Charges	—	—	2,731
Total Assets	**1,284,761**	**1,211,454**	**1,130,800**
Liabilities			
Current Liabilities			
Accounts Payable	281,631	257,113	234,379
Short/Current Long-term Debt	8,236	7,500	—
Other Current Liabilities	21,250	62,098	104,970
Total Current Liabilities	**311,117**	**326,711**	**339,349**
Long-term Debt	135,000	143,236	131,182
Other Liabilities	16,732	17,082	16,990
Deferred Long-term Liability Charges	26,611	10,879	—
Total Liabilities	**489,460**	**497,908**	**487,521**
Stockholders' Equity			
Common Stock	605	596	589
Retained Earnings	208,797	140,431	79,425
Capital Surplus	587,240	575,300	566,624
Other Stockholder Equity	(1,341)	(2,781)	(3,359)
Total Stockholder Equity	**795,301**	**713,546**	**643,279**
Total Liabilities and Stockholders' Equity	**1,284,761**	**1,211,454**	**1,130,800**

Source: Adapted from public domain information at finance.yahoo.com.

and appears capable of meeting its upcoming financial obligations. In fact, the ratio analysis reveals no unusual concerns in any area. Any negative changes in the financial ratios, specifically the modest declines in the activity ratios, are due

Table 3.2 Orbital Sciences income statement

Period Ending	Dec 31, Current Year	Dec 31, Previous Year	Dec 31, Two Years Ago
	All numbers are in thousands		
Total Revenue	1,365,271	1,436,769	1,345,923
Cost of Revenue	1,062,466	1,097,190	1,074,389
Gross Profit	302,805	339,579	271,534
Operating Expenses			
Research Development	89,233	114,205	102,751
Selling, General, and Administrative Expenses	100,027	112,803	88,989
Operating Income or Loss	113,545	112,571	79,794
Income from Continuing Operations			
Total Other Income/Expenses Net	(5,368)	(9,512)	19,335
Earnings before Interest and Taxes	108,177	103,059	99,129
Interest Expense	4,556	11,275	11,096
Income before Tax	103,621	91,784	88,033
Income Tax Expense	35,255	30,778	20,639
Net Income from Continuing Ops	68,366	61,066	67,394
Net Income	**68,366**	**61,006**	**67,394**

Source: Adapted from public domain information at finance.yahoo.com.

largely to a decrease in sales from one year to the next. Most other ratios shifted in the desired direction or remained unchanged.

One area that often provides interesting insights comes from a deeper dive into the current asset section of the balance sheet. Here, current assets far exceed current liabilities, which, taken by itself is a good thing. But, do not stop there. Are the current assets the *right* kind of assets? What if few of the current assets are cash or near-cash instruments? What if most of the assets are comprised of inventories?

A closer looks reveals that Orbital Sciences maintains a relatively small amount of inventory in terms of total dollars. The company's quick ratio is well over the 1.0 target and has even improved from one year to the next. Excessive inventories can be problematic from a financial point of view, which a later part of this book explores more thoroughly.

Something that stands out is Orbital Sciences receivables compared to its payables. In fact, its receivables are almost half (45%) its annual sales. While this might be typical for this industry, a comparison to Lockheed Martin, another company that makes space vehicles, reveals that its receivables are only 15% of

Table 3.3   Orbital Sciences financial ratio analysis

	Ratio	Preferred Direction	Current Year Ratio Value	Previous Year Ratio Value
Liquidity	**Current ratio:** current assets – current liabilities	Higher	$951,073/$311,117 = 3.06	$848,823/326,711 = 2.60
	Cash ratio: cash/ current liabilities	Higher	$265,837/$311,117 = .85	$232,324/$326,711 = .71
	Quick ratio: (current assets – inventories)/ current liabilities	Higher	($951,073 – $61,675)/ $311,117 = 2.86	($848,823 – $61,251)/ $326,711 = 2.41
Activity	**Asset turnover:** sales/ total assets	Higher	$1,365,271/$1,284,761 = 1.06	$1,436,769/$1,211,454 = 1.19
	Current asset turnover: sales/current assets	Higher	$1,365,271/$951,073 = 1.44	$1,436,769/$848,823 = 1.69
	Inventory turnover: sales/inventory	Higher	$1,365,271/$61,675 = 22.1	$1,436,769/ $61,252 = 23.5
	Inventory days outstanding: 365/ inventory turnover	Lower	365/22.1 = 16.5	365/23.5 = 15.5
Leverage	**Debt to equity:** total liabilities/equity	Lower	$489,460/$795,301 = .62	$497,908/$713,546 = .70
	Current debt to equity: current liabilities/equity	Lower	$311,117/$795,301 = .39	$326,711/$713,456 = .46
	Interest coverage: earnings before interest and taxes/interest	Higher	$108,177/$4,556 = 23.7	$103,059/$11,275 = 9.14
Profitability	**Net profit margin:** net income/sales	Higher	$68,366/$1,365,271 = .05 or 5%	$61,006/$1,436,769 = .04 or 4%
	Gross margin: (sales – cost of goods sold)/ sales	Higher	($1,365,281 – $1,062,466)/$1,365,271 = .22 or 22%	($1,436,769 – $1,097,190)/$1,436,769 = .24 or 24%
	Operating margin: operating income/sales	Higher	$113,545/$1,365,271 = .08 or 8%	$112,571/$1,436,769 = .08 or 8%
	Return on assets: net income/total assets	Higher	$68,366/$1,284,761 = .05 or 5%	$61,066/$1,211,454 = .05 or 5%
	Return on equity: net income/equity	Higher	$68,366/$795,301 = .09 or 9%	$61,006/$713,546 = .09 or 9%

(figures are in thousands)

its sales. It is reasonable to ask if Orbital Sciences could do a better job at accelerating the collection of its receivables. Other financial tools focus on the credit worthiness of customers, something that would tell us if there is a concern with customers paying their obligations on time.

Financial ratio interpretation is an art and a science. We can interpret some ratios simply from their value. Current and quick ratios, for example, should be over 1.0. Other ratios should be compared to benchmark values within an industry. This is something that, in actual practice, should be part of the analysis. Various sources provide third-party financial benchmarks, including Hoovers (www.hoovers.com), Bizminer (www.bizminer.com), bizstats (www.bizstats.com), Factiva (www.factiva.com), and Mergent Online (www.mergentonline.com).

Comparisons should, whenever possible, be against companies within the same or similar industrial segment. If you know a company's NAICS or SIC code, then it is not too difficult to obtain specific industry reports and benchmarks. The North American Industry Classification System (NAICS) is the standard used by federal statistical agencies in classifying business establishments for the purpose of collecting, analyzing, and publishing statistical data related to the United States business economy.[4] An SIC code is a company's standard industrial classification code. The SIC code for Orbital Sciences, for example, is 3663 while its NAICS codes are 336415, 332993, and 334220.[5] This information is also useful when searching other potential suppliers within a specific industry group.

Keep in mind that our motivation for conducting ratio analyses is not the same as it is for financial investors. A financial investor conducts a ratio analysis to determine if a company represents a worthy investment. The investor would like to see, for example, high profit margins. Assuming we are not investing in the supplier, the supply manager conducts this analysis to gain insight into the financial risks associated with entering into a purchase contract. The supply manager likely views high margins as an indication that the supplier is making too much money at the buyer's expense!

Final Thoughts on Financial Ratio Analysis

Some words of caution are in order when calculating ratios. Data access and the reliability of that data is often a concern, particularly for private and foreign companies. Furthermore, ratio analysis is simply a tool that should be part of a broader supplier evaluation and selection process. Like measurement, ratio analysis is not a substitute for good management or sound decision making.

Care must also be taken when comparing companies from different industries. While the numerical values of some ratios are interpreted similarly across industries, the value of other ratios may not be as comparable. Some industries have different perspectives about the assumption of debt versus equity (i.e., stock), for example. When this is the case, an attempt should be made to identify industry benchmarks for comparisons.

Finally, financial statements, which are the basis for most ratios, represent only a point in time for a balance sheet or a relatively short period of time for income and cash flow statements. And, they are backward-looking with some degree of time lag before they are issued. Conversely, forward-looking financial statements are called *pro forma* statements. Pro forma is a Latin term meaning *for the sake of form*. It describes a method of calculating financial results in order to emphasize either current or projected figures. Pro forma financial statements are designed to reflect proposed changes, such as the expected effect of a merger or acquisition.[6]

Let's go back to Orbital Sciences. The company had a spectacular explosion of one of its unmanned rockets as it attempted to lift off from its launch pad in Virginia. And, the company has merged with the aerospace defense group of Alliant Technologies (also known as ATK). Any financial impact of major risk events or mergers would not yet be reflected in the company's financial statements. This is always a challenge when performing financial assessments. Current events are rarely factored into financial statements because of a time lag. Backward-looking financial statements would have provided minimal insights into the rocket explosion or merger.

Multiple time periods should be considered during a ratio analysis to identify possible trends. A supplier may appear less than ideal in terms of its financial statements currently but may have improved dramatically over the last several years. One advantage of financial statements is that many periods of data may be available for trend analysis and period-by-period comparisons.

SUPPLIER BANKRUPTCY PREDICTORS

The financial crisis of 2008 put a big spotlight on the need for supply managers to assess the financial health of suppliers, both during the selection process and during ongoing management. As a result, we continue to witness a growing number of third-party providers, offering sophisticated tools for assessing company health. Predicting supplier financial health is also something we can perform ourselves.

Whether we realize it or not, bankruptcy predictors are one of the earliest uses of predictive analytics. Predictive analytics is the practice of extracting information, usually from large data sets, to identify patterns to predict future outcomes and trends.

Predictive analytics applied anywhere is by no means perfect. The process provides a forecast or prediction of what might happen in the future with what we hope is an acceptable level of reliability. At times, the prediction may involve what will happen in the next few minutes or hours. This might be the case when smart sensors are modeling real-time data from high speed production processes. As the predictive model captures data that is trending in a nonrandom way, estimates about when the process ceases to be in control can be made. Or, a transportation company may have telematics units installed on its vehicles. These units monitor and transmit engine and other vehicle performance indicators in real time to identify anomalies that lead to performance problems. Predictive analytic tools often include what-if scenario analysis and risk assessment.[7]

The time frame when using predictive analytics for monitoring supplier financial health is longer than hours or days. Here, we may be looking out a year or two when evaluating the expected health of suppliers. A longer time frame allows actions to be taken to mitigate the risk of poor financial performance.

The "I Am Your Father" of Bankruptcy Predictors—the Altman Z-Score

Perhaps the most cited bankruptcy predictor is the Altman Z-Score. The Z-Score provides a well-established approach for assessing financial health that requires relatively few financial ratios. Edward Altman, an NYU Stern Finance Professor developed the Z-Score formula in 1967. In 2012, he released an updated version called the Altman Z-Score Plus for evaluating public and private companies, as well as manufacturing and nonmanufacturing companies in U.S. and non-U.S. companies.[8] The Z-Score combines a series of weighted ratios for public and private firms to predict the likelihood of financial bankruptcy. While sources sometimes differ on the predictive validity of the Z-Score, most users operate under the assumption that the Z-Score is almost 90 percent accurate in predicting bankruptcy one year in advance, and 75 percent accurate in predicting bankruptcy in two years.

The Z-Score has several features that make it popular. The first is its relative simplicity. Only four ratios are needed to calculate the Z-Score for private firms— and five ratios for public firms. The challenge with private companies is obtaining the data to populate the model. The second popular feature is that the Z-Score can be interpreted with a red, yellow, and green scoring format. A score in the red zone means a supplier is financially at risk; a yellow score indicates some area of financial concern; and a score in the green zone means the supplier is financially sound.

Supply chain managers will find that the Z-Score, as with other bankruptcy predictors, supports some worthwhile objectives. Perhaps foremost, the Z-Score is ideal as a screening tool at the earliest stages of supplier evaluation and selection. This assessment helps provide a *go* or *no-go* concerning whether to continue viewing that supplier as a possible sourcing option.

There are at least two other times after supplier selection when Z-Score calculations are valuable. The first is during the supplier risk assessment process. Better firms will update their suppliers' Z-Scores whenever financial information becomes available. And, this update should be shared with all relevant parties. This approach is useful for tracking financial changes over time. Supply chain risk managers should calculate supplier Z-Scores at least quarterly.

The Z-Score is also beneficial when rationalizing the supply base. Recall from Chapter 1 that rationalization means finding the right mix and number of something to maintain, usually for a specific item or commodity group. While technically speaking, supply base rationalization can result in adding suppliers, historically it has often resulted in suppliers being eliminated as buying companies pared down the number of suppliers they maintain. The Z-Score, along with other supplier performance indicators, provides guidance regarding which suppliers to keep or eliminate from the supplier selection pool or from the supply base.

Z-Score Formulas

The following are the Z-Score formulas for private and public firms. Notice that a company's total assets appear in three out of the four ratios for a private company—and four out of the five ratios for a public company. Clearly, total assets comprise an important part of this tool. Furthermore, the heaviest weight (3.3) for public companies is placed on the EBIT/Total Assets (EBIT is earnings before interest and taxes). For private companies, the Working Capital/Total Assets and the EBIT/Total Assets ratios are weighted heavily (6.56 and 6.72).

Private Company:

$$\text{Z-Score} = 6.56 \times \frac{\text{Working Capital}}{\text{Total Assets}} + 3.36 \times \frac{\text{Retained Earnings}}{\text{Total Assets}} + 6.72 \times \frac{\text{EBIT}}{\text{Total Assets}} + 1.05 \times \frac{\text{Net Worth}}{\text{Total Liabilities}}$$

Where:

Z-Score < 1.1	Red Zone—Supplier is financially at risk
Z-Score between 1.1 and 2.6	Yellow Zone—Some area of financial concern
Z-Score > 2.6	Green Zone—Supplier is financially sound

Public Company:

$$\text{Z-Score} = 1.2 \times \frac{\text{Working Capital}}{\text{Total Assets}} + 1.4 \times \frac{\text{Retained Earnings}}{\text{Total Assets}} + 3.3 \times \frac{\text{EBIT}}{\text{Total Assets}} +$$
$$0.6 \times \frac{\text{Net Worth}}{\text{Total Liabilities}} + 1.0 \times \frac{\text{Net Sales}}{\text{Total Assets}}$$

Where:

Z-Score < 1.8	Red Zone—Supplier is financially at risk and is likely to enter bankruptcy
Z-Score between 1.8 and 3.0	Yellow Zone—Some area of financial concern
Z-Score > 3.0	Green Zone—Supplier is financially sound

The required data for the Z-Score ratios appears in either the balance sheet or income statement. The cash flow statement is not required for this analysis. The following explains the financial location of each piece of data required for the Z-Score calculation.

- **Total assets:** This is a straightforward figure taken directly from the balance sheet. The assets section is the first section of the balance sheet.
- **Working capital:** Working capital is not a figure that appears on the balance or income statement. This figure requires a calculation on the user's part. From an accounting standpoint working capital represents the difference between current assets and current liabilities. These figures appear on the balance sheet. Be careful—this is the difference between current assets and current liabilities, not total assets and total liabilities. This figure could be negative if a company's current liabilities exceed its current assets.
- **Retained earnings:** Retained earnings are the net earnings that are not paid as dividends. Instead, these are earnings retained by the company for reinvestment or to pay debt. Retained earnings appear directly on the balance sheet within the *stockholders' equity* portion of the balance sheet. No additional calculation is required.
- **Earnings before interest and taxes:** This figure may require some calculation since EBIT is often not presented directly as a line item on the income statement. When this is the case, take the *net income* figure and add back *interest expenses* and *taxes*. Both of these figures will appear in the bottom portion on the income statement. Earnings before interest and taxes could be a negative calculation.
- **Net worth:** The net worth figure is presented as shareholders equity on the balance sheet for publicly traded companies.[9] It is possible, even likely, that you will not see a line item listed as *net worth*. Use the *total stockholders' equity* figure for net worth.
- **Total liability:** This figure appears between *total assets* and *total stockholders' equity* on the balance sheet. This item requires no additional calculation.
- **Net sales:** This is the top line of the income statement. It is likely this will not appear as *net sales* but rather as *sales*. Use the sales figure from the income statement.

The Z-Score Illustrated

It is beneficial to not only present the Z-Score formulas but also to illustrate their use. Table 3.4 provides three years of Z-Scores for Orbital Sciences, the company that was featured during the financial ratios section of this chapter. As with

Table 3.4 Three-year Z-Score analysis for Orbital Sciences

Z-Score Ratio	Current Year	Previous Year	Two Years Ago
1.2 × working capital*/total assets =	($951,073 – $311,117)/ $1,284,761 = .498 × 1.2 = **.6**	($848,823 – $326,711)/ $1,211,454 = .43 × 1.2 = **.52**	($755,399 – $339,349)/ $1,130,800 = .37 × 1.2 = **.44**
1.4 × retained earnings/total assets =	$208,797/$1,284,761 = .163 × 1.4 = **.23**	$140,431/$1,211,454 = 1.4 × 1.4 = **.16**	$79,425/$130,800 = .07 × 1.4 = **.1**
3.3 × EBIT*/ total assets =	$108,177/$1,284,761 = .084 × 3.3 = **.28**	$103,059/$1,211,454 = .09 × 3.3 = **.3**	$99,129/$1,130,800 = .09 × 3.3 = **.29**
.6 × net worth*/ total liabilities =	$795,301/$489,460 = 1.62 × .6 = **.97**	$713,546/$497,908 = 1.43 × **.86**	$643,279/$487,521 = 1.32 × .6 = **.79**
1.0 × net sales/ total assets =	$1,365,271/$1,284,761 = 1.06 × 1.0 = 1.06	$1,436,769/$1,211,454 = 1.18 × 1.0 = **1.19**	$1,345,923/$1,130,800 = 1.19 × 1.0 = **1.19**
Z-Score =	**3.14**	**3.03**	**2.81**

*Working capital = current assets – current liabilities
*EBIT = earnings before interest and taxes
*Net worth = stockholders' equity

financial ratio analysis, Z-Score analysis benefits from using more than one time period.

Perhaps the first thing to notice is the improvement in the company's Z-Score over this three-year period. Overall, we should conclude the company is not in immediate danger of financial insolvency since its Z-Score is over 3.0. The company's Z-Score trend has been one of improvement.

Why has the Z-Score value changed from the current period compared with two years ago? The largest, but not the only effect on the score is due to changes in the company's retained earnings. As mentioned, retained earnings are earnings retained by the company for reinvestment or to pay debt. Retained earnings also affect the company's net worth (i.e., stockholders' equity) since they reside in that part of the balance sheet. Overall, this analysis reveals no dangerous trends or causes for alarm at this point in time (but not losing sight of the risk issues raised earlier about this company). Even for financially strong companies it would be a mistake not to update the Z-Score whenever new data become available. Otherwise, the risks associated with complacency will likely set in.

Final Z-Score Thoughts

Keep in mind that the Z-Score is a financial risk indicator; it does not tell us if the supplier has adequate capacity or can meet quality or delivery requirements. It also tells us nothing about a supplier's labor relations, how well that supplier manages its supply chain, or its design capabilities. And, as mentioned, it is backward-looking with a time lag. The bottom line is—bankruptcy predictors are a necessary, but not sufficient, indicator of a supplier's overall qualifications. It is but one piece of a giant puzzle.

It would be a mistake to place undying faith in the Z-Score (or any bankruptcy predictor, for that matter), just as it is a mistake to rely on a single indicator for almost anything. Some observers argue strongly that the Z-Score has limitations. It was originally developed for industrial companies (i.e., manufacturers) and not for industries such as financial services, utilities, or hospitality. Furthermore, a study by Shumway purports to show that some of the variables included in the Z-Score are no longer predictive of bankruptcy.[10] He and other researchers claim to have developed bankruptcy models that exceed the effectiveness of the Altman model. And, the Z-Score might not be valid when a shock hits the financial system. After the financial meltdown of 2008, any models that were backward-looking, which includes most financial statements and forecasting models, became questionable in terms of validity.

In response to these concerns, Dr. Altman introduced Z-Score Plus in 2012, in conjunction with Business Compass. Z-Score Plus covers non-U.S. companies, including those in emerging markets such as China; nonmanufacturing firms, both public and private (Z"-Score); and privately-held industrial manufacturing firms (Z'-Score). Enhancements include the assignment of a 1- to 10-year probability of default; a percentile ranking likelihood of bankruptcy by industrial category; and a bond-rating equivalent (BRE) for each company that compares its most recent Z, Z' or Z"-Score with the average score for appropriate bond rating classes from AAA to D (default).[11]

The Z-Score is ingrained as a bankruptcy predictor in the minds of practitioners and academics. Relying on a single bankruptcy predictor, however, is probably a risky strategy. You would not go to a doctor for a physical and then have only your temperature taken. Or, if you had a serious illness you might not want to rely only on one opinion. Combining the Z-Score technique with other third-party bankruptcy indicators and a full set of financial ratios will help to reach a more enlightened conclusion. Having more than one set of eyes looking at the same situation is a good thing.

Other Third-party Supplier Bankruptcy Predictors

Not every company has the resources or expertise to evaluate hundreds, or even thousands, of suppliers from a financial risk perspective. It is also safe to assume that financial data about suppliers will not always be easy to obtain. For these reasons, buyers often rely on third-party assessments to support their efforts. The following discusses two external services that provide predictive ratings of financial health—Rapid Ratings and Dun & Bradstreet. (The author has no connection to either of these companies.)

Rapid Ratings (www.rapidratings.com) provides a multipart report that provides extensive financial data and analysis of companies. The first part of the output report is a detailed discussion of a company's Financial Health Rating (FHR). The FHR, which is a number that ranges from 0 to 100, includes multiple years of trend data for comparison purposes.

The second part of a Rapid Ratings report contains six sections. These sections include (1) an executive summary, (2) a return on capital employed (ROCE) analysis, (3) FHR history and performance category scores, (4) areas of strength and weakness in relation to other sector participants, (5) the company's balance sheet, and (6) the company's income statement. This represents not only data in the form of financial statements, but also value-added analysis using proprietary company algorithms.

Dun & Bradstreet (www.dnb.com) has built its reputation on collecting and disseminating information about companies. Over time it has progressively figured out new ways to leverage the data that it collects. The company now offers a suite of risk management products under a category called *Supplier Risk Manager.* Two analytic tools are available that use predictive scores, including the Supplier Stability Indicator (SSI), a predictor of near term (90-120 days) financial and operational stability, and the Supplier Evaluation Risk (SER) Rating, which predicts the likelihood that a company will obtain legal relief from creditors or cease operations without paying creditors in full over the next 12 months. These reports are especially useful when evaluating private suppliers. They are also useful as part of a suite of assessments that use data from multiple sources. When relying on third-party data for supplier financial assessments, a buying company is essentially outsourcing this analysis to companies that specialize in this type of work.

QUALITATIVE INDICATORS

Not all supplier financial assessment is quantitative. In fact, the best approach will feature a combination of ratio analyses, bankruptcy predictors, and qualitative assessments. While ratio analysis is a powerful tool, the technique still relies on data that are updated infrequently, difficult to obtain, or sometimes unreliable. At times, clues in the marketplace become available that cause us to wonder if perhaps a deeper investigation is in order. The following presents a checklist that might provide hints that a supplier is struggling from a financial perspective:[12]

- A supplier is overly dependent on sales to customers in a single industry; on sales to customers in depressed or declining industries; or on customers who are financially distressed
- A supplier cannot meet the agreed-upon lead times because of problems with placing purchase orders for materials to its suppliers

- A supplier is shipping early due to a lack of business
- A key executive at a supplier becomes ill
- A supplier hints at or announces facility shutdowns, closings, and/or layoffs
- A supplier has reduced its investment in research and development (R&D), IT, equipment, or resources
- Unusual turnover occurs at the executive level
- A supplier's payable's period is lengthening
- A supplier's quality is deteriorating
- Additional discounts are offered to customers for early payment or payments are required in advance
- A supplier is restating negative financial reports and projections
- A supplier's product is labor intensive, requiring large payrolls
- A supplier has absorbed up-front research and development and tooling costs on new products that are delayed in getting to the marketplace
- An unusual amount of company stock is being sold by executives
- A supplier becomes the subject of an investigation due to accounting irregularities
- Rumors of problems begin to emerge on the street

While qualitative indicators are not modeled quantitatively, they can still provide valuable insights. The challenge becomes one of obtaining intelligence in a systematic way rather than receiving it on an ad-hoc basis. One way to make qualitative assessments more systematic is to establish Internet alerts that forward information as soon as it enters the public domain. Of course, the risk always exists of information overload. Another method is to rely on distributors and other channel members, such as sales personnel, to pass along information. Like forecasting, which benefits from a combination of quantitative and qualitative approaches, assessments of supplier financial health should also benefit from a combination of quantitative and qualitative approaches.

ROUGH CUT CAPACITY ANALYSIS

Another supplier selection risk that buyers should consider, besides financial distress, involves supplier capacity. Here we will employ a technique developed by the author called *rough cut capacity analysis*. It is called *rough cut* because precision is not our primary goal here. Close enough is good enough—something we should never say when pursuing Six Sigma initiatives.

A rough cut capacity analysis relies on three important pieces of information. While the technique is straightforward, obtaining the data may not be. The following steps are required to arrive at a rough cut capacity figure:

Step 1:   Divide total sales by the capacity utilization rate to identify what one point of capacity generates in sales.

Step 2:   Multiply what one point of capacity is worth in dollars (or whatever currency you are dealing with) by the points available. This indicates what the total capacity available could generate in new sales.

Step 3:   Divide total capacity available in dollars by the quoted unit price to arrive at capacity available in units.

Step 4:   Compare available capacity to needed capacity.

Table 3.5 presents financial and capacity utilization data for two suppliers. This table also explains step-by-step, how to arrive at a rough cut estimate. As the

Table 3.5 Rough cut capacity analysis

	Windra	Specialty Features	Devlin Industries
Quoted price per pound	$12.20	$11.98	$12.06
Current installed capacity utilization	97%	98%	95%
Current annual sales	$6,500,000	$5,500,000	$12,355,000

For our purposes here, current installed capacity utilization indicates that portion of the supplier's production capacity that is currently utilized for the production of the item of interest. For example, if current installed capacity is 98%, then this supplier is utilizing 98% of its normal production capacity and therefore has 2% of its capacity available for new business. This does not indicate how many available pounds this represents.

Step 1: Divide total sales by the capacity utilization rate to identify what one point of capacity generates in sales.

Windra: ($6,500,000/97) = $67,010
Specialty Features: ($5,500,000/98) = $56,122
Devlin Industries: ($12,355,000/95) = $130,052

Step 2: Multiply what one point of capacity is worth in dollars (or whatever currency you are dealing with) by the points available. This indicates what the total capacity available could generate in new sales.

Windra: $67,010 × 3* = $201,030
Specialty Features: $56,122 × 2 = 112,244
Devlin Industries: $130,052/5 = $650,260

Step 3: Divide total capacity available in dollars by the quoted unit price to arrive at capacity available in units.

Windra: $201,030/$12.20 = 16,478 pounds of capacity available
Specialty Features: 112,244/$11.98 = 9,369 pounds
Devlin Industries: $650,260/$12.06 = 53,919 pounds

Step 4: Compare available capacity to needed capacity.

* Since 97% of capacity is being used, 3 capacity points are available.

analysis reveals, we should have concerns whether the supplier has enough capacity to satisfy our requirements.

Several important assumptions underlie this technique. First, this technique assumes a supplier will not suddenly drop its other customers to make additional capacity available for a prospective customer. Second, it assumes a supplier is not planning to alter its capacity capability in the short term and that it operates in a steady state. And third, it assumes that any available capacity is not being pursued at that moment by another customer.

Even with these assumptions, along with the *roughness* of this technique, attention should be given as to whether a supplier can satisfy a purchase requirement. This analysis will open the door for a serious conversation about a supplier's capacity availability, if a buyer has doubts. If we simply ask a supplier if it has the capacity to satisfy our needs, 99% of the time the answer will be *yes*. While the slogan at one supplier is, "We would rather turn you down than let you down," most suppliers do not buy into that slogan. While trust is nice, there is something to be said about verification.

CONCLUDING THOUGHTS

The evaluation and selection of suppliers is a critical business process. Errors made here can have long and painful consequences. Performing this process correctly means conducting assessments that combine financial ratio analysis, bankruptcy predictors, and qualitative intelligence gathering to ensure that, at least from a financial perspective, a supplier does not arrive with some unpleasant surprises. As economic conditions improve, supply managers must also avoid the tendency to become complacent by focusing less on this important part of the selection process. While complacency is not one of the seven deadly sins, from a business perspective it probably should be.

REFERENCES

1. www.investopedia.com/terms/l/leverageratio.asp.
2. From www.money-zine.com/investing/investing/market-ratios/.
3. From www.wikipedia.com, Orbital Sciences Corporation, founded in 1982, is an American-based company specializing in the design, manufacture, and launch of small- and medium-class space and rocket systems for commercial, military, and civil government customers. The company's rockets include the Antares, Minotaur, Pegasus II, and Minotaur-C.

4. www.census.gov.
5. www.zoominfo.com.
6. www.investopedia.com/terms/p/proforma.asp.
7. Adapted from www.webopedia.com/TERM/P/predictive_analytics.html.
8. www.investopedia.com/terms/a/altman.asp.
9. www.investopedia.com/terms/s/shareholdersequity.asp.
10. http://www-personal.umich.edu/~shumway/papers.dir/forcbank.pdf.
11. http://www.stern.nyu.edu/experience-stern/faculty-research/altman-launches-zscore-plus.
12. "10 Warning Signs of a Supplier in Peril." *Industry Week*, April 2009: 38.

4

EVALUATING AND SELECTING SUPPLIERS— APPLYING FINANCIAL TECHNIQUES

As with each section of this book, the third chapter in each section contains exercises pertaining to the financial tools, techniques, and concepts presented in the previous chapter. This chapter contains hands-on exercises for conducting financial ratio analyses, calculating bankruptcy predictors, and calculating a rough cut capacity analysis using financial data.

CALCULATING FINANCIAL RATIOS

The exercises in this section require you to calculate and interpret financial ratios using a set of financial statements.

Financial Ratios Exercise A: Carpenter Technologies

Carpenter Technologies (NYSE: CRS), headquartered in Reading, Pennsylvania, develops, manufactures, and distributes cast/wrought iron and powder metal stainless steels and specialty alloys. Assume you are part of a commodity team that is evaluating suppliers for a future contract for the kinds of items that Carpenter supplies. Using the following financial statements and ratio template (see Tables 4.1, 4.2, and 4.3), perform a three-year financial analysis on Carpenter.

Table 4.1   Carpenter Technologies balance sheet

Period Ending	June 30, Current Year	June 30, Previous Year	June 30, Two Years Ago
			All numbers in thousands
Assets			
Current Assets			
Cash and Cash Equivalents	120,000	257,500	211,000
Short-term Investments	—	—	—
Net Receivables	339,600	344,700	364,800
Inventory	699,200	659,200	642,000
Other Current Assets	35,700	20,100	31,900
Total Current Assets	**1,194,500**	**1,281,500**	**1,249,700**
Property, Plant, and Equipment	1,407,000	1,168,400	924,600
Goodwill	257,700	257,700	260,500
Intangible Assets	80,600	95,000	109,900
Other Assets	117,700	80,300	83,100
Total Assets	**3,057,500**	**2,882,900**	**2,627,800**
Liabilities			
Current Liabilities			
Accounts Payable	430,600	421,200	453,200
Short/Current Long-term Debt	—	—	101,000
Total Current Liabilities	**430,600**	**421,200**	**554,200**
Long-term Debt	604,300	604,200	305,900
Other Liabilities	407,600	481,100	623,200
Deferred Long-term Liability Charges	110,700	73,300	31,400
Minority Interest	—	—	9,300
Total Liabilities	**1,553,200**	**1,579,800**	**1,524,000**
Stockholders' Equity			
Common Stock	275,800	274,600	274,000
Retained Earnings	1,311,600	1,217,300	1,109,600
Treasury Stock	(101,400)	(107,500)	(120,000)
Capital Surplus	263,500	254,400	252,700
Other Stockholder Equity	(245,200)	(335,700)	(412,500)
Total Stockholder Equity	**1,504,300**	**1,303,100**	**1,103,800**
Total Liabilities and Stockholders' Equity	**3,057,500**	**950,400**	**733,400**

Adapted from public domain information retrieved at finance.yahoo.com.

Table 4.2 Carpenter Technologies income statement

	All numbers in thousands		
Period Ending	June 30, Current Year	June 30, Previous Year	June 30, Two Years Ago
Total Revenue	**2,173,000**	**2,271,700**	**2,028,700**
Cost of Revenue	1,774,100	1,838,200	1,637,700
Gross Profit	**398,900**	**433,500**	**391,000**
Operating Expenses			
Selling, General ,and Administrative Expenses	186,900	200,800	169,200
Non-recurring	—	—	11,700
Operating Income or Loss	**212,000**	**232,700**	**210,100**
Total Other Income/Expenses Net	1,400	5,100	2,300
Earnings before Interest and Taxes	213,400	237,800	212,400
Interest Expense	17,000	21,000	23,800
Income before Tax	196,400	216,800	188,600
Income Tax Expense	63,600	70,300	67,000
Minority Interest	—	(400)	(400)
Net Income from Continuing Ops	132,800	146,100	121,200
Net Income	**132,800**	**146,100**	**121,200**

Adapted from public domain information retrieved at finance.yahoo.com.

Table 4.3　Financial ratios analysis template: Carpenter Technologies

	Ratio	Preferred Direction	Current Year Ratio Value	Previous Year Ratio Value	Two Years Ago Ratio Value
Liquidity	**Current ratio**: current assets – current liabilities	Higher			
	Cash ratio: cash/ current liabilities	Higher			
	Quick ratio: (current assets – inventories)/ current liabilities	Higher			
Activity	**Asset turnover**: sales/ total assets	Higher			
	Current asset turnover: sales/current assets	Higher			
	Inventory turnover: sales/inventory	Higher			
	Inventory days outstanding: 365/ inventory turnover	Lower			
Leverage	**Debt to equity**: total liabilities/equity	Lower			
	Current debt to equity: current liabilities/equity	Lower			
	Interest coverage: earnings before interest and taxes/interest	Higher			
Profitability	**Net profit margin**: net income/sales	Higher			
	Gross margin: (sales – cost of goods sold)/sales	Higher			
	Operating margin: operating income/sales	Higher			
	Return on assets: net income/total assets	Higher			
	Return on equity: net income/equity	Higher			

Using the information obtained from your ratio analysis, prepare a financial report about this supplier.

Financial Ratios Analysis Exercise B: Breeze-Eastern Corporation

A major aerospace defense contractor is considering a modification to its heavy-lift helicopter. This modification will involve adding a new feature to the product; specifically, a rescue hoist and cargo hook system. One supplier under consideration for this contract is Breeze-Eastern Corporation (NYSE: BZC) of Whippany, New Jersey. Breeze-Eastern designs, develops, manufactures, sells, and services engineered equipment for specialty aerospace and defense applications. It is a designer, manufacturer, service provider, and supplier of rescue hoists and cargo hook systems. Breeze-Eastern also manufactures weapons handling systems, cargo winches, and tie-down equipment. These products are sold primarily to military and civilian agencies and aerospace contractors.

Using the following financial statements and ratio template (see Tables 4.4, 4.5, and 4.6), perform a three-year financial analysis for Breeze-Eastern.

Table 4.4   Breeze-Eastern balance sheet

	All numbers in thousands		
Period Ending	March 31, Current Year	March 31, One Year Ago	March 31, Two Years Ago
Assets			
Current Assets			
Cash and Cash Equivalents	6,021	6,688	12,683
Net Receivables	28,799	22,712	28,264
Inventory	18,909	17,790	13,974
Other Current Assets	1,868	1,506	759
Total Current Assets	**55,597**	**48,696**	**55,680**
Long-term Investments	—	—	—
Property, Plant, and Equipment	10,132	10,486	11,420
Goodwill	402	402	402
Other Assets	9,465	9,540	7,782
Deferred Long-term Asset Charges	4,197	4,289	4,567
Total Assets	**79,793**	**73,413**	**79,851**
Liabilities			
Current Liabilities			
Accounts Payable	10,675	9,592	9,089
Short/Current Long-term Debt	—	—	2,464
Other Current Liabilities	5,214	5,070	4,979
Total Current Liabilities	**15,889**	**14,662**	**16,532**
Long-term Debt	—	—	8,215
Other Liabilities	13,420	15,679	16,952
Total Liabilities	**29,309**	**30,341**	**41,699**
Stockholders' Equity			
Common Stock	101	100	99
Retained Earnings	(41,344)	(46,985)	(51,061)
Treasury Stock	(6,983)	(6,972)	(6,831)
Capital Surplus	98,707	97,113	96,019
Other Stockholder Equity	3	(184)	(74)
Total Stockholder Equity	**50,484**	**43,072**	**38,152**
Total Liabilities and Stockholders' Equity	**79,793**	**73,413**	**79,851**

Adapted from public domain information retrieved at finance.yahoo.com.

Table 4.5 Breeze-Eastern income statement

			All numbers are in thousands
Period Ending	March 31, Current Year	March 31, Previous Year	March 31, Two Years Ago
Total Revenue	**85,933**	**79,956**	**84,942**
Cost of Revenue	54,802	47,143	49,728
Gross Profit	**31,131**	**32,813**	**35,214**
Operating Expenses			
Research Development	8,162	9,377	12,531
Selling, General, and Administrative Expenses	13,880	15,246	15,661
Operating Income or Loss	**9,089**	**8,190**	**7,022**
Income from Continuing Operations			
Total Other Income/Expenses Net	(89)	(93)	(109)
Earnings before Interest and Taxes	9,000	8,097	6,913
Interest Expense	49	227	396
Income before Tax	8,951	7,870	6,517
Income Tax Expense	3,310	3,794	2,741
Net Income from Continuing Ops	5,641	4,076	3,776
Net Income	**5,641**	**4,076**	**3,776**

Adapted from public domain information retrieved at finance.yahoo.com.

Table 4.6 Financial ratios analysis template: Breeze-Eastern Corporation

	Ratio	Preferred Direction	Current Year Ratio Value	Previous Year Ratio Value	Two Years Ago Ratio Value
Liquidity	**Current ratio**: current assets – current liabilities	Higher			
	Cash ratio: cash/ current liabilities	Higher			
	Quick ratio: (current assets – inventories)/ current liabilities	Higher			
Activity	**Asset turnover**: sales/ total assets	Higher			
	Current asset turnover: sales/current assets	Higher			
	Inventory turnover: sales/inventory	Higher			
	Inventory days outstanding: 365/ inventory turnover	Lower			

Table 4.6   Continues

	Ratio	Preferred Direction	Current Year Ratio Value	Previous Year Ratio Value	Two Years Ago Ratio Value
Leverage	**Debt to equity**: total liabilities/equity	Lower			
	Current debt to equity: current liabilities/equity	Lower			
	Interest coverage: earnings before interest and taxes/interest	Higher			
Profitability	**Net profit margin**: net income/sales	Higher			
	Gross margin: (sales – cost of goods sold)/sales	Higher			
	Operating margin: operating income/sales	Higher			
	Return on assets: net income/total assets	Higher			
	Return on equity: net income/equity	Higher			

Using the information from your ratio analysis, prepare a financial report about this supplier.

CALCULATING BANKRUPTCY PREDICTORS

A buyer is evaluating three suppliers for a longer term purchase contract. These suppliers will be asked to provide a specialty chemical to support the production of an important new product. Given the following financial data (see Tables 4.7 and 4.8), answer the questions that appear at the end of the financial statements.

Table 4.7 Selected supplier balance sheet data (U.S. $ in millions) for the most recent year end

	Crest Materials	Facet Chemicals	MMX, Inc.
Assets			
Current Assets			
Cash	$95.9	$35	$54.3
Marketable Securities	$122.5	$9	$27.7
Accounts Receivable	$889	$45	$174.5
Inventories	$1,057.7	$75	$135.4
Total Current Assets	$2,165.1	$164	$391.9
Property, Plant, and Equipment	$2,472.9	$146	$507.5
Goodwill	$300	$40	$80.4
Total Assets	**$4,938**	**$350**	**$979.8**
Liabilities			
Current Liabilities			
Current Portion of Long-term Debt	$525.5	$11	$35
Accounts Payable	$525.9	$75	$125
Taxes Due on Income	$245	$23	$48
Accrued Payroll and Employee Benefits	$484.2	$13.5	$139
Total current liabilities	$1,780.6	$122.5	$347
Long-term Debt	$1,243.5	$55	$165
Total Liabilities	**$3,024.1**	**$177.5**	**$512**
Shareholders' Equity			
Common stock	$300	$30	$57.8
Retained earnings	$1,613.9	$142.5	$410
Total Shareholders' Equity	$1,913.9	$172.5	$467.8
Total Liabilities and Shareholders' Equity	$4,938	$350	$979.8

Table 4.8 Statement of income data (U.S. $ in millions) for the most recent year

	Crest Materials	Facet Chemicals	MMX, Inc.
Net Sales	$6,500	$550	$1,355
Cost of Goods Sold	$5,325	$407.5	$948.5
Gross Profit	$1,175	$142.5	$406.5
Selling, General, and Administrative Expenses	$475	$65	$250
Operating Profit	$700	$77.5	$156.5
Other Income/Expenses	$25	$5	$12
Earnings before Interest and Taxes	$725	$82.5	$168.5
Interest Expense	$300	$12	$55
Income Tax Expense	$100	$28	$45
Net Income	$325	$42.5	$68.5

Calculate and Interpret the Z-Score for Each Supplier:

Supplier Name	Crest Materials
Working capital/total assets × 1.2 =	_____
Retained earnings/total assets × 1.4 =	_____
EBIT/total assets × 3.3 =	_____
Net worth/total liabilities × .6 =	_____
Net sales/total assets × 1.0 =	_____
Z-Score =	_____

Interpretation of the supplier's Z-Score:

Supplier Name:	Facet Chemicals
Working capital/total assets × 1.2 =	_____
Retained earnings/total assets × 1.4 =	_____
EBIT/total assets × 3.3 =	_____
Net worth/total liabilities × .6 =	_____
Net sales/total assets × 1.0 =	_____
Z-Score =	_____

Interpretation of the supplier's Z-Score:

Supplier Name:	MMX, Inc.
Working capital/total assets × 1.2 =	_____
Retained earnings/total assets × 1.4 =	_____
EBIT/total assets × 3.3 =	_____
Net worth/total liabilities × .6 =	_____
Net sales/total assets × 1.0 =	_____
Z-Score =	_____

Interpretation of the supplier's Z-Score:

ESTIMATING SUPPLIER CAPACITY

A pharmaceutical company forecasts that it will require 20,000,000 pounds of a raw material next year to support a new product introduction. Given the following data (see Table 4.9), calculate a rough estimate of the amount of capacity in pounds available from these three suppliers. What do you conclude about each supplier's ability to satisfy next year's demand requirement?

Table 4.9

	Foster Technologies	Andrea Materials	Focus Industries
Quoted price per pound	$4.55	$5.45	$5.05
Current installed capacity utilization	99%	94%	95%
Current annual sales	$6,500,000,000	$550,000,000	$1,355,000,000

For our purposes here, current installed capacity utilization indicates that portion of the supplier's production capacity that is currently utilized for the production of chemicals. For example, if current installed capacity is 98%, then this supplier is utilizing 98% of its normal production capacity and therefore has 2% of its capacity available for new business. This does not indicate how many available pounds this represents.

Calculations:

A company forecasts that it will require 10,000 units of a steering mechanism next year to support its new line of riding lawn equipment. Given the following data (see Table 4.10), calculate a rough estimate of the amount of capacity in units available from these suppliers. What do you conclude about each supplier's ability to satisfy next year's demand requirement?

Table 4.10

	Drive-Train Systems	Helix, Inc.	Xenox Applications
Quoted price per unit	$42.50	$40.78	$41.33
Current installed capacity utilization	97%	92%	94%
Current annual sales	$9,500,000	$6,250,000	$8,266,000

For our purposes here, current installed capacity utilization indicates that portion of the supplier's production capacity that is currently utilized for the production of chemicals. For example, if current installed capacity is 98%, then this supplier is utilizing 98% of its normal production capacity and therefore has 2% of its capacity available for new business. This does not indicate how many available units this represents.

Calculations:

STEEL CORP CASE DISCUSSION QUESTIONS

The following questions apply to the Steel Corp case presented at the end of Chapter 2.

1. What is driving the need to manage assets more effectively at the railroads?
2. The return on net asset (RONA) measure is a superordinate measure. What is a superordinate measure? What are some other examples of superordinate measures?
3. How might different functional groups contribute to various parts of the formula?
4. What is the process used at Steel Corp to coordinate the various initiatives that may affect the RONA?
5. Even though the railroads receive most of their revenue from their parent corporation, how can the railroads grow the numerator of the RONA equation?
6. What is consignment? How does it affect the RONA equation financially?
7. What is systems contracting? What was the previous model for contracting in this industry?
8. Why might a supplier resist systems contracting as it is presented in this case? Why might a supplier want to enter into a systems contract as presented in this case?
9. What kind of negotiating factors or issues should Steel Corp consider when developing a systems contract?
10. How do the railroads forecast their annual requirements? What role does the purchasing group play in this process?
11. How are internal users at the individual railroads involved in the systems contracting process?
12. What factors do you think are most critical to the success of this process at Steel Corp?
13. What are the advantages of a centrally led purchasing group (versus decentralized purchase decision making at each railroad)?
14. What benefits have the railroads realized due to systems contracting?

15. How do suppliers know when and what to invoice the railroads? How has the system-contracting approach improved or streamlined the payments process?

16. What future enhancements besides those mentioned in the case might the railroads pursue?

5

BEST PRACTICES IN SUPPLIER MANAGEMENT AND DEVELOPMENT

The first section of this book stressed the importance of the supplier evaluation and selection process. And, it is safe to say that few knowledgeable observers would argue against the importance of this process. Few observers would also argue against the importance of what comes after. The selection of a supplier, which represents the end of one process, is also the start of something very special. That something special is the commencement of the buyer-seller relationship, a relationship that could continue for many years, possibly even decades. Never forget that a natural order of events takes place here. Supplier evaluation and selection comes first, followed by supplier management and development.

This chapter begins the section of the book that shifts our thinking from supplier evaluation and selection to supplier management and development. Specifically, the chapter provides an overview of supplier relationship management before moving to the main focus of the chapter—supplier performance development.

MANAGING SUPPLIER RELATIONSHIPS

One of the most important responsibilities of supply managers is the cultivation and nurturing of supply chain relationships. And while any discussion of relationships sounds likes we should be sharing our feelings with Dr. Phil, this seemingly intangible area can lead to very tangible benefits. Supplier relationship management can result in favorable treatment from suppliers, access to supplier-developed innovation, and a heightened willingness of suppliers to make investments that only benefit certain customers.

Supplier relationship management (SRM) is a broad-based management methodology describing how a firm interacts with its supply base. It is a philosophy about supplier relationships that is shared throughout an organization by purchasing and supply management professionals. How a buying company manages its suppliers can be a source of competitive advantage.

When managing suppliers, it is important to appreciate that not all supplier relationships are equally important. Knowing when, where, and how to pursue a specific kind of relationship with a supplier is an important part of the procurement process. Figure 5.1 presents a continuum of supplier relationships.

Counter-productive relationships, also called antagonistic relationships, feature the parties working against each other's interests. In addition, neither party feels a need to assume responsibility for what transpires. This scenario clearly is detrimental to the longer-term success of a relationship. While this type of relationship is not recommended, they do occur. A buyer who sues a supplier to prevent a price increase that the buyer contends violates a contractual agreement is a clue that a relationship is moving toward counter-productive.

Competitive relationships—also known as distributive, win-lose, or adversarial relationships—feature supply chain members competing over a fixed amount of value (which is the definition of a win-lose relationship). This contrasts with working jointly to create new opportunities that lead to new value for the parties (which defines win-win). For many items the relationship with suppliers should be competitive. Beyond the arms-length activities taking place, few benefits will

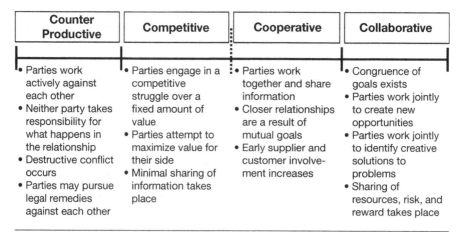

Counter Productive	Competitive	Cooperative	Collaborative
• Parties work actively against each other • Neither party takes responsibility for what happens in the relationship • Destructive conflict occurs • Parties may pursue legal remedies against each other	• Parties engage in a competitive struggle over a fixed amount of value • Parties attempt to maximize value for their side • Minimal sharing of information takes place	• Parties work together and share information • Closer relationships are a result of mutual goals • Early supplier and customer involvement increases	• Congruence of goals exists • Parties work jointly to create new opportunities • Parties work jointly to identify creative solutions to problems • Sharing of resources, risk, and reward takes place

Figure 5.1 Continuum of supplier relationships

result from a closer relationship. While a majority of a buying firm's relationships should be competitive, these relationships usually do not comprise a majority of total purchase dollars.

Cooperative relationships, also referred to as integrative relationships, recognize the value of working jointly on a common business-related assignment or purpose. These relationships feature open sharing of information. They are most often associated with suppliers who are expected to be longer-term members of a supply base.

Cooperative relationships with suppliers are often formalized through longer term contracts that lead to discussions about how to improve cost, quality, delivery, packaging, inventory management, product innovation, and service, all factors that can affect performance. These relationships may feature, for example, early supplier involvement during product development.

Collaborative relationships, sometimes called creative relationships, involve a limited number of suppliers that provide items or services that are essential or unique to a firm's success. A willingness to work jointly to identify better ways to compete in a global marketplace is characteristic of a collaborative relationship.

These relationships, which should be relatively few, represent the most intensive relationship possible between a buyer and seller. They feature executive-to-executive interaction, joint strategy development sessions, and a sharing of resources and risk. Supply chain alliances and partnerships, for example, are collaborative by design. The parties ideally recognize that the value they receive would be far less than if collaboration did not exist.

Cooperative and collaborative relationships should, by definition, be win-win. This means the parties, by working together, can increase the amount of value derived from a relationship. Value is not considered a fixed commodity.

The Role of Trust

Numerous studies have concluded that trust is a major predictor of relationship success. In fact, it is safe to say that the most important factor that affects the success of a buyer-seller relationship is trust. Trust refers to the belief in the character, ability, strength, or truth of the parties in a relationship. While different models of trust exist, a simplified model views trust in terms of two primary dimensions: character-based trust and competency-based trust.

Character-based trust refers to ethics, honesty, and truth of a participant. Relationships that feature a lack of trust are characterized by lengthier contracts, expensive and time-consuming oversight (often by a legal group), and a reluctance to share information. Conversely, the characteristics of trust-based relationships are the opposite of relationships that lack trust. Trust-based relationships are more efficient.

Trust is not automatic in a buyer-seller relationship. It evolves over time and is demonstrated by actions rather than words. To that end, it makes sense for both buyers and sellers to engage in trust-building actions and activities. Examples of trust-building actions and activities include:

- Open and frequent communication across organizations, particularly face-to-face
- Co-locating personnel, which promotes frequent and open communication (frequency of communication is a predictor of trust)
- Following through on promises and commitments
- Acting legally and ethically in all dealings
- Acting on the behalf of the relationship rather than self-interests
- Publicizing success stories and personal narratives, especially those that enhance the standing of the other party
- Treating information and data gathered within the relationship as confidential

Importance of Supplier Relationship Managers

A supplier satisfaction study involving 300 suppliers revealed that over 90 percent of suppliers agree strongly that it is critical for the customer's personnel, whom they deal with on a regular basis, to be knowledgeable about their product, processes, business, and industry.[1] Almost all suppliers also indicated they have assigned an individual at their organization to be the primary contact with their customer. And, almost every supplier indicated they are aware of a specific individual assigned by the customer to manage the buyer-seller relationship. Suppliers overwhelmingly agree that it is important to interact regularly with their customers through specific and knowledgeable individuals. They also agree about the importance of face-to-face interactions with these individuals.

When tasking specific individuals with the responsibility of working with a supplier, it is not sufficient to simply assign an individual with that responsibility. In the eyes of suppliers, that individual must also be highly qualified. Without question, relationship management demands effective relationship managers.

DEVELOPING SUPPLIER PERFORMANCE CAPABILITIES

A key component of supplier management is supplier development. Supplier development represents any activity or effort on the part of a buying firm to improve the performance of its suppliers. At times, although rare, we may also witness a supplier working to improve the performance of its customers. A supplier engages in customer development because it understands the concept of *co-destiny*. That concept maintains that what happens to one party affects the other, and vice versa. So, if a customer becomes healthier and grows its business, the supplier grows along with it.

The logic behind supplier development is actually quite clear. Most companies have reduced the size of their supply base dramatically, at least at the tier-one level, compared with historical levels. While at one time the practice was to work with many suppliers, the prevailing view today is to work with a smaller supply base in terms of numbers. It is easier to manage and engage in value-creating activities with 100 primary suppliers rather than 2,000 suppliers. Many remaining suppliers are now on longer term rather than short-term contracts—making supplier switching that much harder.

With fewer remaining suppliers, many of which have longer term contracts, supply chain improvement will occur primarily through working with existing suppliers rather than large-scale supplier switching. Engaging in supplier development with existing suppliers is a logical way to pursue continuous improvement. And, as followers of quality management understand well, the need for continuous improvement never goes away.

From an historical perspective, supplier development has been philosophically difficult for many companies, at least in the United States. Traditional or adversarial relationships, which characterized the typical buyer-seller relationship, are not conducive to the kinds of information sharing and cooperation that supplier development requires. And, a lack of trust between buyers and sellers almost ensures that supplier development efforts, if they exist at all, will fall short of performance expectations. Historically, if a supplier experienced problems, the response by a buyer was to warn the supplier that if it did not improve, another supplier was available to take that supplier's business. Today, as suppliers contribute greater amounts of value, such as providing entire systems instead of simply components, the ability to *kick out* these suppliers becomes increasingly difficult.

The philosophical reluctance to pursue supplier development means that most supplier development activities have been reactive. And what are we reacting to? Usually the reaction is to problems that require immediate attention. A preferable approach is to focus on activities that help prevent problems from occurring in the first place. Unfortunately, since most companies view supplier development as an expense, a natural reluctance to take on additional expenses limits our willingness to engage in development activities.

Supplier development has most often been applied to underperforming suppliers, although that does not mean we cannot work with higher performing suppliers. When working with higher performing suppliers, the primary objective is often to develop new supplier capabilities. Supplier development efforts fall primarily into three broad categories:

- Working with a supplier to improve an existing performance capability
- Working with a supplier to resolve a problem with an existing capability
- Working with a supplier to create a performance capability where none previously existed

No single activity defines supplier development. In fact, any initiative designed to improve supplier performance could theoretically fall under the development umbrella. Examples of development activities include providing education or training programs; enhancing working relationships with suppliers to promote joint improvement efforts and information sharing; and providing direct financial support. Other types of development include assigning personnel to work on-site at a supplier, providing process equipment, and providing technology. There is no shortage of ways to practice supplier development.

Supplier development also presents risk. What if a buying company makes a financial commitment to a supplier and the development effort fails to produce anything of substance? Nowhere is it written that supplier development has to succeed. Why is a buying company improving the performance of a supplier when other customers of that supplier, perhaps even competitors, will likely benefit from the supplier's improved performance? This line of thinking elevates the risk that supplier development will not be undertaken. And, what if supplier development, particularly when the focus is on developing new capabilities, creates a new and more powerful supplier that eventually becomes a competitor? What if a supplier's enhanced capabilities makes it attractive for a takeover by another company that is not friendly to your company? If you think hard enough about all the potential risks present in supply chains, you might not want to get out of bed in the morning.

Factors Critical to the Supplier Development Process

Supplier development is one of those areas where, if it were easy, every company would routinely engage in it—and we know that is not the case. With any important process we must understand the factors that will help define success. After all, these are called critical success factors for good reason.

Executive Commitment

It should come as no surprise to say that any major initiative will fail if it does not have executive commitment. For supplier development this means commitment at the buyer and the supplier. Executives at the buyer show their commitment by making resources available to support development efforts. Executives at suppliers demonstrate their commitment by buying-in to the goals of supplier development, which they make known in no uncertain terms across their organization. This contrasts with situations where executives at a supplier perceive they have to go along with a buyer's development requests or risk losing their business.

Trust-based Relationships

A number of years ago, a major automotive company began to pursue its own version of supplier development. This involved sending a team to visit suppliers for a week to make plant layout changes. At the end of the week the buyer then demanded double-digit price reductions from these suppliers. Needless to say, suppliers began to fear these visits. A complete lack of trust characterizing the buyer-seller relationship was a major inhibitor to the success of the development effort. As important as any factor, supplier development success requires trust-based relationships. Without trust the probability that open sharing of information will take place diminishes greatly.

Credibility

Any buying company that initiates supplier development effort must have *street cred*. What this means is that the supplier must perceive the buyer actually has expertise in a particular subject area. Years ago a major United States company began to promote its supplier development program. Unfortunately, this company was itself not a strong performer, either in operational or financial terms. This company was no role model. It should come as no surprise that suppliers did not assign much credibility to this company's development process and resisted any development overtures. Privately, some suppliers suggested that the buying company might be better off asking its suppliers for help.

Data and Measurement Capabilities

Financial and other resource constraints ensure that most companies can engage in a limited number of supplier development projects. This means companies have to be cautious regarding where they allocate their resources. What suppliers offer the best payback? What suppliers are not worth the effort and should instead be candidates for elimination? What performance measures are in place to verify the success of any efforts? Some companies will use their supplier scorecards to help identify development opportunities. While in theory this sounds good, the reality is that far too many companies have poorly designed scorecards that are of limited use. Supplier development requires some serious data support from reliable sources.

Commitment of Financial and Human Resources

When all is said and done, supplier development is largely a people business. This process usually relies on engineers, quality experts, logistics personnel, and others to be part of any development effort—often working directly at a supplier's location. Unfortunately, few organizations have people committed specifically to supplier development activities. This means that supplier development competes with other endeavors for human and financial support, including an employee's regular job responsibilities. Without adequate human support, development initiatives will be severely limited or even unsuccessful. On the financial side, supplier development usually requires travel and oftentimes, equipment and supplier financial support. None of this is free.

Time

Many supplier development initiatives require significant time before showing results. If correcting a problem or developing a new capability were quick and easy, then the need for supplier development would not be all that great. In the lean space, even five-day Kaizen workshops require much more than five days when planning activities are taken into account. The challenge is that most managers, particularly in the U.S., are not particularly patient. The quest for quick results often conflicts with our development objectives, which may take months before reaching fruition, if at all. The challenge is to be patient, but not too patient.

A Proper Power Relationship

Power represents the ability to exert influence over another party. Supplier development usually, but not always, features a larger buyer working with a smaller supplier. This size differential enables, at least partly, a buyer to approach a supplier in the first place. While a smaller customer *could* approach a larger supplier, it is not common. The author once worked with a smaller company whose main suppliers were Dow Chemical and DuPont. The power relationship with these suppliers was not conducive to any serious supplier development discussions. On a positive note, having a blue-chip roster of suppliers should limit the need for supplier development—at least for those development efforts that attempt to solve problems. On the flip side, larger suppliers usually have significant leverage over their smaller customers.

This set of success factors, while certainly not the only ones we could list, will influence greatly the success or failure of supplier development.

SUPPLIER DEVELOPMENT BEST PRACTICES

As with supplier selection, it is important to appreciate that a set of best practices exists that defines leading-edge supplier development. Companies that excel at supplier development look and act differently than companies that fall short of the mark. Use these best practices to perform a self-assessment of supplier development at your company. Let's examine the practices that define effective supplier development.

An Executive Steering Committee Helps Identify and Prioritize Development Opportunities

It is hard to imagine a leading supply organization without an executive steering committee or advisory board to provide strategic leadership. These boards or councils, usually comprised of internal executives from various functional and operating groups, engage in some serious work. The following includes the responsibilities of an executive steering committee at a leading company:

- Establish the strategic direction for purchase commodities
- Charter and staff strategy development teams
- Search *outside the box* for new sourcing ideas and methods
- Coordinate strategy development with other functional groups
- Pursue consistent supply policies, procedures, and processes worldwide
- Establish company-wide improvement targets
- Ensure compliance to corporate agreements
- Monitor supply chain risk and support company-wide risk management initiatives
- Identify and support supplier development initiatives

Just as leading supply organizations have a high-level supply executive, these organizations are also supported by a high-level steering committee or council that sets the strategic direction for some very important areas. Supplier development just happens to be one of those areas.

A Well-understood Supplier Development Process Is in Place

Like most topics that fall under the supply management umbrella, supplier development also benefits from taking a process view. And like all processes, supplier development can be displayed generically as a series of steps:

Step 1: Identify improvement opportunities
Step 2: Target specific suppliers that should benefit from development activities
Step 3: Meet with the supplier's leadership to obtain buy-in, agree on the development opportunity, and develop project plans and clear measures of success

Step 4:   Identify the type of supplier development support
Step 5:   Make development resources available, including human and financial resources
Step 6:   Perform the development project
Step 7:   Measure and report the financial return from supplier development

A central part of this process includes having a methodical way to identify supplier development candidates. A typical supply base contains three groups of suppliers.

Budget Is Available to Support the Expenses of Supplier Development Participants

As mentioned, few companies allocate human resources specifically to support supplier development initiatives. This means development activities must rely on functional groups for support. Besides providing human support, functional managers at some companies have also been asked to cover their employee travel and living expenses while their personnel are working on development projects. Any nonprocurement manager who enjoys having these expenses come out of his or her budget is not normal.

Requiring functional managers to support supplier development expenses will only serve as a barrier to supplier development. A partial way to lessen resistance from managers is to create a budget specifically to cover employee travel and living expenses. Best-practice companies anticipate this issue and respond to it by not making the managers, who provide the personnel to support development initiatives, also absorb variable travel and living expenses.

Use Financial Investment Techniques to Evaluate Development Initiatives

It is safe to conclude that most corporate executives, if they think about supplier development at all, view it primarily as an expense. When this is the case, it should come as no surprise that supplier development is not always looked upon favorably. A basic tenet of financial thinking is *expenses are bad, investments are good*. Expenses are a necessary evil, and as such, this evil should be minimized whenever possible.

The easiest way to forgo the expenses associated with supplier development is simply not to perform any development efforts. This is due partly, if not largely, to not applying financial assessment techniques such as payback, net present value (NPV), or internal rate of return (IRR). The next chapter addresses this topic specifically. By the time the reader is done with this section of the book, he or she will be able to frame development projects in ways that excite executive managers.

Manage Supplier Development Initiatives as Projects

Applying project management techniques to supplier development initiatives piggybacks on the inherent value of managing work as projects. Structuring work as projects rather than as continuous work or a set of activities is attractive for several reasons. First, projects have a defined start, and an end date that builds in preestablished goals and milestones. Second, projects contain a defined scope of work that is specified prior to starting the project. Third, project control tools (such as Microsoft Project) are available that help the participants manage time, gauge the progress of a project against preestablished milestones, assign responsibilities, and control a project's budget. Finally, we can visually display a project and its tasks, including the interrelationships among those tasks. Visualization helps participants understand the big picture.

Use a Supplier Performance Measurement System to Identify Development Opportunities and to Track Improvement

Many companies use their supplier performance measurement systems (i.e., scorecards) to identify and rank development opportunities, particularly opportunities that involve performance shortfalls. The reality is that too many companies have poorly designed scorecards. This can be problematic because (1) poor scorecards will constrain a company's ability to identify valid development opportunities, and (2) the ability to measure the effects of any improvement efforts are likely impacted due to poor measurement capabilities.

What are the shortcomings of many supplier scorecard systems? Perhaps the most obvious shortcoming is many scorecards measure suppliers the same way. If suppliers are not all equal, then why apply equivalent measures? Many systems also rely extensively on data collected manually for their input (raising concerns about accuracy), usually monthly or quarterly (raising concerns about timeliness). Few supplier measurement systems feature objective, real-time data. It is not hard to conclude that a lack of data accuracy and timeliness is a severe limiter. Too many systems are also populated with subjective rather than objective assessments of supplier performance. The list of potential shortfalls with supplier scorecards could go on and on.

Best practice companies appreciate the importance of an effective performance measurement system and strive to continuously improve their measurement capabilities. They address the shortcomings that limit the value of supplier performance measurement because they know that measurement and data are key development enablers.

Work with Suppliers to Identify Opportunities and to Gain Support

Let's agree that supplier development efforts are likely to fail if they lack a supplier's complete support. For those who believe that suppliers are always receptive to a company's performance improvement overtures, get over that delusion right now. While a large company may have the power to coerce a supplier into submission, the use of coercion is, at best, a short-term tactic. Leading companies understand that supplier development is a joint activity that features executive-to-executive engagement early on to secure higher-level buy-in. While some development activities may feature lower-level *fixes*, other initiatives will require a greater commitment of time, personnel, and money.

Share Development Savings with Suppliers

This best practice borrows heavily from supplier suggestion programs. Let's illustrate this practice with an example. In the 1990s, Chrysler initiated its supplier development program called SCORE (supplier cost reduction). At its pinnacle, Chrysler received thousands of supplier suggestions a year that resulted in hundreds of millions of dollar in savings annually. The SCORE model was widely cited as the premier supplier suggestion program in United States industry.

What made SCORE so successful? One prominent factor was Chrysler's willingness to share savings with suppliers. The lesson learned was that sharing of savings within a trust-based relationship provides a powerful incentive for suppliers to participate. Suppliers openly brought their best suggestions to Chrysler, often to the chagrin of Ford and GM. As an aside, after Daimler purchased Chrysler, the supplier suggestion program faded away. The Germans apparently did not respond well to the idea of sharing savings.

Some will philosophically argue against the sharing of savings with suppliers, particularly if a supplier development initiative is attempting to solve a problem. While this argument has merit, it ignores the fact that leading companies expect to apply their development efforts less to problems and more to continuous improvement opportunities and the development of new performance capabilities. A willingness to share savings should be a clear indication that a buyer wants to engage in a win-win relationship. It is hard to argue that the sharing of savings is a disincentive for suppliers to participate. Leading companies understand that motivating suppliers to participate, which worked beautifully with Chrysler's supplier suggestion program, should also work with supplier development projects.

Establish a Central System for Controlling and Reporting Supplier Development Projects

Leading companies have a central system where projects and other initiatives are uploaded, something that provides visibility across an organization. Tapping into these corporate systems provides legitimacy to supplier development efforts. A central system helps embed a supplier development process into a company's culture, partly through the legitimacy afforded by the system. Across the company everyone can see that development efforts are managed similarly to other important projects and initiatives.

The use of a central system leads to other benefits. A key feature of a central system is its regular updating, thereby promoting accountability and discipline. Creating a central system or repository, whatever its final design, is also a way to avoid confusion about the extent of a company's supplier development efforts. Instead of diffused reporting across divisions, sites, and geographic locations, a company can easily see the extent of its company-wide development efforts. And, it can easily transfer the results from development projects to a company Intranet for widespread sharing. A central system also helps with the compilation of performance reports. Finally, personnel across a company can see if any development efforts are similar to what they are proposing. The central system serves as a repository of supplier development initiatives where learning from previous projects is shared with personnel participating in future projects. Why continuously reinvent the wheel?

Recognize That No Single Development Technique Applies to all Suppliers

As mentioned, supplier development represents a broad array of activities that are designed to improve supplier performance capabilities. Taking a broader view of this topic provides a degree of flexibility that supports creativity. The following examples illustrate this point:

- **McDonalds:** A prime example of supplier development is McDonald's support of Trikaya Agriculture, a supplier of fresh iceberg lettuce. Initially, lettuce could be grown only during the winter months in India. With McDonald's expertise, Trikaya Farms in Talegaon, Maharashtra now grows lettuce year round. McDonald's has provided assistance in the selection of high-quality seeds, exposed the farms to advanced drip–irrigation technology, and helped develop a refrigerated transportation system. Trikaya Agriculture has become a major supplier of iceberg lettuce to McDonald's for its Indian operations.[2]

- **IBM:** IBM has implemented a Commercial Mentoring Program with 6-8 diverse suppliers participating at any given time.[3] Each supplier has an IBM employee assigned as its mentor for 12-18 months. All the participants are incumbent suppliers with long-term relationships that can still benefit from a closer relationship. IBM mentors identify development efforts that will result in advancing the supplier's business intelligence. Each mentoring session begins with a two-day retreat where the top members of the suppliers' management team meet with their mentor and the IBM supplier diversity program manager who is responsible for the program. IBM utilizes several educational programs designed to improve the business skills of diverse suppliers. These programs cover subjects such as quality, financial and management skills, strategic planning, and technology. These businesses also participate in various procurement strategy and cost management courses at IBM.
- **Cocoa:** If there is one item that is the lifeblood of chocolate producers, it is cocoa. And, if there is one item that presents a strategic risk to chocolate producers, it is cocoa. Around 70% of the world's cocoa crop is concentrated in five African countries, a region that is not the most stable of locations. Even on a good day cocoa can be risky to grow; farms experience lower yields compared with other crops, limited access to fertilizer, and an abundance of pests. Not surprisingly, cocoa growers are increasingly shifting to more profitable crops such as rubber while younger farmers are reluctant to become cocoa farmers in the first place. Major chocolate companies have come to the conclusion that they must work with suppliers to manage the risks that may affect their cocoa supply. They are working to develop pest resistance cocoa beans, ensure farmers have access to needed fertilizer, and financially support young farmers to encourage them to grow cocoa.

As these examples show, supplier development comes in different shapes and sizes.

CONCLUDING THOUGHTS

Supplier development represents a viable way to solve supply chain problems or to pursue continuous improvement opportunities. Larger buyers often use their development efforts to help disadvantaged suppliers, such as minority and women-owned suppliers as well as international suppliers that need to be brought up to speed. Given that supplier management is an active rather than passive process, understanding what defines effective supplier development becomes a necessity. The next chapter will present financial techniques for framing supplier development and other supply chain initiatives as investments rather than as expenses. Life takes a different turn when we focus on investments rather than expenses. It is time to change our thought process.

REFERENCES

1. Trent, Robert J. and Zacharia, Zach, "The Wisdom of Becoming a Preferred Customer," *Supply Chain Management Review*, November 13, 2012, 10-18.
2. Adapted from http://www.mcdonaldsindia.com/pdf/fresh-lettuce -supplier.pdf.
3. IBM White paper, "Building a Community of Diverse Suppliers," http:// www-03.ibm.com/procurement/proweb.nsf/7a84535a0acd580885256 b3f000e250a/b575a679cdcab5098525726b006b3c38/$FILE/Supply_ rev16_8_11_06.pdf.

6

SUPPLIER MANAGEMENT AND DEVELOPMENT—THE FINANCIAL PERSPECTIVE

Most would argue that the financial crisis of 2008 was a severe shock to the world economy. At one point, there was concern at the highest levels of government that the U.S. economic system might actually collapse. At the corporate level, the need to reduce expenses quickly took on a tremendous urgency. And, that's exactly what happened as companies cut expenses as rapidly as they could.

Supply managers saw their travel budgets cut, making visits to suppliers suddenly a luxury—and, training was no longer part of the picture. The CEO of a major Midwest equipment manufacturer reduced his company's highly respected supplier development program to almost nothing. He viewed supplier development as an expense, and expenses had to go away. A supply professional later commented that he knew the supplier development program was more than paying for itself, but *we couldn't make the financial case.*

What if you could turn those nasty expenses around and frame them in a way that excites the decision makers at your company? That single question sums up this chapter. This chapter explains three financial investment techniques (also known as capital project evaluation techniques) that will enable you to frame expenses as investments. We will apply these techniques in ways that are not at all typical. By the end of this chapter you will understand the simple payback method, the net present value (NPV) method, and the internal rate of return (IRR) method of financial evaluation.

CAPITAL PROJECT EVALUATION TECHNIQUES

Certain techniques are used whenever a company evaluates capital project expenditures, such as building a new facility, buying a piece of equipment, or installing a new information technology (IT) system. These techniques are also used when evaluating new products. They are presented in the same section of the book with supplier development to illustrate that we can apply these techniques across a variety of settings. Their basic application remains the same regardless of where we use them.

It is not realistic to assume that every initiative in supply chain management (SCM) involves a capital project. In fact, most supply chain initiatives will not be part of a capital project. When the initiative is not part of a capital expenditure it is treated as an expense. And never forget, the prevailing view among most managers is that investments are good and expenses are bad. What we want to do is manage supply chain initiatives, such as supplier development, as investments, and apply financial techniques where they historically have not been applied. The techniques we review in this chapter are robust, which means they work across a wide range of settings. Investments tend to gain the favor of key decision makers much more than expenses.

The following sections describe three financial evaluation techniques—simple payback, NPV, and internal IRR. Chapter 7 will provide the opportunity to work with these techniques directly.

Simple Payback

The first evaluation technique presented here is also the most basic. Simple payback represents the length of time required to recover the cost of an investment without considering the time value of money. If the cash flow or benefits from a project are uniform each year, then the payback formula is simply:

Payback Period = Cost of Project/Annual Cash Flows

Payback may be best suited for projects that are not overly complex or where management wants to get a relatively quick snapshot of an expected payback period. This method does not consider the time value of money, so the calculations are relatively straightforward. The payback method is popular because it is relatively simple and, for a company in a tight cash position, it provides a quick indication of how soon it will recover invested funds.[1] For our purposes, simple payback may not be enough to catch management's attention (i.e., create the *wow* factor) unless a company has a minimum payback threshold in terms of time that the calculated payback easily meets.

Let's provide an example of a simple financial payback. Assume a company decides to put forth a cash outlay of $100,000 to purchase smart sensors for installation at a supplier's work cell. These smart sensors monitor the physical process and quality of products as they are produced. Project planners have identified the relevant savings due to better machine uptime and improved quality to be $75,000 annually over a three-year expected life. A simple payback analysis reveals the payback is one year and four months, or 1.33 years.

How did we arrive at the payback of one and a third years? During year one $75,000 of the $100,000 in investment was realized as savings. That left $25,000 of the original investment still outstanding. Given that the second year savings are also expected to be $75,000, the remaining $25,000 of the investment will be realized after four months ($25,000 is one-third of $75,000, and four months is one-third of a year). This technique assumes that savings are realized in a level manner across the year. Alternatively, since the annual cash flows are expected to be uniform each year, we can use the formula presented at the beginning of this section to calculate the payback period:

$$\text{Payback Period} = \$100,000/\$75,000 = 1.33 \text{ years}$$

The following example illustrates the payback method when cash flows from the investment are not uniform each year.

Simple Payback Illustrated

Table 6.1 illustrates the use of the simple payback method for two projects. From this example we see that Alternative *C* has the fastest payback—at two years. It is important to note that the size of the payback in terms of monetary outcomes is not a factor in this analysis. This analysis is all about how quickly a company recoups its investment. If that is troubling then perhaps a different evaluation technique that explicitly considers financial returns rather than time might be in order.

Interestingly, Alternatives *A* and *C* generate the same amount of funds above their investment (each alternative returns $150 above their investment amount). However, Alternative *A* has a lower investment amount compared with Alternative *C* ($300 investment compared with a $400 investment). A technique such as NPV or IRR would show that Alternative *A* has a slightly higher rate of return. All we know from the simple payback analysis is that Alternative *C* is faster at recouping the investment. In this case, is faster better? Or is a higher return better? If we are interested in the return, then we should apply other evaluation techniques.

Net Present Value

A company may require a more complex financial assessment of a proposed project. And, we may need a technique that better grabs the attention of management.

Table 6.1 Simple payback period illustrated

	Alternative A	Alternative B	Alternative C
Cash Outflow Year 0	($300)	($350)	($400)
Cash Inflow Year 1	$100	$100	$200
Cash Inflow Year 2	$125	$100	$200
Cash Inflow Year 3	$225	$200	$150
Pay Back Period:	2.33 years	2.75 years	2.0 years

Figures are in thousands of dollars.

Calculations:

Alternative A: In Year 1, a $100 cash inflow leaves $200 of the $300 Year 0 investment remaining; in Year 2 a $125 cash inflow leaves $75 of the $200 investment amount remaining; in Year 3 a $225 cash inflow will cover the remaining $75 investment amount in four months, ($75/$225 = .33 of a year)

Alternative B: In Year 1, a $100 cash inflow leaves $250 of the $350 Year 0 investment remaining; in Year 2 a $100 cash inflow leaves $150 of the $250 investment amount remaining; in Year 3 a $200 cash inflow will cover the remaining $150 investment amount in nine months, ($150/$200 = .75 of a year)

Alternative C: In Year 1, a $200 cash inflow leaves $200 of the $400 Year 0 investment remaining; in Year 2 a $200 cash inflow leaves $0 of the $200 investment amount remaining

NPV is a well-established evaluation technique in the finance world. It represents the present value of projected future cash flows or benefits discounted at an appropriate cost of capital or hurdle rate less the cost of the investment. The hurdle rate is discussed shortly.

Whenever we see the word *net*, it is safe to conclude that something has been backed out or subtracted to arrive at a final result. NPV, which is a more complex financial evaluation compared with the simple payback method, follows a multistep process:[2]

1. *Estimate the initial cash outlay:* This includes the primary capital expenditures, as well as any other costs to pursue the project. For example, freight costs to receive new capital equipment, when paid by the company that is receiving the containers, should logically be included as part of the investment cash outlay. Unless told otherwise, initial cash outlays occur at *Time 0.*

2. *Determine annual incremental operating cash flows:* This requires quantifying the net savings that result from the project. There are a variety of ways to arrive at the incremental cash flows. One way is to perform a cost-benefit analysis to arrive at annual benefits due to the project. Another way is to prepare an estimated income statement and cash flow with and without the project (what is called *pro forma* statements). The

difference represents the incremental impact due to the project. Both methods require a careful assessment of individual benefits or incremental cash flows.

3. ***Project the terminal cash flow or expected salvage value:*** Add the salvage value of any assets at the final project year's operating cash flow.

4. ***Determine the present value of the future cash flows:*** This represents the value in today's dollars of the benefit stream over each year of the project. Future flows are discounted by some percentage provided by finance, such as a hurdle or discount rate.

5. ***Determine the net present value of the project:*** The project's NPV is the sum of the present values of the flows (benefits received each year), less the outflows (investment cost). A positive number means the current value of the discounted future benefits exceeds the project hurdle rate.

The challenge when using any financial investment technique is arriving at accurate investment costs and incremental savings due to the project. This is not as simple as it sounds. Often, particularly for major capital investments, we are trying to forecast five years or more into the future, which raises the question of data validity. Capital project evaluation techniques are really forecasting techniques. Instead of forecasting future sales we are forecasting future cash flows and benefits. And, we are often forecasting multiple years into the future. It is a well-accepted tenet of SCM that the further we look into the future, the less reliable information becomes.

Most of us have sat through presentations where financial costs and savings are taken as absolutes without question. Oftentimes no one challenges the savings since they appear in a highly regarded financial format. These investment models always arrive at an output number. The question then becomes; are the costs modeled correctly?

Another issue involves the specification of the model. At times, we simply fail to consider an expansive set of benefits, both direct and indirect, that will result from a project. A prime example involves PPL, an electric utility that operates in Eastern Pennsylvania. PPL was the first regulated utility in the U.S. to install automated meter readers at 100 percent of the commercial and residential locations it served. While this was a game-changing project for the company and industry, the reality is—this project almost did not happen. It did not show a positive return when first conceived since the only major savings it considered was the elimination of human meter readers.

PPL failed to include the less obvious benefits from the new system. These benefits fall primarily into four categories, including: enhanced profitability from lower field service costs (such as fewer service calls due to meter problems), operational benefits from improved billing processes and results costs (100 percent of meters are read each month with near-perfect accuracy), better outage management (the system can quickly pinpoint where outages occur), and benefits from using the system as a strategic data management platform. While project costs are usually modeled accurately, the benefits are sometimes understated or hard to quantify. This makes a project appear less viable.

The Hurdle or Discount Rate

An important financial topic is something called the hurdle rate. This rate plays a front and center role in many financial applications, including NPV analysis. In capital project evaluation, the hurdle rate, which is presented as a percentage, is the minimum rate that a company must earn before approving a project.[3] If a proposed investment or project is considered to have an unusually risky outcome, the hurdle rate could be adjusted to reflect higher risk.

Most companies establish their hurdle rate as equivalent to the cost to obtain capital, or the cost of raising cash through equity and debt. Companies with no equity only use the cost of debt, while companies with equity and debt arrive at a weighted average of the two.[4] Calculating the hurdle rate is the responsibility of finance.

Technically, the rate at which we subject investments in an NPV analysis is called the discount rate—it does not necessarily have to be the company's hurdle rate. Companies have different ways of identifying the discount rate, including using the expected return of other investment choices with a similar level of risk.

As mentioned, capital projects are often evaluated by discounting future cash flows to the present (which we call Year 0) by a hurdle or discount rate to determine the NPV of the project, or by computing the IRR and comparing that to the hurdle rate. (The next section discusses IRR.) If the NPV in terms of dollars (or whatever currency is used) of a proposed project is greater than zero, then the expected project return exceeds the hurdle or discount rate. Higher NPVs are better than lower NPVs. A negative net present value means the project is not expected to generate a return that meets or exceeds the hurdle rate. If the IRR method is used, a project where the IRR exceeds the hurdle rate is a candidate for approval. As with NPV, the higher the IRR percentage the better—from a financial return perspective.

NPV Illustrated

An important part of the NPV process is understanding the formula used to take future cash inflows and discount them at an appropriate rate into current values. While tables are available that provide values to discount future flows to the present, we will perform the calculations by hand to better understand the mechanics of the process. The following formula is used to arrive at the present value of a future value:

$$\text{Present Value } (PV) = \text{Future Value } (FV)/(1 + r)^n$$

Where r = the discount or hurdle rate and n = the future value period.

Let's say in three years we expect to have a cash inflow from a project of $400,000. If the discount rate is 12%, what is the present value of the $400,000?

$$\text{Answer: } PV = \$400,000/(1 + .12)^3$$

Note that $(1 + .12)^3$ is simply $(1 + .12)(1 + .12)(1 + .12) = 1.40$. The present value of $400,000 discounted at 12% is ($400,000/1.40) = $285,714. Viewed another way, the future value in three years of $285,714 at 12% is $400,000.

Let's expand our understanding by looking at two separate three-year investments to arrive at the NPV for each investment. Table 6.2 summarizes the data for two investments cleverly named Project A and Project B. As we can see, discounting the future value of cash inflows resulting from the project to the present (Time 0) is a fairly straightforward process. The NPV is essentially the *bottom line* of the investment. For Project A, the NPV is just over $125,000 when the future cash inflows are discounted at a 13% discount rate; the NPV for Project B is just

Table 6.2   Net present value illustrated

	Alternative A	Alternative B
Cash Outflow Year 0	($750)	($675)
Cash Inflow Year 1	$300	$310
Cash Inflow Year 2	$425	$300
Cash Inflow Year 3	$400	$350

Discount rate = 13%; figures are in thousands of dollars.

Project "A" NPV Calculation:

Present Value for Year 1 Inflow: PV = $300/(1 + .13)^1 =	$265.48
Present Value for Year 2 Inflow: PV = $425/(1 + .13)^2 =	$332.03
Present Value for Year 3 Inflow: PV = $400/(1 + .13)^3 =	$277.78

Present Value for Year 1 Inflow: $PV = \$300/(1 + .13)^1 =$ $265.48
Present Value for Year 2 Inflow: $PV = \$425/(1 + .13)^2 =$ $332.03
Present Value for Year 3 Inflow: $PV = \$400/(1 + .13)^3 =$ $277.78

Present Value of Inflows: $875.29
Less Year 0 Outlay: $750

Project "A" Net Present Value: **$125.29**

Project "B" NPV Calculation:
Present Value for Year 1 Inflow: $PV = \$310/(1 + .13)^1 =$ $274.34
Present Value for Year 2 Inflow: $PV = \$300/(1 + .13)^2 =$ $234.37
Present Value for Year 3 Inflow: $PV = \$350/(1 + .13)^3 =$ $243.05

Present Value of Inflows: $751.76
Less Year 0 Outlay: $675

Project "B" Net Present Value: **$76.76**

under $77,000 when the future flows are discounted at 13%. Remember, the 13% figure used here is provided by finance—supply chain managers did not calculate it. If we can only select one project, we would select the one with the higher NPV.

Internal Rate of Return

A similar concept to NPV is the IRR. IRR represents the discount rate that makes the NPV of all future cash flows from a particular project equal to zero.[5] While NPV and IRR are conceptually similar, they have a major difference. The first three of the five steps for arriving at the NPV that were presented earlier are identical for the IRR. With NPV, the rate at which we discount the future cash flows (Step 4) is provided by finance at the onset of the analysis. The NPV analysis cannot happen without knowing that rate. As illustrated, the end result of an NPV analysis is a monetary value. With IRR, the output of the analysis is a rate of percentage return for the project that makes *the present value of the discounted cash flows equal to the cost of the investment or project.* A company's hurdle or discount rate has no direct bearing during the calculations. An example will help clarify this admittedly confusing paragraph.

As a last step, we should compare the IRR against the corporate hurdle rate or against other projects under consideration. Obviously, we want to select projects that have the highest IRR and exceed the company's hurdle rate. It would be foolish to select a project that does not satisfy a minimum return rate.

IRR Illustrated

Table 6.3 illustrates the mechanics for arriving at an IRR. Our objective is to identify the IRR from this project, where the percentage return for the project makes the present value of the discounted cash flows equal to the cost of the investment or project. Please note that the values in this table are subject to some slight rounding.

We will use a trial and error method to identify the return rate where the discounted cash flows equal the initial cash outlay. Admittedly, arriving at the IRR this way is a bit cumbersome. Financial calculators are available that will allow the user to input the data to calculate the IRR with the push of a button. The use of a financial calculator is beyond the scope of this discussion.

In this example, we see that a 22% IRR is too high, while an 18% IRR is too low. The IRR for this project is projected to be around 20%, which is the rate where the return for the project makes the present value of the discounted cash flows equal to the initial cost of the investment or project. Is this a good rate of return? That will depend on a number of factors, including a comparison to a company's required hurdle or discount rate or comparisons to other possible projects. As with NPV, higher values are better.

Table 6.3 Internal rate of return illustrated

	Project
Cash Outflow Year 0	($900)
Cash Inflow Year 1	$300
Cash Inflow Year 2	$325
Cash Inflow Year 3	$425
Cash Inflow Year 4	$350

Project IRR Calculation at 22%:

Present Value for Year 1 Inflow: PV = $300/(1 + .22)^1 =	$245.90
Present Value for Year 2 Inflow: PV = $325/(1 + .22)^2 =	$218.12
Present Value for Year 3 Inflow: PV = $425/(1 + .22)^3 =	$234.05
Present Value for Year 4 Inflow: PV = $350/(1 + .22)^4 =	$158.06

Present value of cash inflows: $856.13

Less Cash Outlay at Year 0 $900

Difference between inflows and outlay: **($43.87) (22%, too high)**

Project IRR Calculation at 18%:

Present Value for Year 1 Inflow: PV = $300/(1 + .18)^1 =	$254.24
Present Value for Year 2 Inflow: PV = $325/(1 + .18)^2 =	$233.81
Present Value for Year 3 Inflow: PV = $425/(1 + .18)^3 =	$259.15
Present Value for Year 4 Inflow: PV = $350/(1 + .18)^4 =	$180.41

Present value of cash inflows: $927.61

Less Cash Outlay at Time 0 $900

Difference between inflows and outlay: **$27.61 (18%, too low)**

Project IRR Calculation at 20%:

Present Value for Year 1 Inflow: PV = $300/(1 + .20)^1 =	$250.00
Present Value for Year 2 Inflow: PV = $325/(1 + .20)^2 =	$225.69
Present Value for Year 3 Inflow: PV = $425/(1 + .20)^3 =	$245.95
Present Value for Year 4 Inflow: PV = $350/(1 + .20)^4 =	$168.79

Present value of cash inflows: $890.43

Less Cash Outlay at Time 0: $900

Difference between inflows and outlay: **($9.57) (IRR = approx. 20%)**

FINANCIAL EVALUATION TECHNIQUE EXAMPLES

Let's remember something important here; there is no law that says financial evaluation techniques apply only to capital projects, and there is no law that says we cannot discount future costs the way we discount future cash inflows. Not all costs occur at Time 0, even in capital expenditure projects.

Let's look at two examples where we might apply financial investment techniques. The first example is a supplier development project. This is an area that would normally be thought of as an expense without much consideration given to the derived benefits, at least from a financial investment perspective. The second example is a more traditional capital expenditure project involving returnable containers. This chapter will not include the financial investment analysis of the cost and benefit data. That is part of the next chapter. Here, we simply describe the projects.

A Supplier Development Project

A number of years ago, an automotive company made a decision to reduce the total number of suppliers it actively maintained. Part of this company's strategy was to work with a smaller set of trusted suppliers and to help them develop new performance capabilities. One such opportunity involved the production of mirrors.

This original equipment manufacturer (OEM) used two suppliers to provide mirrors for a specific car model—one supplier for interior mirrors and one for exterior mirrors. Neither supplier could produce both kinds of mirrors, largely because the technology and tooling required to make each type is different. The OEM's plan was to work with the higher performing supplier (which currently made the exterior mirrors) to develop the capabilities required for also producing interior mirrors. The OEM's goal was to achieve lower costs, a lower parts-per-million defect level, and improved delivery performance.

Higher performance was not the only reason the OEM focused on that particular supplier. The two companies were located relatively close geographically, making visits less of a burden. This is not the case when a supplier's production facilities are located in another country, for example. As an aside, SeaMicro, a company that makes an innovative line of efficient and small data servers, relies on a contract manufacturer located less than a mile from its engineering and design center in California. SeaMicro's engineers are constantly at the supplier trying out new ideas and working on product and performance improvements. The company calls this approach *lean engineering*.

The two companies in our automotive example had a long history of working together. A vice president at the buying company commented that this supplier always supported the OEM's philosophy of continuous improvement and had been a willing participant in previous initiatives. The supplier, for example, is fully capable of delivering its products on a just-in-time basis due to a previous development project. From a cultural perspective the two companies have a good fit, characterized by mutual trust. The foundation for a successful supplier development initiative was in place before this initiative started.

Some companies might provide supplier development funds based simply on a faith that the effort will be successful. But do we know how successful it will be if we don't model it as an investment? Most decisions require more than faith.

Table 6.4 identifies a set of costs and incremental benefits associated with the mirror project. Identifying the costs and benefits for a financial analysis presents two challenges. The first challenge is to ensure that a full set of costs and benefits are identified. As mentioned, many projects fail to include all benefit categories, thereby under-specifying the financial model and making the investment look less attractive. Failure to include all the cost and benefit categories raises serious questions about the validity of the model. Unfortunately, these questions often arise when we are presenting our analysis to executive managers. Any shortcomings become evident at the wrong time.

The second challenge is populating the model with accurate data. On the cost side, direct costs are usually straightforward. In this example, we know that an engineer will be assigned to the supplier for an extended period. While technically that engineer's salary is paid whether he or she is working on this project or not, we must still allocate the salary to the project to ensure accurate cost accounting. The equipment and tooling required for the project should also be known with some certainty.

Some items are not so easily modeled. These are often called soft or indirect costs or benefits. What is the financial benefit of managing one supplier instead of two? How confident are we about our supplier switching costs, which no

Table 6.4 Costs and benefits of a supplier development project

Costs	Benefits
Salary and fringe benefits for an on-site engineer	Reduced quality defects and warranty costs
Travel and living expenses for an on-site engineer	Reduced inventory carrying costs at the buyer due to improved just-in-time delivery performance
Misc. administrative costs (negotiating a new contract, winding down the contract with the other supplier, etc.)	Lower supplier management costs due to reduced supply base
Direct financial support provided to supplier to purchase work cell equipment, including delivery of the equipment and facility change and setup charges	Reduced supply chain costs due to the elimination of one supplier (fewer material releases, less receiving, material handling, accounts payable, etc.)
	Lower per unit purchase price due to purchasing economies at the supplier, machine efficiencies, and reduced material handling costs from improved layout and flow at the supplier

accounting system actually tracks? What is the financial value of fewer defects and improved on-time delivery performance? Are there any indirect or second-order benefits that are not included? For example, would more reliable deliveries lessen the need for safety stock, thereby resulting in lower inventory carrying charges? And, let's not forget, we are looking years into the future. The longer our time horizon becomes, the less confident we are in our projections.

The next chapter will include figures for the items presented in Table 6.4. You will be able to analyze this project from a financial investment perspective and determine its expected gain or loss. Not only will you be able to provide an objective answer regarding the projected worth of this project, you will also feel good about taking another large step toward understanding the combined worlds of finance and supply chain management.

A Returnable Container Project

A second example involves a more complex, but also more traditional type of capital investment project. This example involves a returnable container project, something that would likely be treated as a capital project given the level of expenditures and the expected life of the capital assets.

A returnable container, usually made of steel or reinforced plastic, is a container intended for repeated use. Some will interchange the terms returnable and reusable. Unlike corrugated shipping containers that are intended for a single or relatively few trips before being disposed of or recycled, returnable containers are intended to return to their point of origin in something called a closed-loop system. It is not unusual for returnable containers to have a three-to-five-year useful life span. We will build this life cycle directly into our financial model.

A critical part of this project centers on the required number of containers. This question is important because too few containers moving through a system means that corrugated containers must compensate for any shortfalls. Too many containers will result in holding returnable containers that are not being used efficiently. Perhaps most important, the number of containers purchased is also going to represent the largest part of the capital investment. This question, while important, is outside the scope of this example. Our objective is to illustrate the use of financial investment techniques to model the project costs and benefits. Other sources discuss how to estimate the number of containers to populate within a system.[6]

A major issue involves how to get the containers back to their originating point. After all, these are called *returnable* containers. Let's consider this question using a Midwest company that has an aftermarket distribution network. This company delivers its smaller and medium size replenishment items to its regional centers via trucks using returnable containers. It sends its oversized and large sheet metal parts to these same regional centers via rail cars. After a regional facility puts away the replenishment parts, the rail cars are reloaded with returnable containers, returnable racks, and other miscellaneous items, such as warranty parts. The rail cars then make their way back to the rail yard. The rail cars with the returns and containers are then forwarded to the national facility from which they originated. The returnable containers are then unloaded and refilled with replenishment inventory to make another trip on a truck. In lean terminology this network is called a closed-loop system. Any costs incurred to return containers back to their originating point should be part of the financial analysis, although in this case, there are no specific charges to return rail cars back to their originating location. The charge is embedded in the freight rate.

Identifying Cost and Benefit Categories

By now you should realize that the financial evaluation of any project requires a detailed assessment of the individual cost and benefits associated with that project. Table 6.5 identifies the cost and benefit categories that we should model in our investment analysis for a returnable container project. As this table shows, the expected benefits from returnable containers go far beyond simply eliminating the material and labor costs associated with corrugated containers. We know that many investment projects overlook some benefits or exclude them from the analysis because they are too hard to model quantitatively. A major challenge when evaluating a returnable container project, or any capital project for that matter, is identifying the savings that result from the new system.

Assuming that reliable data are available, the actual assessment of a returnable container project is usually not as complex as other projects or financial investments. In the author's experience, the project is usually not being compared against any other options except the status quo, which is the continued use of corrugated shipping containers. Because corrugated containers and wooden pallets are replaced by returnable containers, it is legitimate to treat the elimination of corrugated containers and pallets as a benefit. This represents a legitimate cost avoidance due to the use of returnable containers, which Table 6.5 includes.

Each benefit and cost from a returnable container system must be quantified or modeled before finalizing the financial evaluation. This will involve, at a minimum, the participation of finance, transportation, purchasing, operations, and industrial engineering. Each will bring some relevant information to the table to help arrive at the net savings from a returnable container project. Chapter 7 will extend Table 6.5 by providing cost and benefit data for this example.

Quantifying Benefits

Consider just one of the benefit categories that we might overlook when crafting a financial investment analysis—better trailer utilization. Better trailer or cube

Table 6.5   Costs and benefits of a returnable container program

Costs	Benefits: At the National Distribution Center
Returnable container costs	Elimination of corrugated container material costs (corrugated, nails, wooden pallets)
Replacement container panels	Elimination of corrugated container labor costs required for constructing the shipping containers
Administrative project costs (packaging, engineering, purchasing, staff time)	Better space utilization of loading lanes at national distribution center due to higher load stacking
Loading returnable containers on rail cars at the regional centers	Reduced trailer loading costs at national distribution center due to fewer trailer setups
Unloading of containers at national distribution center from returning rail cars	Reduced yard congestion and trailer handling at the national distribution center due to fewer trailers
	Benefits: In-transit
	Reduced transportation costs due to better trailer cube utilization
	Reduced in-transit damage
	Benefits: At the Regional Distribution Centers
	Reduced receiving costs due to fewer total trailers processed
	Reduced trailer unloading costs at regional centers due to fewer unloading setups
	Elimination of corrugated disposal costs (labor, container break down, hauling away) at regional facilities
	Reduced yard congestion and trailer handling at regional centers due to fewer trailers
	Corporate Benefit
	Tax savings resulting from depreciation of capital investment

utilization goes a long way toward making the financial case for returnable containers, but only if we include it in the analysis. It would be a serious error to overlook the impact of better trailer utilization, just as it would be a mistake to overlook the other benefit categories presented in Table 6.5.

Why is trailer or cube utilization improved when using returnable shipping containers? Returnable containers allow the stacking of loads three high rather than only two high in a trailer. Corrugated containers affixed to wooden pallets are usually not stacked three high, especially over longer distances because pallets shift during transit or their weight causes loads to collapse. The returnable containers also nest securely on top of each other, somewhat like Lego blocks connected together. This prevents the crushing and shifting of loads, which eliminates the cost of damaged parts, as well as the labor involved with sorting through damaged loads. The bottom line is that better utilization due to returnable containers means fewer trailers shipped to the regional facilities.

Consider the financial cash flow benefits that result from better utilization. One of the regional facilities (out of 14 in the network) received an average of 8 trailers per week, or around 400 trailers per year, from the national distribution center prior to switching to returnable containers. After switching, this facility now receives around 10 percent fewer trailers each week, and the items received are rarely damaged. Transportation freight savings at this facility amounted to $100,000 annually ($2,500 freight cost to ship a trailer × 40 fewer trailers per year). And this is only the savings from one of the smaller facilities in this network! Aggregating the transportation savings across the 14 regional facilities helps justify this company's investment in returnable containers.

CONCLUDING THOUGHTS

The world of finance deals extensively with investments while the world of SCM deals extensively with expenses. If we plan on interacting with finance, then we need to think in terms of investments and investment analysis wherever possible. Doing so means feeling comfortable with applying financial evaluation techniques. The next chapter allows the reader to apply directly the concepts and approaches presented in this chapter. It is time to take another step forward in your growth as a supply chain financial manager.

REFERENCES

1. Sam Weaver and Fred Weston, *Strategic Financial Management: Application of Corporate Finance* (Mason, OH: Thompson Southwestern, 2007), 337.
2. S. Weaver and F. Weston, 382.
3. From http://www.investopedia.com/terms/h/hurdlerate.asp.
4. From http://smallbusiness.chron.com/assessing-projects-hurdle -rate-75860.html.
5 http://www.investopedia.com/terms/i/irr.asp.
6. To see a methodology for calculating the number of containers to populate in a system, see Robert Trent, *End-to-End Lean Management*, (Ft. Lauderdale, FL: J. Ross Publishing, 2008), 189-192.

7

DEVELOPING SUPPLIER PERFORMANCE CAPABILITIES—APPLYING FINANCIAL TECHNIQUES

This chapter provides the opportunity to apply the concepts presented in Chapter 6. Specifically, the problems and cases presented in this chapter all relate to evaluating investment options using the techniques presented in Chapter 6. This chapter reinforces how to calculate a simple payback, net present value (NPV), and internal rate of return (IRR).

CALCULATING SIMPLE PAYBACK, NPV, AND IRR— PROBLEM 1

Use the data in the following table (see Table 7.1) to answer the questions that follow. All numbers are in thousands.

Table 7.1

Project Costs and Benefits	Project
Cash Outflow (costs) Year 0	($735)
Cash Inflow (benefit) Year 1	$200
Cash Inflow Year 2	$300
Cash Inflow Year 3	$375
Cash Inflow Year 4	$325

Given the investment data for this project, calculate and interpret the payback, NPV, and IRR. Assume this company's hurdle rate is 12%.

CALCULATING SIMPLE PAYBACK, NPV, AND IRR— PROBLEM 2

Use the data in the following table (see Table 7.2) to answer the questions that follow. All numbers are in thousands.

Table 7.2

	Alternative A	Alternative B	Alternative C
Cash Outflow Year 0	($500)	($575)	($475)
Cash Inflow Year 1	$220	$300	$175
Cash Inflow Year 2	$380	$330	$275
Cash Inflow Year 3	$350	$350	$300

Given the investment data for this project, calculate and interpret the payback, NPV, and IRR for the three alternative project options. Assume this company's hurdle rate is 14%. If you could only select one project alternative, which one would you choose? Did all three calculations (payback, NPV, and IRR) reach the same conclusion regarding the preferred option?

SUPPLIER DEVELOPMENT INVESTMENT ANALYSIS CASE

This case extends the supplier development example presented in Chapter 6. Recall that an automotive company relied on two suppliers to provide mirrors for a specific car model—one for interior mirrors and one for exterior mirrors. The original equipment manufacturer's plan is to work with a single supplier to develop the capabilities required to produce both kinds of mirrors. The chosen supplier currently produces exterior mirrors only. The other supplier will likely be eliminated from the supply base, or at least from that car model.

The following extends this example by providing cost and benefit data to support the development of a financial investment model. The benefits associated with the mirror project are expected to accrue over a three-year period, at which time the car model will be replaced with a new model.

The automotive company expects the supplier to provide the following volumes over the three-year project life for interior mirrors. During Year 1 the supplier is ramping up its production and therefore does not provide a comparable number of interior mirrors compared with Years 2 and 3:

Year 1:	60,000 mirrors
Year 2:	120,000 mirrors
Year 3:	125,000 mirrors

Cost Information

- **Salary and fringe benefits for on-site engineer:** The buyer plans to assign an engineer to work directly at the supplier during the first year of the supplier development project. The engineer expects to spend three-quarters of his time at the supplier. The engineer makes $125,000 annually with an additional $30,000 in benefits. The engineer will work directly at the supplier over the course of the first year only.

  While costs are normally accounted for at the onset of a project (i.e., Year 0), the buyer has decided to include the engineer's salary and benefit costs in Year 1 and then discount them to Year 0. The engineer will not be assigned to the supplier after the first year.
- **Travel and living expenses:** As with the engineer's salary and benefits, the buyer has decided to include travel and living expenses in Year 1, and then discount them to Year 0. The buyer expects to incur $25,000 in travel and living expenses. No travel and living expenses are expected in Years 2 and 3.
- **Miscellaneous administrative costs:** Due to the relative insignificance of these costs, the buyer has decided to treat this cost category as a Year 0 expense. Miscellaneous administrative costs associated with transitioning work from one supplier to another and terminating the supplier relationship are expected to be $10,000.
- **Direct financial support provided to supplier to purchase work cell equipment, including delivery, facility change and setup charges:** The buyer has decided to support the supplier's capital equipment requirements for producing the interior mirror. Project planners calculate the cost of buying work cell equipment, delivery of the equipment, and any facility changes and setup charges to be $1,250,000. The buyer is sharing these costs 50/50 with the supplier. This is a Year 0 cost.

Benefit Information

- **Reduced quality defects and warranty costs:** The new production process is expected to yield higher levels of product quality. Warranty charges attributed to quality issues with the existing interior mirror are $25,000 per year. The buyer expects to reduce this figure by 10% in Year 1, 25%

in Year 2, and 25% in Year 3. Improved factory quality compared with current levels and improved yield at the factory will provide incremental benefits of $20,000 in Year 1, $35,000 in Year 2, and $40,000 in Year 3.

- **Reduced inventory carrying costs at the buyer:** The buyer expects a more reliable, just-in time delivery system with the supplier to reduce the inventory carrying charges associated with safety stock, as well as lower average inventory levels, by $15,000 in Year 1, $25,000 in Year 2, and $27,000 in Year 3.
- **Lower supplier management costs:** The buyer expects no savings in Year 1 from reduced supplier management costs. The buyer projects savings of $3,000 in Year 2 and $3,000 in Year 3.
- **Reduced supply chain costs due to the elimination of one supplier:** The buyer estimates eliminating one supplier will result in reduced supply chain costs of $4,000 in Year 1, $6,000 in Year 2, and $7,000 in Year 3.
- **Lower per unit purchase price due to purchasing economies at the supplier, machine efficiencies, and reduced material handling costs from improved layout and flow:** The buyer expects to realize a $2 per unit savings in Year 1 compared with the current supplier's price, a $3 per unit savings in Year 2, and a $3.25 per unit savings in Year 3.

Table 7.3 summarizes these costs and benefits.

Table 7.3

Costs	Benefits
Salary and fringe benefits for on-site engineer	Reduced quality defects and warranty costs
Travel and living expenses for on-site engineer	Reduced inventory carrying costs at the buyer due to improved just-in-time delivery performance
Misc. administrative costs (negotiating a new contract, winding down the contract with the other supplier, etc.)	Reduced supplier management costs due to fewer mirror suppliers (fewer supplier performance review meetings, for example)
Direct financial support provided to the supplier to purchase work cell equipment, including delivery of the equipment and facility change and setup charges	Reduced supply chain costs due to the elimination of one supplier (fewer material releases, less receiving, material handling, accounts payable, etc.)
	Lower per unit purchase price due to purchasing economies at the supplier, machine efficiencies, and reduced material handling costs from improved layout and flow at the supplier

Assignment

1. Use the information and data provided to create a three-year cost and benefit table for the supplier development project. Construct this as a table you would present to your executive management.
2. Calculate the simple payback for this supplier development project. If the company has a minimum payback requirement of 18 months, what do you conclude?
3. Calculate and interpret the NPV of this project. The company's hurdle rate for projects is 14%.
4. Calculate the IRR for the project. Compare the IRR to the company's hurdle rate of 14%. What do you conclude?
5. Can you think of any costs or benefits this analysis failed to consider?

RETURNABLE CONTAINER FINANCIAL INVESTMENT ANALYSIS CASE

This case extends the returnable container example presented in Chapter 6. Recall that a company is looking to replace its use of corrugated shipping containers with reusable containers to move goods from its national distribution center to its 14 regional distribution centers. This case is somewhat different than traditional capital investment projects in that several of the expenses are not incurred in Year 0. Instead, they are recurring expenses once the returnable system is operational. While it would be easy to overlook these expenses, the result would be a model that over-specifies the benefits by the amount of these expenses.

Cost Information

- **Returnable container costs:** Each returnable container costs $200. This company expects to purchase 18,000 containers.
- **Replacement container panels:** Damaged containers are easily repaired using replacement panels. These will be purchased at the start of the project and then placed at each location that receives and uses returnable containers. Each replacement panel costs $25. The company expects to purchase 1,500 panels.
- **Administrative project costs:** This project required a detailed analysis of current system volumes, selection of the container supplier, contract negotiation, container stress tests, education at each regional facility about the new program, and other miscellaneous administrative tasks. Administrative project one-time costs are $75,000.

- **Loading returnable containers on rail cars at the regional centers:** While the rail trip for containers returning back to the national distribution center for reuse incurs no additional charge, the cost to process and load containers at each facility has some associated labor costs. The 14 regional centers each expect to commit six hours of employee time per week, on average, to process and load returnable containers. One hour of labor with salary and benefits is $32. This is an ongoing expense that begins in Year 1.
- **Unloading of containers from rail cars returning to the national distribution center:** The cost to unload and transfer containers to their point of use at the national distribution center has some associated labor costs. The national distribution center expects to commit 16 hours of employee labor a week to this task. One hour of labor with salary and benefits is $32. This is an ongoing expense that begins in Year 1.

Benefit Information

- **Elimination of corrugated container material costs:** The national distribution center calculates that $250,000 is eliminated annually due to the reduced need for corrugated material, wood pallets, and nails for assembling corrugated shipping containers.
- **Elimination of corrugated container labor costs:** The use of returnable containers eliminates the need for one employee to build corrugated shipping containers. One employee with salary and benefits equates to $55,000 in annual savings.
- **Better space utilization of loading lanes at national distribution center:** While difficult to estimate, more efficient use of outbound dock space creates savings of $25,000 annually, primarily through the elimination of delays and bottlenecks.
- **Reduced trailer loading costs at the national distribution center:** Fewer outbound trailers mean less dock congestion and greater loading efficiency. The national distribution center expects less loading of trailers to yield savings of $30,000 per year, primarily through the processing of fewer trailers.
- **Reduced yard congestion and trailer handling at the national distribution center:** Fewer trailers means less trailer switching at the outbound docks, greater ease in locating trailers in the yard, and less yard movement and congestion. Annual savings of $40,000 per year are expected at the national distribution facility.
- **Reduced transportation costs due to better trailer utilization:** The national distribution center ships 1,500 trailers a year in total to the

regional facilities. This company expects that, due to better cube utilization within trailers, 20% fewer trailers will be required. The average cost to move a trailer from the national center to a regional center is $2,500.

- **Reduced in-transit damage:** The use of corrugated containers is expected to reduce in-transit damage from the national distribution center to the regional distribution centers by 50% (not all items are shipped in returnable containers). The company calculates that it incurs $500,000 of in-transit damage annually.

- **Reduced receiving costs at regional facilities:** Fewer trailers means less processing of trailers at regional centers. Less processing should save, on average, $5,000 at each regional facility.

- **Reduced trailer unloading costs and dock congestion at regional centers:** Fewer trailers means greater efficiency unloading trailers at the regional centers. Efficiency savings of $7,500 on average are expected at each regional center.

- **Elimination of corrugated disposal costs at regional facilities:** The use of returnable containers eliminates the labor required to break down corrugated shipping containers as well as the hauling fees associated with removing corrugated containers. This company calculates that it spends $350,000 annually for corrugated disposal, including labor.

- **Reduced yard congestion and trailer handling at regional centers:** Fewer trailers means less trailer switching at the inbound docks, greater ease in locating trailers in the yard, and less yard congestion. Annual savings of $8,000 per year are expected at each regional facility.

- **Tax savings resulting from depreciation of capital investment:** Depreciation of the capital investment at the corporate level will result in tax savings of $50,000 annually.

Table 7.4 summarizes these costs and benefits.

Table 7.4   Summary of costs and benefits

Costs	Benefits: At the National Distribution Center
Returnable container costs	Elimination of corrugated container material costs (corrugated, nails, wooden pallets)
Replacement container panels	Elimination of corrugated container labor costs required for unloading trailers from vendor (moving, handling, constructing the shipping containers)
Administrative project costs (packaging, engineering, purchasing, staff time)	Better space utilization of loading lanes at national distribution center due to higher load stacking
Loading returnable containers on rail cars at the regional centers	Reduced trailer loading costs at national distribution center due to fewer trailer setups
Unloading of containers at national distribution center from returning rail cars	Reduced yard congestion and trailer handling at the national distribution center due to fewer trailers
	Benefits: In-transit
	Reduced transportation costs due to better trailer cube utilization
	Reduced in-transit damage
	Benefits: At the Regional Distribution Centers
	Reduced receiving costs due to fewer total trailers processed
	Reduced trailer unloading costs at regional centers due to fewer unloading setups
	Elimination of corrugated disposal costs (labor, container break down, hauling away) at regional facilities
	Reduced yard congestion and trailer handling at regional centers due to fewer trailers
	Corporate Benefit
	Tax savings resulting from depreciation of capital investment

Assignment

1. Use the information and data provided to create a three-year cost and benefit table for the supplier development project. Treat this as a table you would present to your executive management.
2. Calculate the simple payback for this supplier development project. If the company has a minimum payback requirement of 15 months, what do you conclude?
3. Calculate and interpret the NPV of this project. The company's hurdle rate for projects is 12%.

4. Calculate the IRR for the project. Compare the IRR to the company's hurdle rate of 12%. What do you conclude?
5. Can you think of any costs or benefits this analysis failed to consider?

POST-HOC PROJECT ANALYSIS

Investigate a capital investment project related to some aspect of supply chain management, preferably at your company. Interview those involved with the project by asking the following questions:

1. Describe the project, including the primary objectives or outcomes sought from the project.
2. Was a team used to develop the project? If so, who was part of the project team? How was the team selected? Did the team require any special tools or training to complete its tasks?
3. What went right with the implementation of the project? What went wrong? Were there any surprises? What would the participants do differently if they worked on another project?
4. Besides financial indicators, did the project participants rely on any other measures of project success?
5. Was this project subjected to an investment analysis such as simple payback, NPV, or IRR? Or was some other approach used to evaluate the merits of the project?
6. If NPV was used, what was the hurdle rate or cost of capital used during the analysis? How did finance or the participants arrive at that rate?
7. What did the investment analysis conclude specifically about the project's potential?
8. Were there any costs or benefits later found to be overlooked in the original project plan? If so, which ones? Was there an identifiable reason why these costs or benefits were overlooked?
9. Were actual project costs and benefits later determined? If so, were the actual figures compared to those used in the project plan? How close were the actual figures to the projected figures?

8

BEST PRACTICES IN MANAGING SUPPLY CHAIN COSTS

Intense global competition combined with ever-demanding customers has created an environment where the pressure to reduce costs is relentless and severe. The list of entities that can raise prices indiscriminately while failing to control costs is certainly a short one. For the vast majority of organizations, the need to manage costs across a supply chain is a strategic necessity. This chapter begins with an overview of cost fundamentals, followed by the goals of price and cost management. Given that cost management is a never-ending endeavor, this chapter emphasizes a set of best practices that characterize effective cost management.

COST FUNDAMENTALS

Let's begin by presenting some fundamental concepts surrounding costs. Simply stated, a *cost* is a resource sacrificed or forgone to achieve a specific objective. That objective could be the purchase of materials, the hiring of labor, heating a building, or numerous other things that represent costs within a business. Technically speaking, a price that is paid is a cost. A *cost object* is anything for which a separate measurement of costs is desired. Examples include products, services, projects, and departments. A *cost driver* is any factor that affects costs. Any change in a cost driver will cause a change in the total cost of a related cost object. *Cost management* includes the actions that managers take to satisfy customers, while continuously reducing and controlling costs and cost drivers. Supply chain professionals must become cost managers, along with the many other hats they wear.

We can look at costs in terms of how they behave and how they are allocated. *Cost behavior* refers to the way costs change with respect to a change in an activity level. Typical cost behavior patterns include fixed costs, variable costs, and mixed costs. *Fixed costs* (such as management overhead) are costs that do not change with modifications in volume or cost drivers, while *variable costs* (such as material and direct labor) are costs that increase directly and proportionately with changes in volume or cost drivers. *Mixed costs* are costs that have a fixed and a variable component.

Another way to think about costs is through the allocation of cost elements. Cost elements are the components that make up the price of a product or service. The most common cost elements are direct costs; indirect costs; selling, general, and administrative costs; and the profit margin. These elements combine to create a price. *Direct costs* are costs that are related to a cost object and can be traced to that object in an economically feasible manner. Direct materials and direct labor can be traceable to a given product, while *indirect costs* are related to the cost object but often cannot be traced in an economically feasible way (unless a company has an activity-based costing system in place). Indirect costs are sometimes allocated to the cost object using a cost allocation method, such as overhead cost per direct labor hour, overhead as a percent of direct labor cost, or overhead per machine hour.

Another cost element or allocation category is *selling, general, and administrative* (SG&A) *expenses.* These expenses are associated with supporting the interface between a buyer and a supplier, as well as those expenses that are not directly related to the organization's primary operations, but are required to support these operations. SG&A will include sales salaries and commissions, advertising, administrative salaries, and research and development (R&D).

An understanding of these cost concepts is essential when talking about cost management. Different tools and techniques will address aspects of price and cost management. A later section will differentiate between price and cost management.

GOALS OF PRICE AND COST MANAGEMENT

At a broad level, there are some good reasons why we engage in cost management. Few would argue with the need to develop accurate price and cost information to support the negotiating process. Engaging in cost analysis is a key part of the negotiation planning process. We also engage in cost management to promote continuous price and cost improvement. Only a small number of industries or companies can raise their prices at will to cover rising costs—making cost management a central part of supply chain management. And, since market success depends on the ability to remain competitive, we engage in cost management to remain competitive.

Cooperative cost management (versus noncooperative cost management) can also improve supplier relationships through the pursuit of mutually beneficial improvements. Many cost management techniques and approaches are cooperative in nature, which means that parties willingly exchange information and work jointly to improve performance. Cooperative cost management, when performed correctly, can benefit buyers and sellers while enhancing supply chain relationships.

Most supply chain managers understand the need to practice cost management. It would be difficult to come up with any good reasons why a company would not engage in cost management. For the record, ignorance, complacency, and laziness do not qualify as good reasons.

COST MANAGEMENT BEST PRACTICES

Research and experience with hundreds of organizations has resulted in a set of practices that characterize effective cost management. Taking on the responsibilities of a cost manager is one more task for supply chain professionals to assume. This is added to the responsibilities of relationship and risk management, which is in addition to normal job responsibilities. The following is a set of best practices that, when followed, will make the task of managing costs more effective.

Know When to Apply Price versus Cost Analytic Techniques

A major responsibility of a buying company is to ensure that the price it pays for an item or service is fair and reasonable. Evaluation of a supplier's actual cost to provide a product or service, versus the actual purchase price paid, is an ongoing challenge. In many situations the need to control costs requires a focus on the cost elements and drivers associated with producing an item or service versus simply analyzing a quoted price. In other cases, it is not necessary to commit much effort or time to understanding costs. A comparison of whether a price is fair given competitive market conditions is all that may be required.

It is important to recognize that fundamental differences exist between price and cost analysis. Price analysis refers to the process of comparing a price against another price, against external price benchmarks, or against other available information—without in-depth knowledge about underlying costs. Examples of price analytic techniques include competitive bid comparisons, comparisons against published catalog prices, price behavior relative to an external benchmark such as a producer price index, and historical price behavior.

Cost analytic techniques focus primarily on the costs that are aggregated to create a purchase price. By better managing and reducing the elements of cost, a buyer should see the result of these efforts in a lower purchase price compared with prices where cost management did not occur. Cost-driven approaches require the identification and management of cost elements and drivers, which are the factors that directly affect cost levels. A change in an element or driver will cause a change in the total cost (and usually the price) of a related product or service.

A primary difference between price and cost analysis is that cost analysis requires a more technical and detailed understanding of costs. Cost analysis also requires greater cooperation with a seller to quantify costs, identify cost drivers, and develop strategies to improve performance.

The issue of when to apply price versus cost analytic approaches within a supply chain is important. Figure 8.1 presents a modified version of the portfolio matrix that appeared in Chapter 2. This matrix helps us conceptualize when to pursue price versus cost analytic approaches. It helps identify when to apply cost analysis approaches, such as cost-driven pricing, versus traditional price analysis approaches, such as bid comparisons or price comparisons to market indexes.

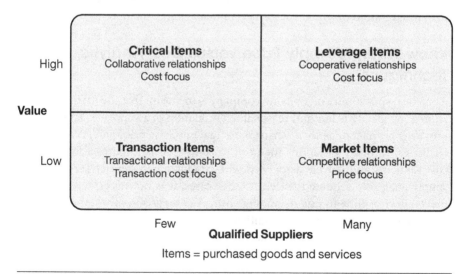

Figure 8.1   Price versus cost focus

Items with a lower total value or standard items that have an active supply market are most conducive to price analysis. The common trait shared by these items is that they have a lower to medium total value, many suppliers that can provide substitutable products and services, and lower supplier switching costs. Price rather than cost analytic techniques usually work best when obtaining these items. Competitive bid or price comparisons, shorter term contracting, reverse Internet auctions, and blanket purchase orders are often-used techniques when obtaining market items. These items are usually part of an active supply market. The competitive market serves as a mechanism for driving costs lower.

Items where consolidating volumes can lead to economic benefit or are critical to a buyer's competitive success are more likely to benefit from cost analytic techniques. For example, leveraging volumes through longer term contracts may lead to discussions with a supplier about quality, delivery, packaging, and service (all factors that can affect cost). Depending on the leveraged item, a cost rather than price focus should be the norm.

At times an item consumes a large portion of total purchase dollars, the item or service is essential to a product's function, and/or the item or service differentiates the product in the eyes of the customer, making these critical items. Although these kinds of items represent relatively few transactions, opportunities exist from collaborative supply chain efforts. This includes a strong focus on cost and cost drivers rather than price. Chapter 9 will present cost-driven pricing, a technique that is ideally suited for managing critical items.

Knowing under what conditions to engage in price analytic techniques and under what conditions to pursue cost analytic techniques is a cost management best practice. Take that to the bank.

Use an Activity-based Accounting System

A large category of costs that are often misunderstood involves the allocation of overhead or indirect costs. Overhead includes business expenses that are not related to direct labor, direct materials, or third-party expenses. Overhead expenses can be fixed, meaning they do not vary as business activity levels change, or variable, meaning they increase or decrease depending on the business's activity level (think of energy consumption to operate a machine cell). They can also be semi-variable, meaning that some portion of the expense will be incurred no matter what, and some portion depends on the level of business activity. We can also have corporate or general overhead that applies to a company's operations as a whole, such as corporate executive salaries. General overhead can also be allocated to a specific project or department.[1] For most organizations there is usually no shortage of overhead.

Far too often overhead is arbitrarily allocated, such as using a rule that assigns overhead at a rate of 150% for every direct labor hour for all products produced on a certain machine. This is usually unsatisfactory because two products that absorb the same direct costs may consume vastly different amounts of overhead, making a generic allocation somewhat problematic.[2] One product within a work area may require significant R&D and engineering support while another product requires minimal engineering resources (and we all know that engineers do not come cheap).

The somewhat arbitrary allocation of overhead can lead to erroneous outsourcing analyses, incorrect product pricing, and misguided cost management efforts. Best practice firms recognize the traditional shortcomings associated with overhead allocation and create cost management systems that allocate overhead based on the overhead actually consumed.

One such system is an activity-based costing (ABC) system. ABC is an alternative to traditional accounting in which a business's overhead (indirect costs such as lighting, heating, and marketing) are allocated in proportion to an activity's direct costs.[3] An ABC method of overhead allocation identifies the activities that a firm performs, and then assigns indirect costs to individual products. An ABC system recognizes the relationship between costs, activities, and products, and assigns indirect costs to products less arbitrarily than traditional methods.[4] While ABC systems are not easy to implement, they do represent a best practice in cost management.

Some companies are naturally reluctant to give up their existing cost accounting system, particularly when internal participants are comfortable with the system. Fortunately, the development of business accounting software programs has made the introduction of ABC systems less arduous.[5]

View Broadly the Domain of Price and Cost Management Approaches

Price and cost management is a broad area where supply chain professionals can be creative. Many tools, techniques, and approaches that have nothing to do with finance and accounting groups are available to help us understand costs. Finance and accounting offer many traditional tools and approaches—even if how we apply them is somewhat untraditional. Asking an accountant to be overly creative can get everyone in trouble.

Let's use Nestlé to illustrate how supply chain costs can be managed creatively.[6] Several years ago the company was under intense pressure as the prices of many of the commodities it purchased increased dramatically. Over a four-year period, each of its major purchased commodities at least doubled in price. In a single year, raw material price changes increased the company's costs by $3 billion. For a company that spends over $30 billion annually on commodities like coffee beans, milk, and cocoa, even a relatively modest 5% increase in costs can have a $1.5 billion impact on the bottom line.

What did the company do to manage these cost pressures? The company now relies on a network of farmers who provide external intelligence that helps the company foresee trends that will pressure commodity prices, particularly in developing countries. If this intelligence indicates future commodity price pressures, Nestlé gradually raises its prices at the retail level, thereby getting a head start on rivals. Retailers are a bit more receptive when you arrive first with a price increase request rather than being the fiftieth company with a request. The company is also slow to reduce prices when commodity prices fall. In their view what goes down (i.e., commodity prices) will eventually go up.

Nestlé also engages in supplier development by helping suppliers manage their costs and increase crop yields. On the packaging front, over a 20-year period the company has reduced its use of packaging materials by over 500,000 tons. Nestlé has reduced the amount of plastic in a Poland Spring water bottle, for example, by 35 percent.

Nestlé has also created more premium priced products where raw materials account for a smaller percentage of the retail price. Packaging its highest quality coffee in single servings for coffee machines allows the company to charge 10 times the price per cup than what its rivals charge for unground beans. Packaging its gourmet ice cream in smaller serving sizes allows Nestlé to charge the equivalent of $15 a quart. And with its purchase of Jenny Craig, the company has moved further away from its dependence on commodities.

As the Nestlé example shows, although a company may not control commodity markets, it can creatively affect the impact of those markets by viewing the domain of price and cost reduction techniques broadly rather than narrowly.

Develop Total Cost Models That Capture More than Unit Price

A clear best practice involves looking beyond unit cost or price to understand all of the cost elements that populate a supply chain. If we are buying a product from China, for example, what are the shipping costs, currency risk costs, duties and customs costs, and inventory carrying charges, to name but a few of the costs associated with international transactions? Best practice firms have developed cost models that help them gain a complete picture of supply chain costs.

Total cost analysis is a subject that supply chain professionals cannot ignore as they search for ways to manage costs. Total cost includes the expected and unexpected elements that increase the unit cost of a good, service, or piece of equipment. The logic behind the development of total cost models is that unit cost or price *never equals total cost*. Furthermore, it is difficult to manage costs when we lack visibility to those costs. Total cost modeling provides that visibility.

The need to understand every element of cost has never been greater. Total cost systems help management identify the magnitude of different cost elements;

track cost improvements in real terms over time; and highlight where cost reduction efforts will have their greatest payback. While there is some agreement regarding the cost elements that should comprise a total cost model, no agreement exists regarding exactly what costs should be part of a particular model. This issue becomes even more complex once we appreciate that, like forecasting models, different types of cost models exist. One type of cost model does not fit every need. Chapter 12 explores total cost modeling in greater detail.

Coordinate with Finance to Validate Savings and Translate Their Impact on Corporate Performance Indicators

The need to involve finance to validate savings is important for several reasons. Perhaps foremost, finance is the one corporate group that has instant credibility when it comes to talking about money. The finance group has internal credibility that can benefit the procurement group in terms of validating cost savings.

Let's face reality here. While hopefully not the norm, procurement groups have been known to make cost savings and cost avoidance claims that raise more than one set of eyebrows. Did you hear about the buyer that padded its bid list with known high price suppliers? After selecting a lower price supplier the buyer was able to claim a cost avoidance. If you are going to make some wild claims about cost savings or avoidances, you better have someone from finance to back you up. Reported cost savings are more believable once finance waves its magic wand and pronounces them to be real.

Another issue regarding the credibility of savings arises when the savings do not make it to the bottom line. Where did those savings go? And, can these savings be real if we cannot follow their path directly to a higher net income? The reality is that savings are often siphoned off by the groups that are responsible for those costs. While procurement buys goods and service, the money to pay for those goods and services is often from accounts that others control. And, other groups often control any savings that are generated. Thank goodness finance blessed those savings before they performed a disappearing act that would impress even Houdini.

What does it mean to say we should *work with finance* to validate savings and translate their impact on corporate indicators? Some companies have assigned finance personnel to commodity teams and other procurement groups to validate savings. This is an important way to show commitment that is likely preferable to running to finance asking for savings to be validated. This may come as a shock, but the finance group has work to do besides waiting for the call from procurement to validate savings.

Procurement can also work with finance to validate the methodology that procurement uses to show the effect of reported savings on corporate indicators.

Earlier chapters in this book addressed this topic more extensively. Here, finance acts as a trainer rather than a validator. Whatever model a company chooses to validate savings and their impact, the need to involve finance is a best practice. Ideally, systems are in place that finance has approved for validating savings. It is not reasonable to expect finance to validate every cost transaction that occurs. Systems support for validating prices paid and savings is a *must have* feature.

Take an Expansive Rather than Narrow View of Lean

Best practice firms endorse lean thinking as a way to better manage costs. Few would argue that waste, which is the central focus of lean, creates higher costs. How could it not? Unfortunately, the vast majority of what has been published on this subject focuses on the internal operations of manufacturing firms. The fact that most firms operate in tightly linked supply chains rather than a self-contained world has yet to register with many lean proponents.

A strict focus on manufacturing firms and internal production is short-sighted. Doesn't every organization, including service providers of all kinds, have waste? And can't waste present itself anywhere within a supply chain? When discussing lean we get inundated with what the Japanese are doing, particularly Toyota and the Toyota Production System (TPS). While the modern roots of lean are in Japan, lean best practices require that we take a broader view of lean than what is typically associated with Japanese industry.

While still recognizing that operations are an integral part of a lean system, effective cost management demands an end-to-end supply chain perspective. This means considering not only lean operations, but also lean supply, lean transportation, lean operations, and lean distribution. In an era when supply chains compete directly against supply chains, the time has come to extend lean thinking beyond our own four walls.

Besides taking an expansive rather than narrow view of lean, best practice firms also expand their horizons in terms of what constitutes waste. Again, the TPS has severely constrained our thinking by focusing and failing to update the seven types of wastes.[7] While understanding these wastes is important, they reveal a perspective that is internal, production-focused, and clearly from an earlier era. When looking across a supply chain, it seems reasonable to add to the list of wastes. Consider these additional kinds of waste:

- Too many bits and bytes—digital waste reflects redundant or unnecessary data that are generated, transmitted, or stored for no value-added reason
- Untapped creativity—failing to utilize human resources, including employees, suppliers, and customers to their fullest potential
- Poor measurement—measuring too much, measuring the wrong things, measuring incorrectly, or promoting unintended behavior

- Excessive overhead—time and cost waste from unnecessary staff and tasks
- Overdesign—waste from designing-in too many components, product features, and variety; relying on too many customized components
- Duplication of effort—developing similar processes across sites or locations, particularly in a decentralized environment
- Poor planning—failing to align the supply and demand segments of the supply chain; poor planning probably creates as much waste as the other types of waste combined

There is usually no shortage of waste across supply chains. In reality, the additional categories of waste presented here are likely an incomplete list. Best practice firms look for lean opportunities across a supply chain and take an expansive view of waste. They find the Toyota approach to lean to be limiting.

Manage Intangible and Hidden Costs

It is a fallacy to believe that all costs within an organization are tangible, easily traceable, or even known. Intangible supply chain costs, for example, are those that traditional cost accounting systems fail to capture, although these costs are real. An intangible cost is an unquantifiable cost relating to an identifiable source.

The problem with intangible and hidden costs is that they are often buried within overhead. The challenge becomes one of partitioning that overhead to better allocate it to its proper source. Because of a failure to quantify or account for those hidden costs, they become difficult to manage or control. Examples include supplier switching costs (related to supplier selection), supply chain transactions costs (related to any supply chain transaction, such as material releases or accounts payable transactions), and poor supplier relationship costs (related to the increased cost of managing a relationship). Another example includes lower employee morale (and eventually lower productivity) due to a reduction in employee benefits. Best practice companies do not ignore these costs—they know that doing so places their company at financial risk.

Best practice firms also attempt to quantify or at least understand hidden costs, particularly when they engage in international purchasing. Chapter 12 will present a set of hidden costs that increase the total cost of doing business with a supplier.

Understand the Differences Between Accomplishments and Activities

An executive at an East Coast company recently sent out an e-mail to everyone in the company proudly announcing that during a recent period, his group made 43 presentations across the company. Unfortunately, the message did not elaborate on any specific accomplishments except to say that these meetings *have been critical in expanding our understanding of certain issues.* This is analogous to a sales representative reporting that she made 25 sales calls (i.e., an activity) in a recent week but offered minimal elaboration. Wouldn't it be natural to ask if these calls generated any actual sales (i.e., accomplishments)?

Many of us have a habit of viewing activities as if they are accomplishments. The political version of this involves candidates who routinely tout their experience, but are much less vocal on what they have accomplished. While activity is important, it matters most if it connects directly to tangible outcomes. Best practice firms understand the distinction between activity and accomplishment well.

In the supply chain space, selecting suppliers, developing supplier performance capabilities, redesigning a supply chain, conducting a reverse auction, benchmarking against industry leaders, forming alliances, and developing supply chain strategies are all *activities.* And, on the surface, there is nothing inherently wrong about feeling good about something the prevailing view says is good. But, in the long run, activities mean nothing unless we can show how they translate directly into tangible outcomes. What did a reverse auction save that a traditional bid could not? What quantified benefits result from a supply chain alliance? Did a supplier development project deliver a positive return? What are commodity teams achieving to justify their expense? In short, what are we *accomplishing*? An important characteristic of best practice firms is that they have the ability to achieve and report accomplishments, particularly cost savings or revenue enhancements, from their supply chain activities. And, they hold individuals and groups accountable for achieving those accomplishments.

Realize Cost Advantages from Early Customer and Supplier Involvement

Early involvement is the process of relying on suppliers or customers early—physically or virtually—to provide support during strategic planning, demand and supply planning, continuous improvement projects, project planning, and when developing new products and technologies. A great deal of early involvement attention focuses on working with suppliers during new product development.

Most firms plan to increase supplier involvement during product development, and most firms indicate that supplier involvement will occur earlier rather than later in the development process. Firms that involve suppliers early in product development indicate they realize greater reductions in material costs, reduced development cycle times, reduced manufacturing costs, greater improvements in material quality, and reduced product development costs compared with firms that involve suppliers later in the development process.

Research also reveals that teams that rely on supplier input and involvement (when a task warrants involvement) are more effective, on average, than teams that do not involve suppliers. Teams that include suppliers as participants also report greater satisfaction concerning the quality of information exchanged between the team and key suppliers, higher reliance on suppliers to directly support the team's goals, fewer problems coordinating work activity between the team and key suppliers, and greater effort put forth on team assignments. And finally, teams that include suppliers as participants report supplier contribution is greater across many performance areas, including suppliers providing cost reduction ideas, quality improvement ideas, actions to improve material delivery, process technology suggestions, and ways to reduce material ordering cycle times.

Research-based findings concerning the value of early supplier involvement are compelling. As a best practice, early involvement is a major contributor of improved performance, including lower material, manufacturing, and product development costs. Early involvement is a cost management best practice. But, like any of the practices listed here, it must be performed correctly.

Benchmark Cost Performance and Techniques Against Leading Firms

Benchmarking is the continuous process of measuring products, services, processes, and practices of a firm against world-class competitors or those companies recognized as industry or functional leaders. A major focus of benchmarking efforts should be cost management and improvement techniques. If another company has lower commodity costs for the same commodities you are purchasing, why is that the case? How does another company routinely validate the cost reductions it achieves while your company struggles in this area?

The key to benchmarking is an understanding of the processes that drive performance rather than simply showing that performance outcomes are different. Even industry leaders should routinely practice performance benchmarking. No supply chain organization is the best at everything. Any organization that believes it has no room for improvement is suffering from a serious condition called arrogance.

Why engage in benchmarking? Supply chain organizations that benchmark have the opportunity to incorporate best practices and technological breakthroughs from other industries, which can drive a culture of continuous improvement. And, engagement with benchmarking studies and visits can stimulate and motivate those who must implement the benchmarking findings. Benchmarking also helps break down resistance to change as participants get to see firsthand the effectiveness of new practices and processes. This also supports the personal growth and development of employees. A benchmarking culture supports a set of long-lasting benefits.

Organizations that make benchmarking an embedded part of their operating culture tend to be grounded in objective evaluation and reality; they search for breakthrough performance opportunities and are externally focused; they understand what defines industry best practices; they are forward thinking, welcoming of new ideas, and have a higher tolerance for change; and they demonstrate superior performance compared with organizations that are inwardly focused with a *not invented here* mindset. While benchmarking is an activity, best practice companies use their benchmarking results to affect meaningful change and improvement. Benchmarking leads to improvement.

Be forewarned that benchmarking can have a darker side. Chapter 15 will talk about the growing tendency of customers to extend, sometimes dramatically, the time they take to pay their suppliers. What does this have to do with benchmarking? In the words of one finance professor, "Investment analysts compare one manufacturer to another and say, 'How come you're not managing your working capital the way that other company is?' It becomes a matter of benchmarking, so if one company does it, then other firms fall in line." In this case benchmarking can lead to an outcome that is not at all desirable to suppliers.

It is also common during a benchmarking study to marvel at what you are seeing at another organization. The tendency is to fall into a dangerous trap by thinking those marvelous results are easily attainable. It is not enough to know the performance outcomes at a company you have benchmarked. It is vital to understand how the benchmark organization achieved that performance.

It is also natural to arrive home and want to achieve better performance in six months or less. Unfortunately, the benchmark organization might have undergone a four-year transformation. Benchmarking can create unrealistic expectations on the home front. An analogy involves comparing yourself to someone who has been participating in CrossFit for two years and then expecting your transformation will require only a month. A disappointment is likely on the horizon.

Engage in Spend Analysis

Spend analysis is the process of collecting, cleansing, classifying, and analyzing expenditure data with the purpose of reducing procurement costs, improving efficiency, developing sourcing strategies, and monitoring contract compliance. Performing detailed spend analysis helps companies find new areas of savings that previously went untapped while holding on to past gains that are already negotiated.[8] The process also helps identify risks and opportunities for performance improvements and savings by applying best practices in purchasing and supply management.[9] It is hard to overestimate how important spend analysis is as a best practice for managing costs.

A study by the Aberdeen Group reached several important conclusions regarding spend analysis. First, spend data management has become a requirement for supply management and business success. Next, the study concluded that successful spend data management initiatives rely on certain critical success factors—access to all spend data sources, a common classification schema, category expertise, efficient and repeatable data cleansing and classification capabilities, advanced reporting and decision support tools, and sufficient resources and executive support. This study also concluded that most enterprises lack sufficient, accurate, and timely insight into corporate spending.[10] Aberdeen estimates that industry loses $260 billion each year in opportunity costs due to an inability to organize and analyze spend data.

Typically, procurement organizations identify a company's expenditures and place those expenditures and items in commodity or category groups for detailed analysis. A commodity or category is simply a like grouping of items, such as printed circuit boards, temporary labor services, or plastic injected parts. Spend analysis should be an integral part of a company's strategic sourcing process. As such, commodity teams should engage in a spirited discussion about how best to obtain and manage an item or family of items. Cost management should be a major part of that discussion.

While many tools and techniques are available to help manage costs, spend analysis represents a rigorous process for managing costs. Specific steps define the spend analysis process:[11]

1. Audit existing spend data management capabilities
2. Access all spend-data sources within and outside the enterprise
3. Adopt a common enterprise-wide classification scheme
4. Establish efficient and repeatable data cleansing and classification capabilities, usually through the use of software
5. Classify spending at a detailed level
6. Enhance core spend data with supply market intelligence
7. Progressively increase frequency and coverage of spend analyses
8. Utilize advanced reporting and decision support tools
9. Continuously expand the use and scope of the spend data management process

Spend analysis allows a company to take a leveraged and coordinated view of its expenditures. It is hard to imagine a supply chain organization that is effective at managing its procurement costs without a well-established spend analysis process in place.

Simplify, Simplify, Simplify

It is becoming widely accepted that supply chains are becoming increasingly complex. And, complexity almost always leads to higher costs. While firms that can manage supply chain complexity can often use that to their advantage, far too often complexity overwhelms our ability to control costs.

Why do supply chains become complex? There is no shortage of blame for increased complexity. The following suggests that the causes of complexity are many:

- Engineers gone wild—why use standard parts or reuse an existing part when an engineer can create a brand new customized part, which, of course, increases costs?
- Marketers gone wild—why do we absolutely need another variation of mint toothpaste?
- Faster product development—the more efficient that companies become at product development, the more products they tend to introduce, which leads to increased supply chain complexity.
- Lack of process thinkers and ill-defined processes—poor processes create waste, which drives up costs.
- Strategic choices—some companies choose to become more complex, particularly as they expand globally or develop increasing numbers of new products.
- Decentralization—a sure way to drive up costs is through a lack of leveraged purchase contracts with few standardized best practices across operating units.
- Continuous reorganizations and new programs—constant organizational change and new programs, many of which quickly fade away, creates individual complexity for employees.
- Bureaucracy—everyone's favorite source for red tape, rules, procedures, and positions creates a breeding ground for complexity.
- Mergers and acquisitions—a guaranteed source of increased complexity as companies try to integrate diverse systems, cultures, procedures, etc.
- Complexity creates job security—would we really need so many accountants if we had a simple tax code?
- Complacency—why would we address complexity when we think everything is just fine?
- Let's go global—make no doubt about it, doing business in a foreign country is exponentially more complex than in one's home country.

A best practice to take costs out of a supply chain is to make it less complex, or what is called simplification. Virtually any aspect of a supply chain can be examined to see if it might benefit from a simpler design or fewer steps. We can have products that are too complex in design, resulting in too many components, too many suppliers, and too high a product cost; too many distribution centers that increase inventory costs; too many suppliers that lead to higher supplier management costs and less opportunity to leverage purchase volumes; and too many customers that cost more to serve than what they provide in profitability. Best practice companies are always searching for opportunities to simplify every aspect of their supply chain.

CONCLUDING THOUGHTS

Effective cost management involves a never-ending pursuit of cost savings. The pursuit of cost savings includes establishing cost targets, developing information systems that capture and report price and cost performance, searching for new and creative ways to manage costs, and holding individuals and groups accountable for achieving specific improvements. This is something that will not change in our lifetime as long as industry after industry is subject to intense global competition. The next chapter will show us that, fortunately, some creative ways exist to manage supply chain costs. Some of these ways will take you out of your comfort zone by introducing techniques that are likely not part of your current skill set.

REFERENCES

1. http://www.investopedia.com/terms/o/overhead.asp.
2. Activity-Based Costing, *The Economist*, June 29, 2009, retrieved from http://www.economist.com/node/13933812.
3. Activity-Based Costing, *The Economist*, June 29, 2009, retrieved from http://www.economist.com/node/13933812.
4. http://www.investopedia.com/terms/a/abc.asp.
5. Activity-Based Costing, *The Economist*, June 29, 2009, retrieved from http://www.economist.com/node/13933812.
6. Tom Miller, "Nestlé's Recipe for Juggling Volatile Commodity Costs," *Business Week*, March 21-27, 2011, 29-30.
7. The traditional set of wastes includes defects, excess inventory, excessive production, unnecessary motion, waiting, overproduction, and unnecessary transport.
8. https://en.wikipedia.org/wiki/Spend_analysis.
9. https://www.kbmanage.com/concept/spend-analysis.
10. https://www.unspsc.org/Portals/3/Documents/Best%20Practices%20in%20Spending%20Analysis%20--%20Cure%20for%20a%20Corporate%20Epidemic.pdf.

11. Adapted from Aberdeen Group, *Best Practices in Spending Analysis*, https://www.unspsc.org/Portals/3/Documents/Best%20Practices%20 in%20Spending%20Analysis%20--%20Cure%20for%20a%20 Corporate%20Epidemic.pdf.

9

MANAGING COSTS ACROSS THE SUPPLY CHAIN—THE FINANCIAL PERSPECTIVE

Death, taxes, rock and roll, and the need to reduce costs are all part of a small set of things we know we can always count on. In fact, it is safe to say that unless you work for a university, the government, or certain parts of the health care system, the need to reduce costs will always be relentless and severe. Fortunately, an abundance of techniques are available to help manage costs across the supply chain.

The time has come to view the set of techniques and approaches for managing costs broadly rather than narrowly. This chapter presents a set of techniques you have likely not seen and do not readily recognize.[1] In no particular order of importance, this chapter presents some creative ways to manage supply chain costs. While these techniques all rely on cost or financial data for their use, this is one chapter where the presented techniques are not taken from finance.

LEARNING CURVE COST MODELS

We have probably all undertaken a task that, as it is performed repetitively, takes progressively less time. What is happening is that learning is taking place. Learning curve models are based on the principle that as individuals become more familiar with a task, the average amount of direct labor required to perform that task or process declines at a predictable rate. The predictable rate is the learning rate or curve. A supplier that experiences learning during production should be in a position to provide a continuous stream of price reductions.

A learning rate is the predictable reduction in direct labor requirements as production doubles from a previous level. A 90 percent learning curve, for example, means that the average direct labor required to produce an item decreases by 10 percent as volume doubles from one level to another. An 80 percent learning curve means the average direct labor to produce an item decreases by 20 percent as production doubles from a previous level. At most firms, learning curve analysis is applied internally. Applying the concept to a supplier's price, particularly during negotiations, is not practiced nearly as often.

Learning curves apply only to the direct labor portion of production costs, even though the term is often used more broadly (and incorrectly). Learning curves also do not apply to simple items or items where the supplier has extensive experience. Even if an item is new to the buyer, it may not be new to the supplier.

Learning curve analysis works best when a supplier is producing a complex item for the first time. Also, the identification of an incorrect learning rate will skew the estimated improvements, as a supplier moves along the learning curve. And, do not expect to go back to a supplier after six months or a year with a new order and expect to see productivity at the same level as where the previous order left off. Something called the *forgetting factor* must be considered.

Table 9.1 shows how to estimate a price change due to learning. While material changes may result due to higher volumes, the learning curve analysis only concerns itself directly with changes due to direct labor requirements. However, the reader might notice several other secondary effects that will further reduce a purchase price. First, if a supplier applies overhead as a percent of direct labor (not an uncommon approach when a supplier lacks an activity-based costing system), the overhead allocation will be reduced since the amount of direct labor is reduced. This is legitimate since the product is consuming less labor and machine time. We might also see a reduction in the amount of profit per unit. Again, this is acceptable since the profit margin, which remains constant, is applied against a lower total cost base.

In this example the buyer calculates an expected price reduction from $209 to $177.10 per unit. Whether the supplier agrees to this price is open to debate and negotiation. This new figure provides a target to work toward with the supplier. Potential improvements in material costs due to greater volumes could further reduce this price.

If learning occurs and the buyer does not capture the cost benefits, then it stands to reason that the supplier will reap the benefits. A buyer must determine if an item will benefit from learning, and then factor that learning into the supplier's pricing. Learning curve is a well-established but not well-understood cost methodology among supply chain professionals.

Table 9.1 Learning curve illustrated

A company submits an order to a supplier for 200 units of an item not previously produced by this supplier. Studies by industrial engineers reveal the learning curve for this type of item to be 90 percent. The supplier provides the following *per unit* information:

Materials	$40
Direct Labor	$60 (3 hours on average per unit @ $20 per hour)
Overhead	$90 (150% of direct labor)
Total costs	$190
Profit	$19 (10% of total costs)

Per Unit Price   **$209**

Several weeks later the buyer submits a new order for 1,400 additional units (making 1,600 total units ordered). What should the buyer expect to pay per unit for the next order of 1,200 units given the effects of a 90 percent learning curve?

Analysis:

Step 1: Estimate the Average Hours per Unit

If the 200 unit order requires an average of 3 hours of direct labor per unit, then a doubling of production to 400 units should require 90 percent (i.e., .9) of 3 hours, or 2.7 average hours per unit.* A doubling to 800 units should require 2.43 average hours per unit (.9 × 2.7 average hours). A further doubling of units to 1,600 units should require 2.19 average hours per unit (.9 × 2.43).

Step 2: Calculate the Direct Labor Hours Required to Make 1,200 Units

Producing 1,600 units should require 2.19 average hours per unit, or 3,504 total hours (1,600 × 2.19 average hours per unit). The first 200 unit order required 600 hours (3 hours on average × 200 units).

The total direct labor hours required for the next order of 1,200 units will be 3,504 (the total hours to produce 1,600 units) – 600 hours (the total hours already consumed to make the first 200 units), or 2,904 direct labor hours.

Step 3: Calculate the Direct Labor Costs for the 1,200 Unit Order

2,904 direct labor hours × $20 per hour direct labor costs means the next order of 1,200 units will consume $58,080 in total direct labor costs. This equals $48.40 in direct labor costs per unit ($58,080/1,200 units).

Step 4: Calculate the Unit Price for the Next Order of 1,200 Units

For the next 1,200 units:

Materials	$40
Direct Labor	$48.40
Overhead	$72.60 (150% of direct labor)
Total costs	$161
Profit	$16.1 (10% of total costs)

New Per Unit Price   **$177.10**

*Recall that the learning curve principle states that average direct labor hours decline by a predictable rate (called the learning curve or rate) as volumes double from one level to another.

THEORETICAL BEST PRICING

This approach requires detailed cost data from suppliers to identify a theoretical best price (TBP). A TBP is the result of combining the best cost elements across a pool of potential suppliers. As with many cost topics, the easiest way to demonstrate this technique is with an example. In Table 9.2 the TBP given this set of costs and suppliers is $45.48 per unit. How was this arrived at? Notice in Table 9.2 that the lowest cost in each row is highlighted. The highlighted cells are added together to arrive at the theoretical price.

The use of this technique serves two purposes. The first is to arrive at a benchmark or target to measure an actual price against. A standardized performance ratio can be created that compares the actual price paid to the TBP. If the price paid for a component, for example, is $14.55 and the TBP is $12, the ratio is 1.21. This means the buyer is paying 21 percent more than the TBP. The second purpose is to identify areas where costs are out of line for each supplier or where possible improvement efforts should be directed.

The second part of Table 9.2 presents a standardized ratio of each supplier's cost within each row, compared with the best cost for that row. For example,

Table 9.2   Theoretical best price

	Supplier A	Supplier B	Supplier C
Direct Labor	$12.55	$12.78	$13.10
Direct Materials	$10.77	$10.33	$9.25
Overhead	$13.12	$12.78	$15.12
SG&A	$5.90	$5.75	$6.55
Profit	$5.05	$5.95	$5.50
Price	$47.39	$47.59	$49.52

Theoretical Best Price = $12.55 + $9.25 + $12.78 + $5.75 + $5.05 = **$45.38**

Standardized against the best cost:

	Supplier A	Supplier B	Supplier C
Direct Labor	1.0	1.02	1.04
Direct Materials	1.16	1.12	1.0
Overhead	1.03	1.0	1.18
SG&A	1.03	1.0	1.14
Profit	1.0	1.18	1.09
Price-to-best-price ratio	1.04	1.05	1.09

Supplier C's ratio for direct labor is 1.04 ($13.10/$12.55). This means Supplier C's direct labor costs are 4% higher than the best cost across the three suppliers. Calculate and interpret all other ratios accordingly. The standardized ratio is an easy way to see what costs are out of line within each row.

Where do we get the data to calculate a TBP? Requests for proposal packages should include a supplier cost form that allows the development of a TBP table. Unfortunately, suppliers sometimes do not know their costs at a detailed enough level to use this approach. And, at times, some suppliers may not be willing to share this kind of information. Nevertheless, this is a technique worth pursuing.

CONFIGURED SOURCING NETWORK

A configured sourcing network is not likely a familiar term to the reader. At times, a buyer will develop contracts with distributors that cover dozens, or even hundreds of items. When configuring a supply network a buyer analyzes price quotations from multiple distributors and configures a sourcing network based on the best quotes from each source. While the buyer may use more distributors than planned, the trade-off of developing a supply network that results in a lower total cost will likely outweigh the costs of maintaining additional suppliers.

Table 9.3 illustrates a configured sourcing network. In this example a buyer has requested quotes for six items from five distributors. (This analysis assumes there are no appreciable differences between the items across suppliers that would create significant price differences.) By analyzing the quotations the buyer can identify the best way (i.e., configuration) regarding how to source these items at the lowest total cost.

An important part of this analysis considers annual volumes, which Table 9.3 illustrates. The importance of accurate demand estimates cannot be overstated. The best annual cost, based on quoted prices is Supplier B at $263,490. Dividing the six items among three suppliers (Suppliers C and D did not qualify for any items) yields an expected configured network cost of $248,260, which is about a 6% price improvement over Supplier B's quotation. The question now becomes whether it is worth the 6% difference to use three suppliers instead of one.

A major assumption when using this approach is that the prices that each supplier quotes are independent of each other. This means a quoted price for one item is not contingent upon agreeing to purchase another item. This independence is what allows a buyer to selectively pick and choose items and distributors. While this example is for a single buying location, the concept can be extended to identify which distributors should supply different buying locations. A buyer may be dealing with hundreds of items from multiple distributors that are being shipped to different locations.

Table 9.3   Configured supply network

Unit Costs:

Item/Part Number	Supplier A	Supplier B	Supplier C	Supplier D	Supplier E
123661 Gloves	$2.45	$2.76	$3.00	$2.40	$2.30
344296 High-density bulbs	$5.40	$4.95	$5.55	$5.32	$5.60
988373 Safety glasses	$6.59	$6.25	$6.75	$6.44	$6.50
746322 Pens	$1.25	$1.33	$1.43	$1.43	$1.20
854471 Soap	$7.70	$7.05	$7.55	$7.35	$7.60
777432 Paper	$3.12	$3.18	$3.23	$3.40	$3.52

Note: Shaded areas represent the lowest price for each part number/item across each row.

Total Dollars Based on Volume:

Annual Volume— Units/Pounds	Supplier A	Supplier B	Supplier C	Supplier D	Supplier E
123661 Gloves 25,000	$61,250	$69,000	$75,000	$60,000	$57,500
344296 Light bulbs 14,000	$75,600	$69,300	$77,700	$74,480	$78,400
988373 Safety glasses 5,000	$32,950	$31,250	$33,750	$32,200	$32,500
746322 Pens 25,000	$31,250	$33,250	$35,750	$35,750	$30,000
854471 Soap 5,000	$38,500	$35,250	$37,750	$36,750	$38,000
777432 Paper 8,000	$24,960	$25,440	$25,840	$27,200	$28,160
Total	$264,510	$263,490	$285,790	$266,380	$264,560

Note: Each cell = (price from the first table) × (volume).
The sum of the shaded areas represents the configured supply network total cost, or $248,260
($248,260/$263,490) = almost a 6% total price improvement.

The benefits from this approach are usually worth the effort. Imagine a company with $100 million in indirect spending with distributors that achieves a 6% total annual savings due to a configured sourcing network. Realizing $6 million in savings (less the increased supplier management costs) is not bad for a few weeks work.

COMPARISONS TO EXTERNAL INDEXES

This approach features the use of objective, third-party information to verify that the prices paid are reasonable, given actual changes in a marketplace. One website that supply chain managers should become familiar with is www.bls.gov. This site, maintained by the U.S. Bureau of Labor Statistics, contains a wealth of free data and information. It is worth exploring; it is, after all, your tax dollars at work.

Along the top menu bar of the bls.gov website is a category called *Data Tools*. Simply click on that icon and scroll down until you see *Prices - Producer*. The user now has the choice to select between industry data and commodity data. According to the Bureau of Labor Statistics, a Producer Price Index (PPI) for an industry is a measure of changes in prices received for the industry's output sold outside the industry (that is, its net output).

The PPI publishes approximately 535 industry price indexes in combination with over 4,000 specific product line and product category sub-indexes, as well as roughly 500 indexes for groupings of industries. The PPI's commodity classification structure organizes products and services by similarity or material composition. This system is unique to the PPI and does not match any other standard coding structure. In all, PPI publishes more than 3,700 commodity price indexes for goods and about 800 for services—organized by product, service, and end use.[2]

Let's illustrate the use of a PPI table and index. Assume you are a buyer of motor vehicle parts to support your company's fleet operations. One of your primary parts suppliers has informed you that his prices will likely go up next year by 6%, reflecting increases in labor and material costs. Without even looking at the supplier's labor and material cost elements, the PPI might provide some insight into whether this increase is realistic.

Table 9.4 presents the PPI for motor vehicle parts. An attractive feature of this tool is that these tables can be easily downloaded for analysis in Excel. A critical point to understand is that the numbers in this table are not prices. They are index numbers for the particular item compared to a base year when the index was established at 100. This particular table was established with an index value of *100* in December of 2003 (Base Date: 200312). The *P* in the table means the data are preliminary and subject to possible revision.

The first thing the reader should notice is the stability of the data index numbers. In fact, from January 2014 (Index = 112.7) to March 2015 (Index = 113.1) there has been almost no change in overall price index for motor vehicle prices. Since the index was established in December 2003 (Index = 100), the net increase in motor vehicle prices over a 12-year period has been a paltry 13.1% ((113.1 − 100)/100). That is just over a 1% increase per year.

Is the supplier in this case justified in seeking a 6% price increase? That request is clearly not in line with what we are seeing in the price index. Perhaps this supplier is not managing costs well or is possibly trying to slip in a price increase. It is possible the supplier might provide an item that uses raw materials that are experiencing pricing pressures. After all, motor vehicle parts are a broad category. The point here is the supply manager now has objective data to have a heart-to-heart talk with the supplier.

Table 9.4   Producer price index for motor vehicle parts

Series Id: WPU141205
Not Seasonally Adjusted
Group: Transportation equipment
Item: Motor vehicles parts
Base Date: 200312

Year	Jan	Feb	Mar	Apr	May	Jun	Jul	Aug	Sep	Oct	Nov	Dec
2005	101.1	101.2	101.1	101.0	101.2	101.1	101.4	101.5	101.6	101.6	101.9	102.1
2006	102.4	102.7	103.2	103.9	103.9	104.3	104.8	105.1	105.2	104.9	105.1	105.1
2007	105.2	105.0	105.0	105.4	105.6	105.8	105.9	106.0	106.0	105.9	106.0	106.1
2008	106.0	106.0	105.8	106.2	106.5	106.7	107.7	108.1	108.5	108.7	108.7	108.7
2009	108.6	108.3	108.3	108.3	108.4	108.2	107.9	107.7	107.9	108.3	108.2	108.4
2010	108.2	108.3	108.3	109.4	109.3	109.3	108.7	109.5	109.5	109.5	109.5	109.5
2011	109.9	110.3	110.5	110.8	110.9	111.0	111.4	111.9	111.5	111.6	111.5	111.5
2012	111.6	111.6	112.0	112.1	112.1	112.1	112.2	112.2	112.2	112.3	112.8	112.9
2013	112.9	112.7	112.8	112.7	112.6	112.6	112.6	112.7	112.6	112.5	112.5	112.5
2014	112.7	112.6	112.6	112.5	112.6	112.7	112.7	112.6	112.7	112.8	112.8	112.6(P)
2015	112.7(P)	113.0(P)	113.1(P)									

P: Preliminary. All indexes are subject to revision four months after original publication.

TARGET PRICING

A traditional approach to pricing generally assumes that the starting point in arriving at a price is the combination of costs associated with producing an item. A traditional pricing approach would be to add up the costs associated with producing an item, add on a desired level of profit, and arrive at a total cost figure that then determines the selling price. Unfortunately, this selling price may not be what the market was expecting. When a company quickly offers rebates or discounts on a new product, this is a clue that perhaps the selling price missed the intended market segment.

A different approach is called target pricing (also called target costing). This method involves (1) identifying the price at which a product will be competitive in the marketplace, (2) defining the desired profit to be made on the product, and (3) computing the target cost for the product by subtracting the desired profit from the competitive market price. The target cost is then given to engineers and product designers, who use it as the maximum cost to be incurred for the materials and other resources needed to design and manufacture the product.[3] It is their responsibility, usually working with procurement and suppliers, to create the product at or below its target cost. Product developers work closely with marketing to identify a selling price that matches customer expectations. Target pricing employs the following formula:

	Traditional Pricing		Target Pricing
	Costs		Selling Price
+	Profit	−	Profit
=	Selling Price	=	Allowable Costs

What happens after arriving at an allowable cost figure? Complex products are broken down into systems, subsystems, and components—each with an assigned cost that rolls up to form the total allowable costs. Eventually costs are managed at the component and production level. Often buyers and suppliers do not even negotiate prices. The price of a component is assigned as part of the target pricing process. The entire focus in target pricing is on cost management.

It is not unusual to find that actual costs are higher than what the cost model says is allowable. This is where the cooperative part of target pricing kicks in. A buyer's design teams and suppliers (internal and external) must work together to simplify a design or production process, search for alternate materials, use standard components instead of custom designed items, or apply any other approach that will reduce cost elements and cost drivers. It is also possible that savings from one part of a project can offset cost deficiencies in another part. A company may also decide to accept a lower profit margin, although that is not a preferred method.

A virtue of target pricing is that it is a disciplined approach to cost management. And, a secondary effect is that the process should result in less time-consuming and costly negotiation with suppliers. Buyers and sellers work cooperatively to achieve allowable costs. Costs are an output of the target costing process, not the negotiation process.

EMPLOYEE AND SUPPLIER SUGGESTION PROGRAMS

A relatively easy way to gain access to cost reduction ideas is through employee and supplier suggestion programs. Thanks to web-based technology, the challenges surrounding supplier suggestion programs are no longer technical. The challenge is in making sure the resources are available to review and then act upon any suggestions. Ideas that remain idle are not valuable.

Firms that are serious about a supplier suggestion program must be willing to commit resources to evaluate the suggestions they receive. Often this means appointing a program manager or steering committee to oversee the process. It also means making engineers available to evaluate the technical merits of suggestions. It takes time to evaluate the hundreds of suggestions that suppliers will hopefully put forth. Suppliers will quickly become disinterested in any program they perceive is a black hole—sucking in ideas that are never seen or heard from again. Another challenge is convincing suppliers to participate.

Progressive firms recognize the important linkage between supplier suggestions and rewards. Rewarding supplier participation should lead to greater involvement with the program. Some firms evaluate a supplier's level of participation and include that in the supplier's scorecard rating. Other firms share any savings realized from the ideas, either directly as payments to the supplier, adjustments to the selling price that reflect the supplier's share, or as credits toward future cost reduction commitments. Direct payments require working closely with accounting since it is often difficult to write a check for suggestions rather than invoices. A later section in this chapter on cost-driven pricing will illustrate how to share savings with suppliers financially.

Best-practice organizations track the suggestions they receive, respond to suggestions in an agreed-upon time frame, and report to executive managers any savings that are achieved through the system. The suggestion system should serve as a central repository for all ideas received from suppliers and employees. Developing a suggestion program can be a cost effective way to manage costs. It is surprising that suggestion programs are not more common.

VALUE ANALYSIS WORKSHOPS

Value analysis (VA), a continuous improvement methodology developed in the 1950s, evaluates the functionality of a product or service against its cost.

Formally defined, VA is the organized and systematic study of every element of cost in a part, material, process, or service, to make certain it fulfills its function for the customer at the lowest total cost. It employs techniques which identify the functionality the user wants from the part, material, process, or service. The VA workshops and process are a combination of group problem solving, project management, kaizen workshops, and process redesign. In equation form, the concept of value is defined as:

$$Value = Function/Cost$$

The objective of VA is to increase value by affecting the numerator and/or denominator of the equation. It is a continuous improvement approach that is applied to existing products and services. (Value engineering is the counterpart of VA and is applied during new product and service development.) Like learning curve, VA has been around for quite a while. This does not mean it is not an effective way to manage costs.

VA benefits from a cross-functional team approach that may involve suppliers, customers, packaging, logistics, supply management, design and process engineers, marketing, accounting, and manufacturing. VA teams ask a series of questions to determine if the value that a customer attaches to a product or service can be improved. The types of questions asked, many of which apply to the cost portion (denominator) of the VA equation, include:

- Are lower cost but equally effective materials available?
- Can the design be simplified?
- Are standard components available to replace custom-designed components?
- Can improvements be made to the production process?
- Can features be added to enhance functionality more than the associated cost increase?
- Are lower cost suppliers available?
- Is there any functionality currently included that the customer does not want?
- Can packaging or logistics costs be reduced?

The VA process has five distinct phases. Results should be tracked closely, with improvements widely reported across the company. In fact, progressive companies establish annual improvement targets to be achieved through their VA process. When performed correctly, VA offers a systematic approach for improving value, functionality, and costs. The five phases include:

- **Information phase:** In this phase executive leadership gathers data and ranks opportunities; establishes preliminary improvement targets;

identifies the function of a part, material, process, or service under study; and creates the VA team.

- **Speculative phase:** This phase includes the questions presented earlier. Creative thinking techniques are employed in this phase.
- **Analytic phase:** The VA team performs cost/benefit analysis on each idea, assesses the effect of a change on internal and external customers, and assesses the reality of any changes. The team will also review improvement targets. Critical thinking techniques are employed in this phase.
- **Execution phase:** A cross-functional VA group works to secure buy-in to proposed change, develops an implementation plan, breaks down resistance to changes across functional areas, and carries out the changes. In this phase it is important to note the date and baseline metrics to assess the effects of changes.
- **Conclusion phase:** In this phase, the VA team verifies the success of changes, documents and reports savings, works to transfer learning throughout the organization, and disbands or assumes a new VA challenge.

A challenge with a process such as VA is maintaining its intensity. One way to do this is to track and report results and initiatives at the highest levels. It is amazing what executive visibility will do in terms of sending a clear message about the importance of this process. Companies can also recognize and reward VA efforts across the organization, as well as across the supply chain. A company can also create VA displays, provide VA updates, report successes from VA, and offer VA training to suppliers. Since VA is really a continuous improvement methodology, embedding a commitment to this process into the corporate culture should provide long-lasting benefits.

COST-DRIVEN PRICING

Cost-driven pricing is a collaborative, but rarely used approach for managing the costs, and therefore the price, of critical items. It is a cutting-edge approach that moves far beyond basic cost analytic techniques. This approach, which offers an opportunity to promote cooperative behavior between a buyer and seller, has as its primary objective continuous cost reductions over the life of a purchase contract. Cost-driven pricing enables buying and selling firms to achieve real cost reductions over time, while simultaneously reducing the conflict typically associated with pricing approaches that promote short-term profit maximization.

Cost-driven pricing contracts differ radically from cost-plus contracting. With cost-plus contracting, profits often increase or decrease based on actual costs incurred. Cost-plus contracting results in conflicting goals because increasing costs eventually benefits the supplier at the buyer's expense.

Cost-driven pricing is also not market-driven pricing. In a market-driven approach, the buyer or seller maintains an advantage depending on supply and demand, the level of product differentiation, or the number of firms involved within a market. Suppliers focus on achieving the highest allowable price, while buyers strive for prices that are often unrealistic. Pursuing individual advantages, unstable pricing, and conflicting goals do not promote cooperative behavior. Furthermore, market-driven pricing typically ignores the cost drivers behind a purchase price.

It becomes necessary to discuss several concepts to understand cost-driven pricing. First, a buyer and seller's joint agreement on the target price, profit, and full cost to produce an item becomes the foundation of a cost-driven price. This requires agreement not only about target prices and allowable profit, but also agreement about standard material, labor, and other direct and indirect costs associated with producing an item. Reasonable administrative, selling, and other general expenses are also recognized as fundamental parts of a supplier's cost base.

Perhaps the most important element of a cost-driven pricing contract is that a supplier's asset investment and return requirements provide the basis for establishing the profit for each item produced. Profit is the result of an agreed to percentage of return on investment employed directly by the seller to satisfy the buyer's contract. This differs from traditional pricing approaches that establish profit as a percentage of the selling price or manufacturing cost. Thus, once a buyer and seller agree upon an appropriate asset base, fluctuations in manufacturing costs (labor, material, etc.) do not affect a supplier's return. Establishing profit based on asset and return requirements should encourage the supplier to commit resources specifically to the buyer-seller relationship. In cost-driven pricing, the buyer explicitly acknowledges the need to satisfy a supplier's financial return requirements.

Joint assumptions and agreement on product cost, production volumes, quality, targeted costs, productivity improvements, and contractual sharing of supplier-initiated savings are also essential to a cost-driven approach. Agreeing on these issues requires higher levels of trust, information sharing, negotiation, and joint problem solving. The complexity of cost-driven pricing ensures it will only be applied as a strategic cost management technique in selected relationships that feature trust and a willingness to share information.

Cost-driven pricing contracts require the establishment of joint improvement targets in areas such as cost, quality, scrap, and delivery. These agreed-upon improvement targets help drive continuous cost reduction over time. Furthermore, shared cost savings take effect only after the supplier achieves initially targeted price/cost improvements. For example, if the buyer and seller target a material content cost reduction of 10 percent per year, shared cost-saving would take effect on any savings beyond the 10 percent level. Productivity improvement targets must be aggressive with both parties developing an action plan to attain targeted goals. Shared cost-savings provide an incentive to accelerate cost improvements beyond those agreed to in the purchase contract.

Not all products or items are candidates for cost-driven pricing. In fact, the vast majority of items would never qualify for a cost-driven pricing approach. A cost-driven approach is most applicable when the seller adds significant value through direct and indirect labor or design capabilities. It is also applicable when sophisticated technologies provide opportunities for product design and process alternatives. Raw materials or other commodity items are least likely to benefit from a cost-driven pricing approach.

The supplier selection decision is usually separate from the mechanics of cost-driven pricing. Supplier selection almost always occurs before the parties even discuss a cost-driven contractual agreement. A willingness to enter into a relationship that, at some point, might feature approaches such as cost-driven pricing, may influence the final choice of a supplier. The chances are good that the buyer and seller have an extensive track record of working together before they consider a cost-driven pricing approach.

Cost-Driven Pricing Example

This section presents a cost-driven pricing example based on the experiences of two companies.[4] Both parties decided to try an innovative approach to contracting that is radically different from anything they had entered into previously. The two parties agreed to analyze jointly the supplier's cost structure for a subassembly, which requires a high degree of trust and confidentiality between the parties. Working together they determined that investment requirements to support this product were $20 million over the contract's expected three-year life. This includes $12 million in working capital requirements and $8 million in capital assets over the projected product life. The parties also agreed to a 20% return on investment target for the supplier. In addition, the supplier committed to annual productivity improvements of 10 percent for direct labor and a 25 percent annual reduction for scrap. The agreement also includes a cost saving sharing agreement for any cost reductions due to design modifications initiated by either party. While not featured here, the agreement also featured a risk sharing formula in the event that demand volumes moved outside of an accepted range of risk. Table 9.5 summarizes the contractual conditions between the buyer and seller.

The two parties agreed to reestablish the subassembly's price at the end of the first and second year of the contract. This review reflected the changes that

Table 9.5   Cost-driven pricing agreed upon contractual issues

Product:	Subassembly		
Negotiated/Analyzed Cost Structure:			
Direct Labor Rate	$20.75 per hour		
Overhead Rate	150% of direct labor		
Scrap Rate	10% of total material, direct labor, and overhead		
SG&A Expenses	12% of total manufacturing cost		
Expected Volume Range	120,000 units per year ± 15%		
Contract Length	3 years		
Agreed to Return on Investment	20%		
Contract Specific Investment:	Year 1	Year 2	Year 3
Working Capital	$4 million	$4 million	$4 million
Net Capital Assets	$3 million	$3 million	$2 million
Total Investment over Three Years	$20,000,000		
Supplier Productivity Commitment:			
Direct Labor Content	10% reduction from previous year level		
Scrap Rate	25% reduction from previous year level		
Joint Effort Design Revision/Cost Reductions:	Savings shared on a 50/50 basis		

occurred over the course of years one and two. Major year-one occurrences included economic increases for material and direct labor. Furthermore, a joint study team developed a substitute material that reduced material costs by $4 per unit, resulting in an equal sharing of savings during year two. Year-two adjustments also reflected positive adjustments due to labor efficiencies and scrap reduction. Tables 9.6 and 9.7 show how each cost element and the unit price were determined for year one and then at the start of year two. While not shown here, a similar review occurred at the end of year two to establish year-three pricing.

This example provides a number of important takeaways. One is that the supplier in this case is motivated to participate because the buyer guaranteed its return on investment requirements. The buyer explicitly recognizes the need for the supplier to maintain a fair profit. Also, a buyer's willingness to share design savings with the supplier in the form of a higher profit per unit certainly supported the buyer's cause.

A second takeaway is an appreciation that even though material and labor costs are increasing during the first year, the price of the item at the start of year two decreases by almost $11.50. This is a direct savings of almost $1.4 million in the second year of the contract, as compared to the first year. And, compared to a market-driven price—which would have increased by almost $5 due to material

Table 9.6   Year one agreement and events affecting year two

	Dollars	Economics	Productivity Commitment and Changes
Material Costs	$40.00	2% increase	$4 per unit joint design saving
Direct Labor Costs	$41.50	3% increase	10% annual improvement
Overhead (Direct Labor × 150%)	$62.25		
Total	$143.75		
Scrap ($143.75 × 10%)	$14.37		25% annual reduction
Manufacturing Cost	$158.12		
SG&A (Mfg. Cost × 12%)	$18.98		
Total Cost	**$177.10**		
Profit per Unit	$11.11		
Selling Price	**$188.20**		

Year One Notes:
- Cost engineers determined each unit requires 2 hours of direct labor ($20.75 × 2 = $41.50 year one direct labor) and material costs are $40 per unit
- Total profit = ($20,000,000 supplier investment × 20% agreed upon ROI)/3 year life of contract = $1,333,333 expected profit per year; $1,333,333/120,000 units per year = $11.11 profit per unit

Table 9.7   Year two agreement and events affecting year three

	Dollars	Economics	Productivity Commitment and Changes
Material Costs	$36.72	4% increase	
Direct Labor Costs	$38.47	2% increase	10% annual improvement
Overhead (Direct Labor × 150%)	$62.70		
Total	$135.90		
Scrap ($135.90 × 7.5%)	$10.19		25% annual reduction
Manufacturing Cost	$146.09		
SG&A (Mfg. Cost × 12%)	$17.53		
Total Cost	**$163.62**		
Profit per Unit	$13.11		
Selling Price	**$176.73**		

Start of Year Two Adjustments:
- Material costs = $36 ($4 material design savings from $40) × 1.02 (2% supplier material cost increase from Year One events) = $36.72.
- Direct labor costs = $41.50 × .9 (reflects 10% agreed upon productivity commitment from Year One level) = $37.35; $37.35 × 1.03 (3% increase in supplier labor costs in Year One) = $38.47
- $13.11 per unit profit includes supplier share of material design saving ($2.00) plus the original $11.11 per unit profit

and labor cost increases with an absence of contractual improvement goals—the buyer realizes a true cost avoidance of $600,000.[5] To sum it up, direct savings and a cost avoidance are close to $2 million in year two. While the calculations are not shown here due to space constraints, year three would also show some unit price savings, although not as great as year two. (Year two, for example, did not feature any design savings.) With a cost-driven pricing agreement, costs are increasing while price is decreasing. It's as if we are violating the laws of physics—and liking it!

This case highlights what real collaboration looks like between two parties. While it sounds cliché, this truly is a win-win opportunity as the parties work jointly to increase the value they each receive. It is not hard to imagine how a lower price for an important subassembly could make the end product more competitive, which could lead to a stronger position within the marketplace. And that stronger position could lead to even greater orders that benefit both parties. Cost-driven pricing, which is a rare form of collaboration, is a cost-management technique that stands apart from the rest.

COST MANAGEMENT WORKSHOPS

Cost management workshops include any methodology in which supply chain members come together with the primary purpose of improving costs. The best way to illustrate one such approach is through a case example.[6]

Achieving continuous cost reductions while expanding a company's global presence are never-ending challenges for multinational corporations. The risk of not exceeding these challenges will have serious consequences for companies that develop highly engineered product systems with long life cycles. Continuous cost improvements often require new ways of doing business that address uncertainty and risk.

This case example features a U.S. defense contractor's efforts at developing a new methodology for identifying every cost element and driver within a complex product. This methodology moves beyond anything previously attempted at this company and combines elements of VA, project management, total cost management, Six Sigma, innovation management, early supplier involvement, and risk management into a coherent cost management process.

This company developed a complex system that was winding down in terms of sales to the U.S. military, presenting an unacceptable financial risk. The company decided to mitigate this risk by targeting a specific international customer to replace the expected loss in sales from its primary domestic customer. The opportunity at the international customer was new and the aerospace company decided this would become a pilot program for developing a new cost management approach. Although this company offered a more superior system than its competition, cost and price reductions were going to be essential to win a contract.

This opportunity became the pilot program for identifying, and then managing, every cost element and driver within a complex system. Doing so required a multiphase process.

- **Phase I: Documenting the current state:** Over its history this company has developed sophisticated approaches for analyzing its products, supplier costs, and quality levels. While providing a solid foundation upon which to carry out an analysis of different cost elements, these approaches did not provide the detail required to dramatically alter product cost structures and win new orders. The company needed a methodology that took cost analysis to an entirely new level.

  A cross-functional team was charged with documenting in detail the *current state* of a complex system, including an extensive analysis of each cost element and driver affecting product cost. A primary objective was to determine where design flexibility, and therefore, potential cost reduction opportunities, might exist. The team examined traditional areas including quality, delivery, and operations to evaluate structural opportunities. The team also broke down cost components to understand manufacturing line costs, machine times, labor rate/times, material costs, and costs of goods sold. The team built extensive cost models, much more so than what had ever been accomplished with existing methodologies. The team developed a detailed understanding of every cost associated with this system—an analysis that revealed that materials, not surprisingly, were 50% of total product costs.

- **Phase II: Internal workshop:** After completing the current state analysis, the company conducted a two-day workshop involving company engineers and designers. High-dollar areas became key areas regarding where to focus engineering and design efforts. The first half of the workshop featured the generation of ideas (creative thinking) while the remainder identified savings and ranked ideas (critical thinking).

  Next, the participants identified the cost to implement ideas by examining two major categories of costs. The first related to the cost to document an idea and verify its feasibility—or what the company calls *characterization costs*. These represent about 20% of total costs. The second category, called implementation costs, included the costs to put an idea in place. These costs include changes to manufacturing, designs, or addressing quality issues. While some costs related strictly to internal manufacturing and control, the majority resided with supplier-provided materials.

- **Phase III: Supplier involvement:** At this point a decision was made to involve suppliers in the cost management methodology. The company has extensive experience in working directly with suppliers, after conducting over 50 supplier cost-reduction workshops, and also through its supplier development efforts. As part of this new process, a conference was conducted involving 20 current suppliers. The company also invited potential suppliers to broaden the domain of innovation. An offsite location hosted the first day of the conference, while the second day took place at a company facility.

At a kick-off meeting that was attended by all participants, company hosts identified the workshop objectives and opportunities. Participants then divided into six smaller groups and were placed in various rooms, according to specific tracks or topics. Electrical suppliers, for example, were placed with the company's electrical personnel, mechanical with mechanical, etc. Buyers, subcontract managers, engineers, quality personnel (as needed), and program management personnel from the company also populated the six rooms.

During the workshops, suppliers identified 165 cost-reduction ideas. A champion at the defense contractor was assigned to own each idea. Each idea needed to be evaluated for feasibility and verification regarding whether suppliers could follow through on what they proposed they could do.

- **Phase IV: Implementation**: During this phase, a group met every Monday for updates about progress on the feasibility and verification of ideas. After several weeks the company decided it was time to update its bid to the international customer. The ideas accepted during the workshop resulted in 20% lower product costs, although the resubmitted bid was only 10% lower to provide a margin of safety.

An issue when using revised cost figures is actually achieving these figures. To mitigate this risk, the company's cost spreadsheets included a risk factor column that reduced the savings percentage that was expected for items that have some risk attached to them. The expected benefits might be reduced for an idea, but the expected costs are maintained as a constant. If, for example, an idea has some technical risk or includes a supplier-provided target that might be too challenging to obtain, characterization and implementation costs would remain constant, but the potential benefit is reduced by an agreed-upon percentage. The reduction is agreed to by a team that has a strong feel for the relative magnitude of potential risks across the various ideas.

Looking Ahead

Much to its disappointment, this company did not win a contract with the international customer. Was all this work a waste of time? While it might be easy to conclude this was a failed effort, this company developed a cost management methodology that will help it better understand and manage costs across its current and future programs. And, for this particular product, the company's primary customer in the U.S. realized cost benefits through better pricing for its remaining orders. While the company was unsuccessful in winning new sales from the international customer, it quickly became evident that this new way of managing costs will allow the company to become increasingly competitive when pursuing future opportunities.

A key lesson learned from this experience involves the benefit of supplier involvement. The company expects suppliers to become involved in future projects earlier—compared with their current involvement—perhaps at the two-day workshop stage that featured only company personnel.

The company also expects to validate its cost models as actual data becomes available, similar to the forecasting models that are updated as actual data becomes available. This will help improve cost model accuracy, thereby allowing the company to become even more aggressive in its bidding as its confidence increases.

Overall, the company will be better positioned to develop competitive pricing proposals, given its better understanding of costs and how they might be reduced. The company will also be better positioned to understand the risks associated with achieving product cost reductions, thereby resulting in improved pricing proposals.

Marketing professionals have a term that reflects learning from failed product launches. They call it *failing forward*. While the proposal featured here failed to land a new contract, the learning gained will be applied to the next opportunity. We all fail at some point. Perhaps the biggest failure is not applying the learning gained to future opportunities.

CONCLUDING THOUGHTS

Competing on a worldwide basis demands progressive approaches for identifying and reducing supply chain costs. It is impossible, here, to address every possible technique or approach available for managing costs. What should have come across clearly is that the domain of cost management techniques is broad—and it benefits, quite literally, from using not only the quantitative side, but also the creative side of our brains.

The need for supply chain managers to be effective cost managers is not even in question today. Because of this, it is necessary for supply chain managers to be comfortable with all facets of price and cost analysis. At times, cost management may involve something as basic as replacing one material with a lower cost, but equally effective material, or rebidding a contract. At other times, it may involve a buyer and supplier working side-by-side to manage a cost-driven pricing contract. Knowing when, where, and how to apply a specific kind of price or cost analytic technique is something that supply chain professionals must bring to the table. The next chapter allows the reader to apply the techniques presented here.

REFERENCES

1. Some material in this chapter is adapted from Robert J. Trent, *Strategic Supply Management*, J. Ross Publishing, 2008, Chapter 12.
2. From http://www.bls.gov/ppi/ppifaq.htm#13.
3. http://www.allbusiness.com/barrons_dictionary/dictionary-target -pricing-4942199-1.html.
4. Both the supplier and buyer have requested that company names not be disclosed. Furthermore, data have been disguised at their request.
5. This figure reflects a new unit price that factors in an increase in material costs (2% in year one) and labor costs (3% in year one) with no offsetting productivity, scrap, or other improvements to offset the cost increase.
6. This case example is adapted from *Implementing Value Chain Risk Management—Case Findings*, Center for Advanced Purchasing Studies (CAPS), Tempe, Arizona, 2012. Robert Trent authored the case adapted for use here.

10

MANAGING COSTS ACROSS THE SUPPLY CHAIN— APPLYING FINANCIAL TECHNIQUES

This chapter provides the opportunity to apply the techniques presented in Chapter 9. Exercises in this chapter include estimating prices by using learning curves, developing a configured sourcing network, and calculating theoretical best prices (TBPs). The chapter also includes an exercise for conducting a value analysis (VA) workshop, interpreting producer price indexes (PPIs), and recalculating price in a cost-driven pricing contract.

LEARNING CURVE ESTIMATE—PROBLEM 1

Your company is buying a new item from a supplier whose process normally demonstrates a 90% learning curve. The buyer placed an order for 5,000 units and received a quote from the supplier of $467.50 per unit. The quote included the following per-unit cost and profit data:

Material	$75	
Direct labor	$140	(10 hours on average per unit at $14 per hour)
Overhead	$210	(Allocated at 150% of direct labor, includes SG&A)
Total costs	$425	
Profit	$42.50	(10% of total costs)
Price per unit	**$467.50**	

Your company now wants to place an order for 35,000 additional units. Your buyer estimates that material costs will decrease by 10% due to larger volumes. How much should your company expect to pay per unit for the second order given the *expected benefit of the learning curve* and the *reduction in material costs due to higher volumes*?

What could cause your estimated price not to be correct?

LEARNING CURVE ESTIMATE—PROBLEM 2

Your company is buying a new item from a supplier whose process normally demonstrates an 85% learning curve. The buyer placed an order for 2,000 units and received a quote from the supplier of $104.61 per unit. The quote included the following per-unit cost and profit data:

Material	$20.50	
Direct labor	$32.40	(2 hours on average per unit at $16.20 per hour)
Overhead	$40.50	(Allocated at 125% of direct labor, includes SG&A)
Total costs	$93.40	
Profit	$11.21	(12% of total costs)
Price per unit	**$104.61**	

Your company now wants to place an order for 30,000 additional units. Your procurement buyer estimates that material costs will decrease by 15% due to larger volumes. How much should your company expect to pay per unit for the second order given the *expected benefit of the learning curve* and the *reduction in material costs due to higher volumes*?

Besides the primary effect that learning has on direct labor, what costs are affected, directly and indirectly, due to learning and higher volumes?

USING EXTERNAL PRICE INDEXES—PROBLEM 1

In June 2012, a buyer entered into a three-year agreement with a supplier that provides plastic water pipe. Among other things, this agreement features fixed pricing over the life of the agreement. It is now March 2015, and the agreement with this supplier is up for review and possibly renewal. While the supplier's overall performance has been excellent, the supplier has already indicated it intends to seek a 3% price increase to cover what it calls *escalating costs*. The time has come to start thinking about renewing this contract. Please answer the following questions using the data in Table 10.1.

Table 10.1

Series Id: WPU072106033
Group: Rubber and plastic products
Item: Plastics water pipe
Base Date: 201112

Year	Jan	Feb	Mar	Apr	May	Jun	Jul	Aug	Sep	Oct	Nov	Dec
2011												100.0
2012	100.4	103.1	105.0	106.7	108.4	110.1	103.4	101.2	102.2	104.5	106.0	105.3
2013	105.8	106.4	107.8	107.3	107.4	106.9	105.8	106.2	105.6	102.6	102.9	102.8
2014	104.4	107.4	109.8	110.7	107.1	105.3	107.7	107.3	107.9	110.2	108.2	105.8(P)
2015	104.3(P)	108.5(P)	106.3(P)									

P: Preliminary. Indexes are subject to revision four months after original publication.

1. What is the average PPI for this item for 2012, 2013, and 2014? Do you believe the price index for this item is relatively stable or volatile?
2. In retrospect, was the decision to pursue fixed pricing with this supplier a good economic decision from the buyer's perspective? Why or why not? Provide quantitative evidence.
3. What was the percent change in the index from June 2012 to July 2012? What was the percent change from January 2014 to April 2014? What could have caused these changes in prices and therefore, the index?
4. If the buyer intends to renew the agreement for another two years with this supplier, do you feel the 3% price increase is reasonable? Why or why not? What other information might you need to know to make an informed decision?
5. What type of pricing arrangements or language would you propose for this contract if it is renewed?

USING EXTERNAL PRICE INDEXES—PROBLEM 2

Assume you are a cost estimator for a landscaping design company. An important part of your company's business involves designing and installing private and commercial patio areas. Decorative concrete blocks comprise a major part of your material cost structure. Use the PPI data that appears in Table 10.2 to answer the following questions.

Table 10.2

Series Id: WPU13312101
Not Seasonally Adjusted
Group: Nonmetallic mineral products
Item: Decorative concrete block
Base Date: 198200

Year	Jan	Feb	Mar	Apr	May	Jun	Jul	Aug	Sep	Oct	Nov	Dec
2005	158.7	160.5	160.3	161.3	161.3	165.4	167.7	167.9	167.9	168.5	168.7	169.5
2006	175.5	179.1	180.1	180.6	180.6	180.6	186.6	186.1	185.3	185.3	185.3	185.3
2007	189.2	189.7	190.2	191.1	192.1	192.1	192.7	192.3	192.8	192.6	192.9	193.1
2008	193.2	193.7	196.4	196.5	198.2	198.2	198.4	198.4	199.4	199.7	199.7	200.2
2009	201.0	200.9	200.9	202.2	201.4	201.4	201.4	201.4	201.4	201.4	201.4	201.4
2010	201.5	203.0	198.2	198.8	198.6	198.6	198.6	198.6	198.6	198.6	198.6	198.6
2011	198.6	199.1	200.2	200.2	201.3	201.3	201.3	201.3	201.3	201.4	201.4	201.4
2012	203.0	202.9	202.9	202.8	203.7	203.7	203.7	204.5	204.5	204.5	204.5	204.5
2013	206.5	206.6	206.7	212.3	212.3	212.3	212.3	212.0	212.0	212.0	212.0	212.0
2014	214.3	214.8	214.8	216.2	216.2	216.2	216.2	216.2	216.9	216.9	216.9	216.9(P)
2015	220.4(P)	220.5(P)	220.5(P)									

P: Preliminary. All indexes are subject to revision four months after original publication.

1. What is the average PPI for 2012, 2013, and 2014 for this item? What is the percent change for the average PPI from 2012 to 2013 and from 2013 to 2014?
2. Do you think the price index (and therefore the price) for this item over the last five years is stable or volatile? Why?
3. If you were preparing customer quotes for landscaping work to be performed in July and August 2015, how confident would you be about the pricing stability of decorative concrete blocks from your supplier for this time period? Is there anything you can do in the customer quotation to protect against the financial risk to your company of a possible price increase?
4. In January 2011, assume you paid $43 for a specific decorative concrete block. What would you pay for that same block in January 2012, given the change in the PPI?
5. In March 2005, the PPI for this item was 160.3. In July 2006 the index was 186.6. What is the percentage change in the index for that period? What might cause a change of this magnitude?

CREATING A CONFIGURED SOURCING NETWORK— PROBLEM 1

Use Table 10.3 to answer Part A.

Part A: Identify the lowest price supplier for each item.

Gloves: Supplier _____

Wax: Supplier _____

Glasses: Supplier _____

Batteries: Supplier _____

Soap   Supplier _____

Part B. Using the information in Table 10.3, complete Table 10.4 and calculate the total cost of the configured sourcing network.

Cost of the configured sourcing network: _____

Part C. Identify the expected savings from the configured sourcing network.

(Lowest total cost supplier) – (Configured sourcing network cost)

= _____Expected savings from the configured sourcing network

Percent of savings compared to lowest total cost supplier: _____

Table 10.3   Quoted unit costs

Item	Supplier A	Supplier B	Supplier C	Supplier D
Gloves	$1.25	$1.65	$1.45	$1.31
Wax	$7.50	$7.61	$6.15	$6.85
Glasses	$2.15	$2.54	$2.41	$2.81
"D" Batteries	$.42	$.30	$.34	$.33
Soap	$4.46	$4.11	$4.45	$4.50

Table 10.4   Total cost

Item/Annual Volume	Supplier A	Supplier B	Supplier C	Supplier D
Gloves—70,000				
Wax—5,500				
Glasses—3,200				
"D" Batteries—31,000				
Soap—8,500				
Total				

CREATING A CONFIGURED SOURCING NETWORK— PROBLEM 2

Use Table 10.5 to answer Part A.

Part A: Identify the lowest price supplier for each item.

Rubber hoses:	Supplier _____
Sealant:	Supplier _____
Replacement glue:	Supplier _____
Tape:	Supplier _____
Brushes:	Supplier _____
Bubble wrap:	Supplier _____

Part B. Using the information in Table 10.5, complete Table 10.6 and calculate the total cost of the configured sourcing network.

Cost of the configured sourcing network: _____

Part C. Identify the expected savings from the configured sourcing network.

(Lowest total cost supplier) – (Configured sourcing network cost)

= _____Expected savings from the configured sourcing network.

Percent savings compared to lowest total cost supplier: _____

Table 10.5   Quoted unit costs

Item	Supplier A	Supplier B	Supplier C	Supplier D	Supplier E
Rubber hoses	$4.75	$4.55	$5.10	$5.00	$5.12
Sealant	$18.50	$22.10	$19.98	$19.98	$21.80
Replacement glue	$7.70	$8.22	$7.40	$7.95	$8.18
Tape	$4.98	$4.98	$4.56	$4.69	$4.72
Brushes	$12.18	$11.50	$11.90	$12.19	$11.78
Bubble wrap	$29.99	$30.50	$30.20	$28.15	$31.25

Table 10.6   Total cost

Item/Annual Volume	Supplier A	Supplier B	Supplier C	Supplier D	Supplier E
Rubber hoses—22,000					
Sealant—13,000					
Replacement glue—5,500					
Tape—14,000					
Brushes—3,000					
Bubble wrap—7,500					
Total					

THEORETICAL BEST PRICE—PROBLEM 1

A buyer is sourcing a new item and has collected the following cost information from three suppliers (see Table 10.7). First, calculate the TBP, given this set of data. Second, complete each row and column of Table 10.8.

Table 10.7

	Supplier A	Supplier B	Supplier C
Direct Labor	$12.55	$12.78	$13.10
Direct Materials	$10.77	$10.33	$9.25
Overhead	$13.12	$12.78	$15.12
SG&A	$5.90	$5.75	$6.55
Profit	$5.05	$5.75	$5.50
Price	**$47.39**	**$47.39**	**$49.52**

TBP: _____

Table 10.8   Standardized against the best cost

	Supplier A	Supplier B	Supplier C
Direct Labor			
Direct Materials			
Overhead			
SG&A			
Profit			
Price-to-best-price Ratio			

How do you interpret the standardized values in this table?

THEORETICAL BEST PRICE—PROBLEM 2

A buyer is sourcing a new item and has collected the following cost information from three suppliers (see Table 10.9). First, calculate the TBP, given this set of data. Second, complete each row and column of Table 10.10.

Table 10.9

	Supplier A	Supplier B	Supplier C
Direct Labor	$18.75	$20.20	$19.90
Direct Materials	$22.18	$22.05	$21.87
Overhead	$25.76	$29.75	$28.34
SG&A	$5.80	$5.20	$6.28
Profit	$7.75	$6.90	$6.50
Price	**$80.24**	**$84.10**	**$82.89**

TBP: _____

Table 10.10　Standardized against the best cost

	Supplier A	Supplier B	Supplier C
Direct Labor			
Direct Materials			
Overhead			
SG&A			
Profit			
Price-to-best-price Ratio			

How can a buyer obtain the cost data necessary to arrive at a TPB?

VALUE ANALYSIS WORKSHOP EXERCISE

VA is a continuous improvement and cost reduction methodology that applies to any part of the supply chain. This exercise requires you to engage in the information and speculative phase of the VA process for an existing product or part at your company. (Recall that VA can also be used to evaluate services or processes.) Use the following template to guide your VA workshop:

Step I: Identify the product or part that will be the focus of the VA workshop

Step II: Identify other participants to involve in the workshop

Step III: Identify the primary function of the product or part in terms of customer usage. Identify any secondary functions of the product or part.

Step IV: Engage in brainstorming (i.e., creative thinking) to improve value in the product or part. Use the following questions to help promote group discussion:

- Are lower cost, but equally effective materials available for the product or part?
- Can the product or part design be simplified?
- Are standard components available to replace custom-designed components?
- Can improvements be made to the production process?
- Can features be added to enhance functionality more than the associated cost increase?
- Are lower cost suppliers available that are capable of producing the product or part?
- Is there any functionality currently included in the product or part that the customer does not want?

- Is there any specific waste that can be targeted for elimination?
- Can packaging or logistics costs be reduced or improved?

Step V: Perform cost/benefit analysis on each idea, assess the effect of a change on internal and external customers, and assess the overall feasibility and timing of changes. Establish performance improvement targets. Identify any potential risks resulting from changes.

Step VI: Develop an implementation plan for carrying out changes. Create a set of baseline measures to assess the effectiveness of the changes. Identify who is responsible or accountable for owning the changes.

COST-DRIVEN PRICING CONTRACT ADJUSTMENT EXERCISE

Using the information provided in Tables 10.11 and 10.12, complete Table 10.13 and identify the new unit price for this subassembly at the start of the second year of this contract.

Table 10.11   Agreed upon contractual issues

Product:	Subassembly for industrial pump		
Initial Expected Price:	$98.50 per unit		
Negotiated/Analyzed Cost Structure:			
Direct Labor Rate	$13.50 per hour		
Overhead Rate	175% of direct labor		
Scrap Rate	10% of total material, direct labor, and overhead		
Selling, General, and Administrative Expense	10% of total manufacturing cost		
Effective Volume Range	100,000 units per year +/– 20%		
Projected Product Life	3 years		
Return on Investment Agreed to	20%		
Contract Length	Life of product with annual pricing recalculation		
Volume Fluctuation Risk	Shared equally if volume fluctuates more than +/– 20% in a year		
Contract Specific Investment:	Year 1	Year 2	Year 3
Working Capital	$2 million	$2 million	$2 million
Net Capital Assets	$3 million	$2 million	$1 million
Total Investment over Three Years	$12,000,000		
Supplier Productivity Commitment:			
Direct Labor Content	10% reduction from previous year level		
Scrap Rate	50% reduction from previous year level		
Joint Effort Design Revision/Cost Reductions:	Savings shared jointly on a 50/50 basis		

Table 10.12   Year one events affecting year two price

	Dollars	Economics	Productivity Commitment and Changes
Material Costs	$36.00	3% increase	$2 per unit joint design saving
Direct Labor Costs	$14.85	2% increase	10% annual improvement
Overhead (Direct Labor × 175%)	$25.99		
Total	$76.84		
Scrap ($76.84 × 10%)	$7.68		50% annual reduction
Manufacturing Cost	$84.52		
SG&A (Mfg. Cost × 10%)	$8.45		
Total Cost	**$92.97**		
Profit Per Unit	$8.00		
Selling Price	**$100.97**		

Year One Notes:

- Cost and procurement engineers determined each unit requires 1.1 hours of direct labor ($13.50 × 1.1 = $14.85 year one direct labor) and material costs are $36 per unit
- Total profit = ($12,000,000 supplier investment × 20% agreed upon ROI)/3 year life of contract = $800,000 expected profit per year. $800,000/100,000 units per year = $8 profit per unit

Table 10.13   Year two revised price

	Dollars	Work Calculations
Material Costs		
Direct Labor Costs		
Overhead (Direct Labor × 175%)		
Total		
Scrap ($72.5 × 5%)		
Manufacturing Cost		
SG&A (Mfg. Cost x 10%)		
Total Cost		
Profit Per Unit		
Selling Price		

BEST PRACTICES IN WORLDWIDE SOURCING

Growth in worldwide trade has increased dramatically over the last 25 years. An increase in the standard of living in emerging countries, generally lower trade barriers, and the rise of the Chinese economy have all contributed to new opportunities on the selling and the buying side of the supply chain. A constant search for what we believe are better sourcing opportunities has taken buyers to just about every square inch of the earth to obtain raw materials, components, capital equipment, and finished goods.

This chapter focuses on worldwide sourcing, an area that has grown dramatically over the last several decades. The first part of the chapter presents worldwide sourcing along a continuum, ranging from basic international purchasing to global sourcing and supply management. The primary focus of this chapter—worldwide sourcing best practices—appears next. The chapter concludes with some predictions about the future of worldwide sourcing.

A CONTINUUM OF WORLDWIDE SOURCING

The findings presented throughout this chapter are derived from two in-depth studies that investigated worldwide sourcing. The first study, conducted by Monczka and Trent, investigated the critical success factors, benefits, progress, risks, methodologies, practices, and lessons learned from the development of global supply processes and strategies. This research included data from 162 larger companies that were headquartered primarily in North America with worldwide operations and buying centers.

A second study, conducted by Monczka, Trent, and Petersen included data from 167 companies. While investigating issues similar to the first study, this project featured a greater number of European firms and emphasized sourcing from emerging countries. Both research projects included respondents who were vice presidents, directors, or managers working at the corporate level rather than at the division or site level. Both studies featured quantitative surveys and detailed on-site interviews.

Figure 11.1 presents worldwide sourcing as a series of evolving levels or steps along a continuum. For purposes of discussion, let's divide worldwide sourcing into two categories—*international purchasing* and *global sourcing and supply management*. International purchasing relates to a commercial purchase transaction between a buyer and supplier that are located in different countries. This type of purchase is typically more complex than a domestic purchase. Organizations must contend with longer material pipelines, greater rules and regulations, language and cultural barriers, currency fluctuations, logistical issues, and increased risk.

An internationalization of the sourcing process takes place as companies evolve or progress from domestic purchasing to the global coordination and integration of common items, processes, designs, technologies, and suppliers across worldwide locations. Companies that operate at Levels II and III exhibit behaviors that are characteristic of international purchasing, while companies that operate at Levels IV and V practice global supply management.

Supply organizations progress, often reactively, toward a basic level of international purchasing (Level II) because they are confronted by some scenario, such

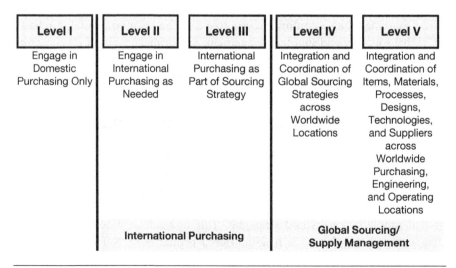

Level I	Level II	Level III	Level IV	Level V
Engage in Domestic Purchasing Only	Engage in International Purchasing as Needed	International Purchasing as Part of Sourcing Strategy	Integration and Coordination of Global Sourcing Strategies across Worldwide Locations	Integration and Coordination of Items, Materials, Processes, Designs, Technologies, and Suppliers across Worldwide Purchasing, Engineering, and Operating Locations
	International Purchasing		**Global Sourcing/ Supply Management**	

Figure 11.1 Worldwide sourcing continuum

as a lack of suitable domestic suppliers, or because competitors are gaining an advantage (usually cost advantages) from their international practices. Strategies and approaches developed in Level III begin to recognize that worldwide buying strategies can lead to major improvements. Most price reductions sought from worldwide sourcing are gained at this level. A key point is that strategies at this level are not coordinated across worldwide buying locations, operating centers, functional groups, or business units.

Supply organizations often begin to realize that it is in their best interest to begin integrating and coordinating their sourcing activities on a worldwide basis. Level IV represents the integration and coordination of sourcing strategies across worldwide buying locations. Operating at this level requires worldwide information systems, personnel with sophisticated knowledge and skills, extensive coordination and communication mechanisms, an organizational structure that promotes central coordination of global activities, and executive leadership that endorses a global approach to sourcing. Level IV features an extensive focus on global contracting.

Level V organizations have achieved the cross-locational integration that Level IV organizations have achieved. The primary distinction is that Level V participants integrate and coordinate common items, processes, designs, technologies, and suppliers across worldwide purchasing centers and with other functional groups, particularly engineering. This integration occurs during new product development, as well as during the sourcing of items or services to fulfill continuous demand or aftermarket requirements. Furthermore, design, build, and sourcing responsibilities are often assigned to the most capable units around the world.

When looking at this model, supply professionals should view global supply management as a process rather than as a set of discrete activities or approaches. Looking at the global business environment leads to a clear conclusion: pressure to improve is relentless and severe. The winners will understand how to manage their supply activities on a global basis; the losers—not so much. Global supply management offers an attractive and largely untapped opportunity to achieve the performance breakthroughs required to compete in intensely competitive markets.

Differences Between International Purchasing and Global Supply Management Organizations

Not only are there definitional differences between international purchasing and global supply management, there are tangible differences between the companies that populate the two segments. The following presents research-based findings concerning the differences between firms along the continuum presented in Figure 11.1:

- Companies that engage in global supply management are larger and more likely to have competitors that are global, compared with international purchasing companies. Global supply management becomes a strategic response to counter global competition.
- Companies that engage in global supply management perceive their strategy implementation progress to be more sophisticated or mature compared with international purchasers.
- Companies that engage in global supply management believe that performance improvement and cost reduction opportunities are more widely available from their worldwide efforts, compared with international purchasing companies. And, global organizations are more likely to have experienced, firsthand, more significant improvements compared with international purchasing organizations.
- Companies that engage in global supply management indicate that the development of global strategies is more important to their executive management compared with international purchasing companies.
- Companies that engage in global supply management indicate they face more rapid changes to product and process technology compared with international purchasing companies. While cost improvements will always remain a primary driver behind worldwide sourcing, the need to manage product and process technology from a global perspective drives some companies to pursue more sophisticated sourcing levels.
- Companies that engage in global supply management rely on a wider array of communication tools to support their worldwide efforts compared with international purchasing companies. This includes a higher reliance on groupware, video conferencing, web-based tools, and phone conferencing at significantly higher levels, compared with the international purchasing segment.
- Companies that engage in global supply management have in place more organizational features to support their worldwide efforts, compared with international purchasing companies. Best practice companies are not surprised by the kinds of features they must put in place to be successful. They know this is what they must do to capture the benefits from global supply management.
- Companies that engage in global supply management rate certain factors as more critical to their success, compared with international purchasing companies. Critical factors include a centralized procurement structure, suppliers that are interested in global contracts, availability of information and data, and site-level participation during global contract development.

The differences between the two segments are clear along many different dimensions.

A Comparison of Benefits Between Segments

Why would any company commit scarce resources toward something as complex as global supply management? The short answer is that companies pursue global supply management to realize benefits that are not as readily available from less sophisticated sourcing practices. Research reveals that extensive differences exist between the benefits that international purchasing and global supply management companies achieve.

Companies that engage in global supply management achieve every benefit evaluated during the earlier-mentioned research projects at a statistically higher level than those that engage in international purchasing. In fact, the overall average across 16 benefit areas is 30 percent higher, on average, for companies that practice global supply management, compared with companies that practice international purchasing. The kinds of benefits that global supply organizations achieve at a much higher level include:

- Better management of supply chain inventory
- Greater supplier responsiveness to buying unit needs
- Greater standardization or consistency of the sourcing process
- Greater access to product and process technology from suppliers
- Improved supplier relationships
- Improved sharing of information with suppliers
- Greater supplier involvement during product development

Besides an impressive array of benefits, is there anything else that helps make the case for pursuing global supply management? Companies that engage in global supply management rate certain areas as more similar across their geographic regions and buying units, compared with those companies that engage in international purchasing. In the longer term, an important outcome from global supply management will be the consistency this process provides. Engaging strictly in international purchasing—which is by definition an uncoordinated activity across worldwide units—cannot create the consistency that a more integrated approach can provide. Areas where the similarity or consistency across units or locations is greater within the global supply management segment, compared with the international purchasing segment include:

- Strategy development process
- Supplier assessment practices
- Purchasing or sourcing philosophy
- Current purchasing strategies
- Problems resolution techniques with suppliers
- Contracting approaches
- Reporting level of purchasing/sourcing

- Similarity of purchase requirements
- Organizational reporting structures
- Supplier performance measures used
- Business ethics

Clearly, the data supporting a global approach to supply management is compelling. If global supply management can be so rewarding, why isn't it commonplace? First, many supply chain managers do not understand the complexities of operating a globally-integrated supply network. Next, many supply organizations lack the vision, leadership, resources, or sophistication to coordinate their activities globally. Many procurement organizations are still reactive or maintain a lower position within the corporate hierarchy. Finally, some companies simply do not have as great a need to pursue a global supply model. Rest assured, however, a slow but steady migration toward higher sourcing levels will continue to occur.

WORLDWIDE SOURCING BEST PRACTICES

It is not enough to proclaim a desire to gain an advantage from your company's worldwide sourcing efforts; we have to understand the characteristics or best practices of firms that capture that advantage. The following provides a set of best practices characterizing firms that operate at the highest levels of worldwide sourcing (Levels IV and V). These practices are not as relevant for firms operating at Levels II and III (from Figure 11.1).

Access to Qualified Human Resources

A theme that consistently emerges when working with leading companies is the important relationship between qualified personnel and successful worldwide sourcing. Effective sourcing, particularly at the highest global levels, is not a process that can be automated or outsourced. When companies are asked during research projects to identify the most important factor that contributes to global success, access to personnel with the right knowledge, skills, and abilities rises to the top. But, when asked to identify the seriousness of problems that may affect global success, a lack of qualified personnel is the most serious of problems identified. This is why access to qualified human resources is a best practice.

What kinds of skills and abilities are required to support worldwide sourcing? Unfortunately, everyone seems to have a different viewpoint regarding the knowledge and skills that define today's supply professionals. Obviously, the need to communicate well, manage conflict, and demonstrate ethical behavior will always be on the list. The following knowledge and skills are based on focus group research with leading companies. Ideally, individuals involved with worldwide sourcing should have the ability to:

- Take a strategic rather than operational or transactional view of supply management
- Manage nontraditional procurement areas, including services
- Manage critical supply relationships worldwide
- Understand strategic cost management, including total cost of ownership models
- Work virtually and across time zones and cultures
- Understand the global supply management process and its objectives
- Be comfortable with using, and perhaps even developing, electronic sourcing and contracting systems
- Understand statistical analysis and fact-based decision making
- Work cross-functionally and across locations
- Understand how to do business in different cultures
- Negotiate and manage worldwide contracts

Supporting the sourcing process with personnel who have the right skills will require the development of high potential individuals, the recruitment of talent from other functional groups or companies, and the recruitment of promising college graduates. Regular assessments of employee knowledge and skill sets must also occur with training tailored to the needs of individual employees. This is all done to ensure that qualified participants are available to support worldwide sourcing. Access to the right people is even more important when companies take a global view of their supply chain.

A Well-defined Process Guides Worldwide Strategy Development

Best practice firms develop a well-defined process or approach to guide their global strategy development efforts. Some organizations have taken their commodity or regional strategy development process and adapted it for global sourcing. When that is the case, the global process usually places more emphasis on risk factors (currency, longer material pipelines, supplier switching) as well as the total landed cost.

Table 11.1 presents a generic strategy development process. What's the big deal about having a defined process? A defined process provides a means to monitor and report strategy development progress. And, a defined process helps accelerate learning across a company as participants become familiar with a single process. A well-understood process also facilitates members moving easily to new projects, since they do have to learn new processes. A defined process also

Table 11.1 A sample global strategy development process

Step 1: Identify Global Sourcing Opportunities

Step 2: Establish Strategy Development Teams

Step 3: Evaluate Sourcing Opportunities and Propose Strategies

Step 4: Identify Internal Requirements and Develop Supplier Proposals

Step 5: Forward Requests for Proposals to Pre-qualified Suppliers

Step 6: Evaluate the Technical and Commercial Merits of Proposals

Step 7: Negotiate with Qualified Suppliers

Step 8: Award Contract

Step 9: Manage Transition to New Contract and/or New Suppliers

Step 10: Monitor Performance and Review Expiring Contracts

avoids duplication of effort across teams and locations. Best practice companies that have a defined process also develop documents, templates, and tools that appear on a company's intranet. Finally, this process, like any other organizational process, can be continuously improved.

Research reveals that the presence of a defined, well-understood process and access to individuals who are capable of taking a global rather than narrow view of supply chains are two powerful predictors of global success.

Organizational Design Features Support Worldwide Sourcing

Best practice firms understand the connection between an effective organizational design and worldwide sourcing success. Organizational design is a broad term that refers to the process of assessing and selecting the structure and formal system of communication, division of labor, coordination, control, authority, and responsibility required to achieve an organization's goals.[1] Important design features that directly support worldwide sourcing success include (1) centrally led decision making supported by strong executive leadership, (2) the use of cross-functional teams, (3) an executive steering committee to guide the process, and (4) strategy review and coordination sessions. Another important design feature—international purchasing offices—is discussed later.

Centrally Led Decision Making Supported by Strong Executive Leadership

Higher-level worldwide sourcing (i.e., Levels IV and V from Figure 11.1) is a process best managed from a centrally led level. The terms *centrally coordinated* or *centrally led* do not necessarily mean the presence of large corporate staffs. In fact, best practice firms are sensitive to the concerns of operating units as they think about a loss of control and a bureaucracy that is far removed from day-to-day activities. Central coordination can be achieved across regions, business units, sites, and other functional groups through the use of organizational design features that do not require individuals residing in a central location.

The trend toward centrally led decision making has been evident over the last 15 years. Research findings reveal that almost 60 percent of mostly larger companies say their procurement organization is structured and governed centrally, while 39 percent say the business unit is decentralized with some coordination. Only 2 percent indicate their business unit is decentralized. Over 70 percent of companies indicate that purchasing and supply management decision-making authority, in general, is centralized or highly centralized.

Separation of Strategic and Operational Responsibilities

A shift toward centrally led, centrally coordinated, and/or centralized worldwide sourcing is only part of the story. In many supply chain organizations, strategic and operational responsibilities often take place at different locations. At no time is this truer than when firms pursue higher levels of worldwide sourcing.

Separating strategic and tactical groups makes sense for several reasons. Few people can operate comfortably in a strategic and tactical environment, or switch easily between one mode and another. Furthermore, in a decentralized model, operational or tactical activities must be satisfied first, leaving less time for longer term planning and strategy development.

Activities that are usually centralized or centrally led include developing category or commodity strategies, negotiating and establishing contracts, locating potential supply sources, evaluating and selecting company-wide suppliers, managing important supplier relationships, and managing supplier development and early involvement activities. Responsibilities that generally are decentralized include executing schedules and inventory plans, expediting goods and services, issuing releases or purchase orders, planning inventory levels, and developing requirements schedules. Care must be taken to avoid the perception that one group is better or more important than the other.

Use of Cross-functional Teams

Companies that pursue the highest levels of worldwide sourcing almost always use teams to develop strategies and to coordinate their worldwide activities. Executive managers should plan for and use teams selectively, always keeping in mind any barriers to their use as well as the factors that affect team success. Teams are destined to fail, for example, if they have poor team leadership or lack the time to commit to their tasks. Research findings are clear that teams with the time to pursue their tasks are more effective, on average, than those that did not have the time. The challenge becomes one of making scarce resources more readily available to team members.

Executive Steering Committee

The formation of an executive steering committee or council to oversee worldwide sourcing is an important way to show commitment to the process. These committees engage in some serious work. The following highlights the duties of a worldwide steering committee at a leading U.S. company:

- Identify and prioritize worldwide sourcing opportunities
- Form project teams and develop team charters
- Establish worldwide sourcing project objectives and broad improvement goals
- Provide required resources to project teams
- Meet with teams to update in-process sourcing projects
- Support the development of worldwide systems
- Validate and report the success of global initiatives
- Manage post-project lessons learned
- Coordinate worldwide sourcing initiatives with new product development teams and engineering groups

Strategy Review and Coordination Sessions

Best practice firms also promote the use of strategy review and coordination sessions. These sessions, which can be face-to-face or virtual, attempt to align different participants from around the world with a common global vision. Colgate, a company with operations in almost 80 countries, relies heavily on these sessions as part of its organizational design to create a common set of global objectives.

International Purchasing Offices Are Established

Most supply managers recognize that their ability to manage activities that happen thousands of miles away is usually quite limited. An important element of worldwide sourcing that does not receive much attention is the use of an international purchasing office (IPO). An IPO provides a company with a day-to-day presence in any supply market or region where the buying company has suppliers. It is wrong to conclude that IPOs are located only in emerging countries, although Eastern Europe and China are well represented as locations.

Just under half of the firms participating in the earlier mentioned research projects maintain IPOs. One thing that is certain is the overwhelming agreement about the value these offices provide. Just over 85% of firms with IPOs say they are extremely important to global sourcing success; around 10% of firms with

IPOs say they are moderately important; and only 5% say they are less than moderately important. No company indicated these offices are of limited importance.

Some companies simply refer to their IPOs as foreign or international buying offices, international procurement centers, or international procurement organizations. No industry standard exists regarding what to call these offices.

IPOs are usually a formal part of a company's organizational design and will increase in importance as global supply management expands. Some companies hire IPO service providers as needed rather than maintaining dedicated offices that increase fixed costs. These companies have taken what is essentially a fixed cost and turned it into a variable cost.

The kinds of services that an IPO provides are varied. At least 70 percent or more of companies with at least one IPO say these offices somewhat or extensively identify suppliers and evaluate their capabilities, negotiate and execute contracts with suppliers, resolve quality and delivery problems directly with suppliers, develop supplier capabilities, measure supplier performance, evaluate product and service designs and samples provided by suppliers, facilitate import and export activities, and perform logistical coordination. These kinds of tasks simply cannot be managed well from a home office located thousands of miles away.

The use of IPOs should increase as supply organizations continue to search worldwide for buying opportunities. However, challenges could also increase as new IPOs are staffed with foreign nationals who have been hired away from other IPOs. Anecdotal evidence has emerged that some companies are experiencing unhealthy turnover in their IPO's due to the *poaching* of staff by other companies. This will have the inevitable effect of increasing the cost of operating an IPO, as well as affecting its performance.

Able to Measure Worldwide Savings

Best practice firms have the capability to measure and validate the savings realized from worldwide sourcing. Reporting the savings from global supply initiatives usually necessitates meeting three key requirements. The first is a system that captures data from around the world—something that is easier said than done. The second is the active involvement of finance. The need to validate savings makes finance involvement a necessity. The third requirement is a higher set of metrics that show the impact that global initiatives have on corporate performance indicators. Traditional purchasing indicators will be ineffective in this kind of environment.

An important part of measurement when engaging in worldwide sourcing is the use of total cost measurement systems. Best practice companies know that total cost of ownership is a topic they cannot ignore as they search for new sources of supply. Total cost models include the expected and unexpected elements that increase the unit cost of a good, service, or piece of equipment.

The reasons for measuring total cost are persuasive. An earlier study found that over 80 percent of companies that created total landed cost models did, in fact, reduce their total cost.[2] These models help to: identify the impact of different cost elements, including supplier nonconformances; track cost improvements over time; identify the areas where cost reduction efforts will have their greatest payback; target specific areas for improvement or elimination; support fact-based rather than subjective supply chain decisions; and provide a better overall understanding of supply chain costs. Chapters 12 and 13 provide greater insight into this important topic.

Access to Information Technology and Communication Tools

There is no question that information technology (IT) enables global success, something that best practice companies know quite well. While it seems intuitive to say that data and information are vital to worldwide sourcing, the reality is that many companies still struggle in that area. While the situation is improving, companies with worldwide operations can still have systems that do not seamlessly transfer data from one platform to another, or from one business unit to another.

Industry leaders address this need by creating global data warehouses that rely on common coding schemes for easier aggregation of worldwide purchase requirements. The ability to perform a global spend analysis is likely just a dream without access to data and systems (refer to Chapter 8 for an overview of spend analysis). These systems should also serve as contract repositories that provide advance notification of expiring regional and global agreements.

Besides data warehouses and contract repositories, leading supply organizations rely extensively on web-based systems and intranets to make information available to worldwide participants. A best practice company recognized for its use of IT has placed a wide range of global support documents on its intranet, including an online manual that describes its global supply management process; a global strategy development template; a contract terms and conditions checklist; a report that identifies the status of completed, in-process, authorized, and future global opportunities; a request for proposal template; and currency risk management guidelines. Participants anywhere in the world can also access information about approved suppliers.

Best practice firms also know that sourcing initiatives have a reduced chance of success without access to communication tools, particularly when participants are located in geographically dispersed locations. Real-time communication tools include web-based meeting software, electronic mail, video conferencing technology, telephone conferencing, and face-to-face meetings. Research findings reveal a clear link between access to state-of-the-art communication tools and a set of desirable global outcomes. IT has become a great enabler of supply chain success.

Risk Management Is Embedded within Worldwide Sourcing

An emphasis on worldwide sourcing has contributed to greater supply chain risk. Longer material pipelines, currency issues, child labor and environmental infractions, quality issues, cultural and language difference, and a host of other issues seem to come to the forefront when expanding globally.

Best practice firms consider risk directly when developing sourcing strategies, whether the strategy involves a domestic or international supplier. To date, most risk initiatives have been separate from normal job responsibilities. As companies understand the true costs of supply risks and disruptions, risk management will increasingly become an embedded part of supply management—much like supplier audits, supplier development, and supplier relationship management are now part of supply management.

Embedding risk management directly into a supply manager's responsibilities does not mean that the importance of risk management will diminish. In fact, the opposite is likely to be the case. As risk management becomes an accepted part of an organization's operating culture, risk issues will be considered early when making sourcing decisions. Supplier selection teams will consider not only a supplier's operating capabilities; they will also consider a potential supplier's financial condition, as well as its risk plans and capabilities. This will be especially true when evaluating suppliers in emerging countries. Selection teams will also consider geographic location to ensure that a supplier is not clustered with other suppliers or located near known hazards. The bottom line is that to be a best practice company, supply managers must become risk managers, particularly when engaging in worldwide sourcing.

Critical Resources Are Available

A factor that is easy to overlook is the resources that support the attainment of global objectives. The availability of needed resources has the potential to separate marginally performing from exceptionally performing worldwide sourcing organizations. The question becomes which resources are critical to success? Best practice companies methodically assess their resource requirements when pursuing worldwide sourcing opportunities.

Figure 11.2 presents a set of resources modified from original work by Peters and O'Connors. While any resource category can affect a global initiative, the resources that are usually the most critical include executive commitment; access

Job-Related Information
The information and data required to support team analysis and performance

Tools and Equipment
The specific tools, equipment, and technology required to support team efforts

Materials and Supplies
The routine materials and supplies required to support team activities

Budgetary Support
The financial resources, not including salaries, required to support a team's task

Required Help from Others
The services and assistance needed from others external to the team but within the organization

Team Member Task Preparation
The personal preparation and experience of team members as it relates to the team's assignment

Time Availability
The amount of time that members can commit to team activities

Work Environment
The physical aspects of the team's work environment

Executive Management Commitment
The overall support that executive management exhibits toward work teams and teaming

Customer and Supplier Participation
The support that critical customers and suppliers provide when involvement is beneficial

Figure 11.2   Resources that affect worldwide sourcing success

to qualified participants; required services and help from others; time, budget, and information; and data. The availability of time remains important since most organizations rely on team members to pursue global opportunities. These team members often have other job responsibilities.

Let's expand on a resource category that is critical to effective worldwide sourcing—information and data. Crafting a worldwide strategy requires all kinds of information and data, including insight into:

- Existing contracts and suppliers
- Existing supplier capabilities and performance
- Purchased commodities and categories, including part numbers that comprise each commodity or category
- Current and future expenditures by part, commodity group, location, etc.
- Potential new suppliers by region, and their capabilities
- Quantitative improvements sought from a worldwide contract
- Internal customer contract requirements
- Macroeconomic conditions of worldwide supply markets

Clearly, it takes a great deal of data to feed this beast called worldwide sourcing. It also takes a host of other resources to ensure this process is successful.

LOOKING TOWARD THE FUTURE

Something we know for certain is that companies will continuously strive to improve their global capabilities, including in the area of worldwide sourcing. With that in mind, let's make some predictions. Only time will tell whether these are correct or not.

Companies that are less proficient at global supply management will stress four enabling areas. In fact, an organization cannot pursue more sophisticated supply chain initiatives without focusing on four key areas: the development of measurement systems, including total cost of ownership systems; access to qualified personnel who have the ability to view the supply network from a worldwide perspective; a supportive organizational design; and IT systems. These areas create the foundation for global excellence.

Another prediction is that the pressure to improve costs will remain severe, resulting in an ongoing search for innovative and aggressive ways to reduce supply chain costs. This includes a continuous search for qualified suppliers in emerging and low-cost supply markets. While economic and risk factors will result in some sourcing shifts across regions, don't expect a mass exodus of work from foreign suppliers back to domestic suppliers. Estimates by the Boston Consulting Group that millions of jobs are coming back to the United States due to reshoring are not realistic. Supply managers will continue to broaden their search to consider a broad mix of countries.

A country that is seeing a benefit from shifting trade is Mexico. A desire by some U.S. companies to nearshore their operations due to the increased cost and hassle of doing business over great distances, a government-industry collaboration that is producing more highly skilled Mexican workers at a reasonable cost, and changing currency values have combined to make Mexico an attractive sourcing spot, even with the country's drug violence. We also expect leading firms to use their supplier development process to improve the capabilities of promising suppliers, particularly in emerging countries.

Looking forward, we expect a continued development and refinement of global supply management processes. Since a majority of supply organizations do not yet practice the highest levels of worldwide sourcing, it is safe to conclude they do not have in place company-wide processes to guide their efforts. If an emphasis on globalization continues to occur, and there is a high probability this is the case, it is almost a given that a continued development and refinement of global supply processes will occur.

We also expect major industrial customers to continue their search for suppliers with global capabilities. The pressure to become a global supplier is partly behind a wave of mergers and acquisitions across certain industries, including the automotive, aerospace, and electronic industries. These mergers and acquisitions are occurring primarily for two reasons. The first reason is to broaden a supplier's geographic reach. A supplier that is North American-centric could find itself at a disadvantage when it competes for contracts against suppliers that have global reach. The second reason is to be better positioned to respond to customer pressure to provide an expanded set of capabilities and services globally.

A somewhat countervailing trend, at least in some industries, is to shift from a reliance on suppliers with global capabilities to a reliance on suppliers with strong regional capabilities. For a variety of reasons, such as logistical issues and trade restrictions, buying companies are showing a preference to use suppliers that are located in the same geographic region as their operations. It seems that corporate strategy is shifting toward a regional perspective and away from a pure global perspective. Sourcing strategy is shifting accordingly.

A shift toward centrally led supply management should continue. Too many companies have experienced firsthand the value of taking a coordinated approach to sourcing to shift back toward a decentralized structure. The challenge will be to create an organizational model that captures the benefits of centrally led supply management, while still being responsive to internal customers at operating sites.

Here is a prediction that is near and dear to this book. Supply managers and finance managers will become better acquainted. Closer interaction between supply, supply chain, and financial managers is inevitable over the next decade. As mentioned repeatedly, a big part of supply chain management is about managing the flow of funds.

It is probably safe to predict that a strict emphasis on global contracts that feature components should gradually evolve toward subsystem and system sourcing. This will involve relying on global suppliers for greater design and engineering support, something that did not happen during the initial stages of globalization. This evolution is a natural extension of global supply management, particularly as leading companies gain confidence in their supply management abilities, as well as the capabilities of their worldwide suppliers.

A safe prediction is that supply managers will increasingly develop global supply strategies for indirect items and services. Whether a manufacturer takes a regional or global perspective, direct items almost always receive more attention than indirect items. As supplier capabilities expand, and as supply managers continuously search for cost reduction opportunities, expect indirect items and services to receive greater attention.

We expect global supply management to move beyond an emphasis on contracting to an emphasis on process consistency. A growth in the percentage of companies practicing Level V global supply management is expected to continue. A defining characteristic of Level V is a movement beyond global contracting to developing standardized global processes and practices. Examples exist (such as

Air Products, Colgate, and Whirlpool) of companies that are developing processes and practices that provide consistent practices across worldwide locations. Worldwide consistency, rather than simply worldwide contracts, will define the new normal for companies that compete globally.

Organizationally, the use of global supply teams will increase, making cross-cultural and communication issues more challenging. No evidence appears on the horizon that the use of teams to manage global commodities will diminish. In fact, we expect continued growth in this area, which will create pressure to develop state-of-the-art communication systems. It is safe to conclude that a supply model that features geographically dispersed team members will become more common over the next decade. It is also safe to conclude that a supply model that features dispersed teams will be exponentially more complex to manage compared with ones that feature co-located participants.

A set of predictions also relate to the risk aspects of globalization, which the following summarizes:

- As companies increasingly recognize the interdependencies between global events and global risk management, global supply strategies will increasingly incorporate risk management strategies
- Expect a shift toward the greater use of total cost models to support global risk management
- Supply organizations will increasingly rely on IPOs as a means for managing supply risk in specific regions
- As smaller companies pursue worldwide sourcing, they will expose themselves to greater supply chain risk due to a lack of global sophistication
- Environmental performance, compliance to rigorous workplace standards, and supplier quality will become more important during the evaluation of suppliers in emerging countries

This set of predictions is certainly not exhaustive. It will be interesting to see how close they are to reality.

CONCLUDING THOUGHTS

Worldwide sourcing, if managed properly, should provide a steady stream of benefits as firms evolve from basic international purchasing to the more complex process called global supply management. Even those companies that are relatively mature from a global perspective can never stop improving or extending their capabilities. A company that coordinates the purchase of its direct materials globally will want to extend its efforts into indirect materials, services, and capital equipment. Or, a company that is effective at managing global contracts will want to apply a consistent set of practices across its buying centers. Underlying this view must be a solid appreciation of risk management.

It is a simple reality that the need to improve, especially from a cost management perspective, is never-ending. And, the search for new and innovative ways to compete, including when sourcing worldwide, is also never-ending—believing otherwise is an invitation for trouble.

REFERENCES

1. G. Hamel and C. K. Pralahad, *Competing for the Future* (Cambridge, MA: Harvard Business School Press, 1994) as referenced in D. Hellriegel, J. W. Slocum, and R. W. Woodman, *Organizational Behavior* (Cincinnati, OH: South-Western College Publishing, 2001): 474.
2. G. Chow, "Getting Back to Basics," *Canadian Transportation Logistics* 111, no. 10 (October 2008), 40.

12

WORLDWIDE SOURCING— THE FINANCIAL PERSPECTIVE

Over the years companies have made many sourcing decisions based solely on price. And why not? After all, price is the easiest and most obvious factor to identify. Everyone knows what they paid for something. Unfortunately, a not-so-well-known truth is that unit price (i.e., what we think we paid) never equals total cost (i.e., what we actually end up paying). Although basing decisions on price is easy, it is not always the right thing to do.

While the need to understand total cost is important whether we are dealing with a domestic or foreign supplier, the complexity that surrounds worldwide sourcing underscores the need to understand an expansive set of cost elements. This wider set of elements is what widens the gap between a price paid and a total cost realized. While total cost information is *out there*, with so many cost elements to consider, the job of consolidating this information into a useful analysis can be intimidating.

Total cost of ownership (TCO) is a topic that combines supply chain and financial thinking. The primary focus of this chapter is to explore TCO, particularly within the context of an international supply chain. This chapter also explains how to calculate inventory carrying charges. The chapter concludes with one company's reliance on total cost modeling to enhance its financial position.

UNDERSTANDING TOTAL COST

Total cost includes the expected and unexpected elements that increase the unit cost of a good, service, or piece of equipment.[1] The logic behind the development of total cost models is that the unit cost or price of something never equals its total cost. If we believe this to be true, then we need to understand the size of the gap between a unit price and its true total cost.

Those who are involved in worldwide sourcing should understand the notion that variables, such as longer lead times and distances, carry additional costs and risks that are not as relevant to domestic purchases. The bottom line is we need to quantify these costs wherever possible.

Measuring Total Cost

It should be obvious why almost every purchasing measurement system includes price-related measures rather than total cost measures. Price is by far the easiest of any metric to identify across a supply chain. Without a total cost system, however, it is difficult to make decisions that do not contain a fair amount of subjectivity.

The reasons for measuring total cost are persuasive. It becomes next to impossible to select a higher price option (but a lower total cost option) without some way to support that decision. Having a *gut feeling* that a higher price supplier will result in a lower total cost is usually not enough justification for going with a higher price. Our confidence in decisions becomes higher when we have total cost data.

Total cost models also help companies identify the relative impact of different cost elements, allowing management to see what affects total cost. These systems also help us track the effectiveness of changes over time. And, total cost systems help us gain management's attention regarding the areas where cost reduction efforts will have their greatest payback. This enables us to develop plans to target specific areas for improvement or elimination. Total cost data also support fact-based rather than subjective decision making, something that makes the quality purists gleeful beyond belief. The truth is it would be hard to identify a set of reasons why we would not want to capture total cost data, at least for the more critical or high cost items.

A survey by Archstone Consulting and the *Supply Chain Management Review* reported that 35 percent of manufacturers experienced a 25 to 50 percent increase in material and component costs from foreign suppliers over a certain three-year period. Over 50 percent of survey respondents reported up to a 25 percent increase in product costs. Similar increases were reported for logistics and transportation costs.[2] How many companies failed to understand the effect of these increases because they lacked total cost measurement systems? In uncertain times, the need to understand every element of cost is a necessity.

The Hidden Costs

As mentioned in Chapter 6, investment models are often underspecified because they fail to account for the benefits that result from a project. The reverse is true with total cost models. These models often underspecify costs rather than benefits. The obvious costs are only part of the equation, particularly in an international transaction. Most sourcing experts recognize that international purchasing contains hidden costs that can undermine the validity of any total cost model. Table 12.1 identifies a set of hidden costs that can affect a total cost analysis.[3]

Traditional purchasing models reveal that the savings derived from international sourcing averages 25 percent, when considering price differentials. Under a revised model that considers a fuller accounting of total cost elements, including hidden costs, actual savings realized from international sourcing tend to be in the 4 to 6 percent range. This is well within a normal margin of error for these kinds of models, meaning the savings from international sourcing could be zero or even negative. This data shows why total cost calculations that include a wide range of cost elements must be an integral part of every sourcing analysis.

Table 12.1 Hidden costs when sourcing internationally

Hidden Cost	Description
Internal expenses	The higher skills, communication, and time required to evaluate and work with foreign suppliers are not free
Quality breakdowns	Managing quality problems offshore can be more costly and complex to resolve
Logistics volatility	Managing the rapid changes in shipping rate changes, port delays, and variable shipping lead times adds an element of complexity
True inventory costs	While longer pipelines increase inventory carrying charges, few companies fully account for these charges in their cost models
Contract noncompliance	Internal noncompliance with a foreign contract can reduce total anticipated savings
Technology	Extended supply changes require greater tracking capabilities
Duty and tariff changes	Employing resources to determine correct duties and monitor changes adds to total cost
Supplier health	Gaining visibility into the financial stability of foreign suppliers is not always easy, particularly in countries where suppliers maintain "two sets of books"
Post-contract lull	Failing to monitor supplier and contract performance after signing an agreement can result in "cost creep"

Adapted from D. Hannon, "9 Hidden Costs of Global Sourcing," *Purchasing*, March 2009.

FOUR A'S OF TOTAL COST DATA

Regardless of where a company applies total cost models, these models all attempt to capture data beyond unit price. A popular misconception is that total cost models must provide better information than not having a total cost model. The reality is that total cost models, like forecasting models, almost always have some degree of unreliability. The question becomes how much unreliability is embedded in the model. This section explains how the categories of information that populate total cost models contribute to inaccuracies.

The elements that populate total cost models can be segmented into four categories that conveniently start with the letter A. The first A category, and the one that provides the highest degree of confidence, includes actual data. Unit price, transportation charges, and tariffs are examples of actual cost data. We know these costs with certainty. Few, if any, total cost models have the luxury of including only actual data. The ones that do include only actual data are likely missing some cost elements.

The second most reliable A category includes approximations or averages. The key feature here is the data are at least based on figures derived from your own internal sources. The challenge with many cost elements is that work involved with identifying the true cost of something sometimes outweighs the value of the data. Should we conduct a detailed study to identify the true cost of every late delivery? Who has the time or resources to undertake a study every time a supplier nonconformance occurs?

Overcoming this issue often results in the use of costs categories or accounts with standard or average charges. The following illustrates this point. In a recent year, 100 late supplier deliveries cost a buying company an estimated $500,000 in total nonconformance costs. The average standard charge in the total cost system for a late delivery becomes $5,000 ($500,000/100) per occurrence.

The usual warnings about using averages apply here. A wide dispersion of true costs around an average cost creates a concern that the average charge may not reflect reality. It is always a good idea to know the standard deviation of a data set to understand the dispersion of occurrences around a mean. Wide dispersions indicate potential issues with averages.

Moving down the spectrum, the next A category includes data that is based on assumptions. Assumptions come from external sources that form the basis for applying a total cost. Let's say a university study concluded that it costs $169 every time a buyer issues a material release. Therefore, every time a buyer issues a material release to a supplier a $169 charge is applied to the total cost for that item under *ordering costs*. But does the $169 have anything to do with what really occurs at your organization? What if your company relies extensively on electronic data interchange (EDI) to reduce ordering costs, while others in the study do not? Be careful not to develop total cost models that are loaded with external assumptions. This will make the model highly suspect.

A fourth data category that starts with A includes data that are absent from a total cost model. The challenge with any cost model is that, at times, the cost to collect data outweighs the value of the data. At other times the sheer number of possible cost elements that could be part of the model is overwhelming. And, at times, a company simply fails to include a relevant cost.

Regardless of the type of cost model used, the need to understand the data that populate the model is critical. Making decisions based largely on assumptions is asking for trouble. And, making decisions using models with missing data is also problematic. Like forecasting models, total cost models will always generate output. A question concerns the accuracy of that output.

No agreement exists regarding the cost categories or specific elements to include in a total cost model. While there is some overlap (almost everyone includes price somewhere in their models) no agreement exists regarding what these models should contain. Models that attempt to measure cost elements from point of origin to final point of consumption can be quite broad. Other models may be narrower in their scope.

A search of the total cost literature leads to several conclusions. First, a wide variety of cost elements are included in total cost models. Literally dozens of cost elements could populate a total cost model, particularly when dealing with international transactions. Second, except for price and transportation costs, no clear consensus exists regarding what elements to include. One study revealed, for example, that only 40% of companies included inventory carrying charges in their total cost models.

TYPES OF TOTAL COST MODELS

Total cost models are part of a family of measurement systems called cost-based systems. Two other kinds of measurement systems are categorical and weighted-point systems. A primary objective of cost-based systems is to replace subjective measurement or assessment with data that are more objective. While this sounds like a great reason to take a cost-based approach, cost-based systems are more challenging and expensive to develop compared with other measurement systems.

No agreed upon typology of total cost systems exists. As it relates to supply chain management, we should see total cost models applied within three areas. This includes total landed cost models, supplier performance index models, and life cycle cost models. While at first glance this may appear as three unique or independent types of models, they can have overlapping cost categories.

Total Landed Cost Models

A total landed cost model is often used when evaluating suppliers prior to making a selection decision, although, that is not the only time they are used. Landed cost is the sum of all costs associated with obtaining a product, including acquisition planning; unit price; inbound cost of freight, duty and taxes; inspection; quality; and material handling, storage, and retrieval.[4] Each of these cost categories can contain subcategories.

While the word *landed* assumes we are dealing with international shipments, we also apply total landed cost models to domestic suppliers. In that case, some of the cost elements (such as tariffs) simply have no costs assigned to them. Some companies will use landed cost models when they are evaluating whether or not to shift work from one supplier to another, or when evaluating whether to insource work that was previously outsourced. The next chapter presents an exercise that combines total cost modeling with insourcing/outsourcing.

Total landed cost models should also be used when doing business with suppliers on an ongoing basis. After all, the factors that affected the sourcing decision in the first place are dynamic and subject to change. Ideally, a company will update its total landed cost models whenever cost factors, such as transportation and exchange rates, change. Keeping these models current is challenging, yet important.

When developing total landed cost models, it is best to start with unit price and build up the total cost, as the goods move from origin to destination. Ideally, every cost element is presented in the same unit of measure. If a product is priced by the pound, then every corresponding cost element in the model should appear as a cost per pound. Costs for discrete parts may be calculated at the per unit level.

There is a potential issue regarding whether to include only costs that the buyer incurs or whether to include all the costs incurred from the point of origin to the point of destination. One way to reconcile this issue is to have parallel cost models. One model can include the costs where the buyer has direct responsibility. The second model, which will have a higher total landed cost, includes all costs across the supply chain. The benefit of managing total supply chain costs is having visibility to all supply chain costs, regardless of who incurs that cost directly.

As it applies to total landed cost models, cost elements are often divided into categories that reflect a logical progression of material through the supply chain. The following illustrates these categories, along with examples of costs that fall within each category:

- **Within country of manufacture:** unit price, storage, labor, quality, overhead, obsolescence, packaging, risk or disruption, exchange rates, inventory carrying charges

- **In transit to country of sale:** transportation charges, fuel surcharges, insurance, port charges, handling, security, banking fees, broker fees, potential detention charges, duties, handling agency charges, inventory carrying charges
- **Within the country of sale:** local transportation and handling, storage fees, taxes, safety stock, inventory carrying charges, production yield, maintenance, quality, overhead allocation, payment terms

Spreadsheet software is ideal for developing total landed cost models. If your company does not base its international purchasing decisions on total landed cost, then it is time to assemble a team to develop these models. Table 12.2 provides a sample of a total landed cost table with specific cost elements. Chapter 13 includes a case that requires the development of a spreadsheet similar to Table 12.2.

Companies looking to begin total cost modeling might want to check out a free total cost estimator developed by the Reshoring Initiative.[5] According to their website:

> "Most companies make sourcing decisions based solely on price, oftentimes resulting in a 20 to 30 percent miscalculation of actual offshoring costs. The Total Cost of Ownership (TCO) Estimator is a free online tool that helps companies account for all relevant factors—overhead, balance sheet, risks, corporate strategy and other external and internal business considerations—to determine the true total cost of ownership. Using this information, companies can better evaluate sourcing, identify alternatives, and even make a case when selling against offshore competitors."

Supplier Performance Models

Various models attempt to capture the true cost of doing business with a supplier on an ongoing basis. Perhaps the best known of these models is something called the supplier performance index (SPI). Let's be clear about something—SPI models are essentially quality-related models. These models measure the additional costs incurred when doing business with a supplier on an ongoing basis. SPI calculations are helpful when tracking supplier improvement over time, when quantifying the severity of performance problems, when deciding which suppliers should stay or exit the supply base, and when establishing minimum levels of supplier performance. This model applies to domestic and international suppliers.

The SPI is a total cost model that presents its output in the form of a standardized index or ratio. It assumes that any quality or other infraction committed by

Table 12.2   Example of a total landed cost calculation

Cost Element	Explanation of Cost Calculations	Cost per Pound	Individual Percent	Cumulative Percent
Unit price per pound	Supplier quoted unit price per pound	$.78	66.7%	66.7%
Ocean shipping	$3,500 per container/50,000 lbs. per container	$.07	5.98%	72.7%
Tariffs and duties	17% × unit price ($.78)	$.13	11.1%	83.8%
Transfer charge from U.S. port to warehouse	$250 per container/50,000 lbs. per container	$.005	.43%	84.2%
Warehouse storage charge	$10.50 per pallet/2,500 lbs. per pallet	$.004	.36%	84.6%
Warehouse handling fee	$8.25 per pallet/2,500 lbs. per pallet	$.003	.28%	84.9%
Inventory Carrying Charge	50,000 lbs. held in inventory each month × unit price ($.78) = $39,000 inventory value; $39,000 × 22% inventory carrying charge = $8,580 annual carrying charge; $8,580/600,000 lbs. annual demand = $.01 carrying charge per lb.	$.014	1.2%	86.1%
Local freight from warehouse to plant	$350 per container/50,000 lbs. per container	$.007	.6%	86.7%
Receiving and quality control	$12 per pallet/2,500 lbs. per pallet	$.005	.48%	87.2%
Product loss before production	2% loss × unit price ($.78). This reduces the annual available product for use during production to 588,000 lbs.	$.016	1.37%	88.6%
Production yield loss	3% × 588,000 lbs. = 17,640 lbs. lost during production; 17,640 lbs. × $.78 unit price = $13,759 yield loss; $13,759/588,000 lbs. = $.023 per lb.	$.023	1.97%	90.2%
Administrative Overhead	15% × unit price ($.78)	$.117	10%	100.2% (due to rounding)
Estimated Total Landed Cost		**$1.17**	**100%**	

Notes: Supplier delivers one container each month; each container has 20 pallets with 2,500 lbs. per pallet; annual usage is 600,000 lbs.

a supplier increases the total cost of doing business with that supplier. It applies after supplier selection, because it is populated with cost occurrences that have happened rather than are expected to happen. If a company can track each supplier nonconformance and assign a cost to it, the calculation of a standardized SPI becomes relatively straightforward. The SPI calculation for a specific period uses the following formula:

SPI = (Cost of material + Nonconformance costs)/(Cost of material)

Assume a supplier delivers $100,000 worth of parts to a company in the third quarter of a year. The supplier also commits four infractions that quarter—a late delivery, missing documentation, and some defective units with two of its shipments. The buying company assigns $11,000 in total nonconformance charges for these infractions. The supplier's SPI for the third quarter is 1.11, or (($100,000 + $11,000)/$100,000).

An SPI of 1.11 means the total cost of doing business with this supplier is 11 percent higher than the unit price, at least in terms of quality-related issues. If the unit price of a supplier's good is $80, then the estimated adjusted cost of that item is $88.80 ($80 × 1.11). Because the SPI is a standardized metric it allows comparisons between suppliers. A supplier with a higher SPI has a higher total cost than one with a lower SPI. It is important to compare suppliers within the same commodity to ensure valid comparisons.

SPI Bias

Unfortunately, the SPI is not as straightforward as just presented. The base SPI calculation has a built-in bias against suppliers that provide deliveries with a lower total value. Assume that two suppliers commit the same infraction that resulted in a $2,000 nonconformance charge. The first supplier provided $15,000 worth of goods during a quarter and the second supplier provided $30,000 worth of goods. The SPI for the first supplier is 1.13 (($15,000 + $2,000)/$15,000). The SPI for the second supplier is 1.07 (($30,000 + $2,000)/$30,000). While each supplier committed the same infraction, the smaller volume supplier appears worse from a total cost perspective.

We overcome this bias with the calculation of a "Q" adjustment factor. The "Q" factor allows valid SPI comparisons by removing the inherent bias against suppliers with a lower total value of deliveries, which are often smaller suppliers. If we want to make our total cost models as accurate as possible, then we have to consider the Q adjustment factor.

Table 12.3 shows how to calculate the SPI along with an adjusted SPI (referred to as SPI/Q). This example assumes that each supplier committed a comparable infraction that resulted in a nonconformance charge of $2,500. Mathematically,

Table 12.3   Supplier performance index with volume adjustment

	Supplier A	Supplier B	Supplier C
1st quarter deliveries	15	12	16
Total value of deliveries	$7,500	$15,000	$30,000
Average delivery	($7,500/15) = $500	($15,000/12) = $1,250	($30,000/16) = $1,875
Nonconformance charges	$2,500	$2,500	$2,500
1st quarter SPI	($7,500 + $2,500)/$7,500 = 1.33	($15,000 + $2,500)/$15,000 = 1.17	($30,000 + $2,500)/$30,000 = 1.08
Average delivery from all suppliers	$1,500	$1,500	$1,500
Q adjustment factor (Avg. delivery/Avg. delivery from all suppliers)	$500/$1,500 = .33	$1,250/$1,500 = .83	$1,875/$1,500 = 1.25
Adjusted SPI	1.11	1.14	1.10

Adjusted SPI (SPI/Q) for Supplier A = $7,500 + ($2,500 × .33)/$7,500 = 1.11
Adjusted SPI (SPI/Q) for Supplier B = $15,000 + ($2,500 × .83)/$15,000 = 1.14
Adjusted SPI (SPI/Q) for Supplier C = $30,000 + ($2,500 × 1.25)/$30,000 = 1.10

we can see how this affects the SPI calculation, particularly for Supplier A given the different volumes provided by the three suppliers. SPI users can compensate for this bias by calculating a "Q" adjustment factor for each supplier:

Q = (average delivery by supplier)/(average delivery from all suppliers within a commodity)

The average delivery from all suppliers should be within a commodity family. That may include deliveries from more suppliers than the three listed here. SPI comparisons and average lot calculations should be between suppliers within comparable groups. It does not make sense to group suppliers that are different in terms of what they provide. The adjustment factor, which is a weight, is then applied against the nonconformance charges within the SPI calculation, as illustrated at the bottom of Table 12.3. After removing the lot-size bias, the SPI/Q shows that the three suppliers are roughly comparable in terms of their adjusted index. The "Q" factor removed the lot size bias.

The SPI does not require a major information technology effort. Like total landed cost models, the development of SPI spreadsheets is not an unreasonable burden. The challenge is to identify the nonconformances that occur and then assign a charge to those infractions. Failure to record nonconformances when they occur results in an underspecified SPI model. A supplier will appear to be a better performer simply due to missing data. This will raise issues regarding the validity of the model.

Life-cycle Cost Models

Life-cycle cost models are usually what comes to mind when thinking about total costs analysis. This type of model is most often used when evaluating capital decisions that cover an extended period, often for equipment and facilities. Life-cycle models are similar conceptually to the net present value models presented in Chapter 6. Most life-cycle cost models are used (or should be used) to evaluate capital decisions rather than the purchase of everyday components and services. The other models described in this chapter are more applicable for repetitively purchased goods and services.

Life-cycle costs apply whether equipment is sourced domestically or internationally. This type of model should not be a "one and done type of thing." Companies should compare the assumptions made during the development of life-cycle estimates with actual data as it becomes available. This will help validate the life-cycle model.

Developers of life-cycle cost models often allocate their cost elements across four broad categories that reflect usage over time:[6]

- Unit price—This is the price paid including purchase terms
- Acquisition costs—This includes all costs associated with delivering equipment, such as buying, ordering, and freight charges to the customer
- Usage costs—Includes all the costs to operate the equipment, including installation, energy consumption, maintenance, reliability, spare parts, and yield and efficiency during production
- End-of-life costs—Includes all costs incurred when removing equipment from service less any proceeds received for resale, scrap, or salvage

The flow through a life cycle is essentially one of buying, shipping, installing, using, maintaining, and disposing.

INVENTORY CARRYING CHARGES

While readers are familiar with many of the cost elements that populate total cost models, one category of costs likely requires further explanation. That category is inventory carrying charges. At times it seems as if only 20 people on earth understand how to account properly for these charges. To most supply chain professionals carrying charges remain a mystery.

Carrying charges are real and occur at any part of a supply chain where inventory is present. It is a fact of life that wherever inventory resides, someone holds title (i.e., ownership) to that inventory. In fact, until the final customer purchases an item someone in the supply chain has title to the goods and therefore accrues carrying charges, whether those charges are explicitly accounted for or not.

Carrying charges are especially important when sourcing internationally because material pipelines are longer in terms of time and distance. Most companies disregard these charges because they don't seem real, are hard to quantify, or are simply unsure of how to handle them.

Three categories of costs comprise an inventory carrying charge. The first category is the cost of capital. Inventory consumes capital that could have been put to other productive uses. The second category reflects the cost of storage, which can include insurance, heat, lighting, rent, and cycle counting. The final category includes the combined costs of obsolescence, deterioration, and loss. Factors such as expired shelf life, scrap, and theft are usually part of this category.

Finance is responsible for combining these components to arrive at a carrying charge that is expressed as a percent of the inventory's unit cost. At a simple level, a unit of inventory, whether it is a raw material, work-in-process, or finished good worth $20 per unit with a carrying charge of 20% results in an annual carrying charge of $4.00 per unit ($20 × .2). Inventory that is held less than a year is prorated accordingly. If the inventory is held for six months, the carrying charge per unit becomes $2.

How exactly are carrying charges calculated? Tables 12.4 and 12.5 illustrate carrying charge calculations under two scenarios. The first scenario considers the carrying charge for inventory used during normal operations. This assumes inventory replenishment occurs on a regular basis. It also employs what we call the "average inventory" method. Average inventory is:

(Beginning Inventory + Ending Inventory)/2 = Average Inventory for a time period

This method assumes that inventory is depleted on a consistent basis over a period of time. Of course, the inventory could have all been consumed on the first or even the last day of a period. But, realistically, who has time to determine the exact time every piece of inventory is used? For most firms simply thinking about calculating carrying charges represents major progress.

The second scenario considers the carrying charges for inventory that is carried as safety stock. This example illustrates that while safety stock is often used as a buffer for risk, that buffer is not free. While it seems strange to think about it in these terms, inventory that sits around and does nothing all day actually accrues costs. Perhaps you have some coworkers that fit that description. While the safety stock may be used at some point, we usually do not know exactly when it will be required. Still, we should calculate the carrying charge when developing supply chain plans or budgets.

Some companies do not take ownership of goods until they receive them physically at their facility. When this is the case it is tempting to ignore any carrying charges for inventory that is inbound from a supplier. And for international

Table 12.4   Calculating inventory carrying charges for replenishment inventory

• Item: chemical raw material • 120,000 pounds of this raw material used each year • Cost: $31.75 per pound • Demand occurs at a steady rate throughout the year • Inventory is received at the start of each month and used throughout the month until it reaches zero at the end of the month • Inventory carrying charge is 22% annually • The average inventory method is used: ((BI + EI)/2) = Average inventory for a period
Total carrying charges for this item: 1. 120,000 lbs./12 = 10,000 lbs. monthly inventory usage 2. (Beginning inventory + ending inventory)/2 = (10,000 + 0)/2 = 5,000 average pounds held each month as inventory. This is the same as saying 5,000 lbs. of inventory are held for a year. 3. 5,000 lbs. × $31.75 cost per pound = $158,750 value of average inventory 4. $158,750 × .22 (annual carrying charge %) = **$34,925 annual carrying charge for this item**
Total carrying charge per pound for this item: $34,925 annual carrying charge/120,000 lbs. annual demand = **$.29 carrying charge per pound**

Table 12.5   Calculating inventory carrying charges for safety stock inventory

• Item: support bracket used in a subassembly • 300,000 units required of this item each year • Cost: $8.75 per unit • One month worth of annual demand to be held as safety stock • Inventory carrying charge is 18% annually
Total charges for carrying this item in safety stock: 1. 300,000 units/12 = 25,000 units per month 2. 25,000 units to hold as safety stock × $8.75 cost per unit = $218,750 value of safety stock inventory 3. $218,750 × .18 (annual carrying charge %) = **$39,375 annual carrying charge for this safety stock**
Total carrying charge per unit for this item: $39,375 annual carrying charge for safety stock/300,000 units annual demand = **$.13 carrying charge per unit**

shipments, this inbound process could takes several months. Is ignoring carrying charges when we do not own the inventory really the best policy?

Let's think about this scenario in financial terms. The supplier that owns the inventory while it is in transit likely knows it is assuming the carrying charges. The supplier will want to recoup these charges by building these costs into its unit price. The higher price will now increase the value of the buyer's current assets since inventory is part of that calculation. A higher asset base with no corresponding increase in income will reduce the buyer's return on assets (ROA). Once the buyer does take title, it will be paying a higher per unit carrying charge since the inventory has an inflated value. As economists like to say, there is no such thing as a free lunch. The buyer could very well be paying for that "free lunch" through higher unit costs, higher inventory carrying charges, and a lower return on investment. Welcome to the world of supply chain financial management.

TOTAL COST MODELING AT DELPHI

A company that knows it is in serious financial trouble tends to approach things differently than a company that is awash in cash.[7] Even before the 2008 financial meltdown, Delphi, a major tier-one supplier to the automotive industry, was in survival mode after filing for bankruptcy protection in 2005.

From a financial and operating perspective, Delphi is a far different company today than it was a decade ago. After shedding assets and costs, the company's return on invested capital (ROIC) now stands at an impressive 34% compared with an 18% industry average. And, profits are now the expectation rather than the exception. (Chapter 1 discussed ROIC.)

Delphi's CEO says that the company now monitors every piece of new business to certify it is equal to or better financially than what it has today. The company focuses on higher margin, innovative products, particularly in a product segment called "active safety." If the order doesn't raise Delphi's ROIC, then the company may decline that order.[8] You know that times are better when you can pick and choose your orders.

As part of its reinvention, Delphi has focused extensively on total cost modeling.[9] Delphi's Cost Management group (a function within Supply Management) developed a desktop tool that is user friendly, requires few manual inputs, and has reduced the time required to estimate the total cost of buying a part from five days to several minutes. Perhaps best of all, the training required to use the tool only takes about 40 minutes. Ease of use helps ensure internal customer acceptance.

Delphi's Cost Management group worked with logistics, manufacturing, engineering, and research and development to develop the model. This entailed collecting data about transportation and logistics costs, capital costs, and currency and risk issues. A critical part of developing any cost or financial model is the identification of the cost elements that populate the model. The development team took almost 18 months to validate the model's accuracy by subjecting it to actual sourcing scenarios. This tool is accepted internally because it replaced a much more cumbersome system. And, it has also demonstrated itself to be reliable.

The risk of a near-death experience resulted in dramatic changes at Delphi. One of these changes is reflected in how the company thinks about managing supply chain costs. Like many companies that require new tools and applications, Delphi realized that managing costs sometimes means developing your own tools. Waiting for third parties to develop commercial applications just might take too long.

CONCLUDING THOUGHTS

This chapter shows how costs can be reported to provide a more complete picture of a supply chain. After completing a total cost analysis it becomes possible to compare costs across common cost categories, identify cost elements that are unusual or require attention, compare the total cost for obtaining similar products from different suppliers and regions, and make better decisions.

Managing supply chain costs from a total cost perspective is also one of the best ways to manage supply chain risk. Unfortunately, the development of total cost models is a best practice that too many companies have yet to do well. Given the growth in international purchasing and the uncertainty that surrounds supply chains today, we should make sure these models are on our "to do" lists.

REFERENCES

1. This chapter is based partially on work by Robert J. Trent and Llewellyn Roberts, *Managing Global Supply and Risk*, J. Ross Publishing: Fort Lauderdale, FL, Chapter 4, 2010.
2. J. Ferreira and L. Prokopets. "Does Offshoring Still Make Sense?" *Supply Chain Management Review* 2009 Jan/Feb: 13(1): 22.
3. D. Hannon, "9 Hidden Costs of Global Sourcing, Purchasing," March 2009, www.purchasing.com.
4. K. Cowman, "Material Costs", *Materials Management and Distribution* 49, no. 7 (September 2004). 73.
5. http://www.reshorenow.org/tco-estimator/.

6. R. M. Moncka, R. J. Trent, and R. H. Handfield, *Purchasing and Supply Chain Management* (Mason, OH: Thomson-Southwestern, 2005), 364-365.

7. This case example is adapted from Greg Schlegel and Robert Trent, *Supply Chain Risk Management: An Emerging Discipline,* CRC Press, 2014, Chapter 14.

8. Bennett, Jeff. "Delphi Roars back from the Brink." *The Wall Street Journal,* November 11, 2013: B1.

9. Siegfried, Mary. "Precision Tool Tackles Complex Task." *Inside Supply Management,* (April 2011): 24.

13

WORLDWIDE SOURCING— APPLYING FINANCIAL TECHNIQUES

This chapter provides opportunities to apply the concepts presented in Chapter 12. Most of what appears in this chapter is not found in finance textbooks. We are using financial data but applying primarily supply chain management tools and techniques. Specifically, this chapter allows the reader to develop a total landed cost model, calculate supplier performance indexes, apply total cost modeling in an insourcing/outsourcing analysis, and calculate inventory carrying charges for normal replenishment and safety stock inventory. This chapter also includes several qualitative exercises.

QUALITY FOODS—TOTAL LANDED COST CASE

Randall Cox is a senior buyer at Quality Foods, a major U.S. multinational food processing company. This company, based in Los Angeles, uses a wide variety of fruit concentrates in many of its popular food products. One of Randall's responsibilities is to negotiate purchase contracts for Vitamin C fruit concentrate. Randall is undertaking an analysis to determine the total cost of doing business with one of his existing suppliers, a Chinese producer of Vitamin C concentrate. Quality Foods has used this supplier's product for a number of years and is generally satisfied with the supplier. However, since Vitamin C concentrate is available from various sources, and since it is a commodity item with minimal differentiation, the need to understand total costs is vital to ensure that Quality Foods is working with the lowest total cost supplier.

The supplier packages the concentrate (currently priced at $0.38/pound, FOB vessel[1]) in sterilized bags, with each bag containing 60 pounds of product, which workers then place into corrugated boxes. (One 60 pound bag goes into one corrugated box.) The boxes are stacked on wooden pallets, 20 to a pallet, for loading into overseas containers. Each container holds 24 pallets and arrives via ocean freighter at the port of Long Beach. The ocean freight charge is $3,000 per container. Once the containers reach the U.S. port, a trucking company moves each container to a local warehouse for storage at a charge of $350 per container. U.S. Customs calculates import duties to be 20% of the shipment's original purchase price. Quality Foods has a demand requirement of one container load per month.

Quality Foods stores each container in a public warehouse until needed for processing (average storage is one month). This is the company's version of maintaining safety stock. The monthly storage charge is $7.50 per pallet. In addition, the warehouse charges a one-time transfer fee of $6.50 per pallet to cover administrative costs. The inventory carrying charge at Quality Foods is 22%, which it applies against the unit prices of material in storage at the warehouse, but not for material in-transit from China. Material planners assume that, for planning purposes, the demand for Vitamin C concentrate will be relatively constant over the year.

When a container of concentrate is required at the plant, a local freight company moves the container from the warehouse, which costs $200 per container. The company estimates that receiving and quality-control procedures for incoming products cost $5 per pallet. Because of the nature of the product and the distance involved in purchasing and storing the concentrate, supply chain planners estimate they lose 2% of the total concentrate purchased. Manufacturing engineers calculate the budgeted factory yield of the concentrate when blending into company products is 98%; this means the company wastes another 2% of the product by volume during production. This is not recoverable.

Occasionally, quality-related issues, such as spoilage, will require removing the product completely from production. Out-of-pocket costs typically total $30,000 for each incident; these costs are not recoverable from the supplier. On average, such incidents with this supplier occur twice a year.

In addition to the costs noted here, accounting requires that cost estimators add a 15% assessment to the concentrate's *unit cost* to cover general and administrative overhead costs at Quality Foods when working with international suppliers. (The assessment when working with domestic suppliers is 10%.)

Case Assignment

Management has requested that Randall develop a cost estimate to identify the true total cost of buying Vitamin C concentrate from the Chinese supplier.

1. Create a total landed cost model that (a) provides a logical build-up of costs as the concentrate flows across the supply chain, (b) identifies the costs for each cost element and its expected per unit cost, and (c) identifies the total estimated landed cost per pound of the concentrate.
2. Graphically map the supply chain for this item, including where different costs are incurred. Identify ways to take costs out of the supply chain.
3. Are there any costs missing from your model? If so, what are those costs?

CREATING A SUPPLIER PERFORMANCE INDEX (SPI) MODEL

Given the following information (see Table 13.1), perform the necessary calculations for the shaded areas within the table to arrive at each supplier's SPI and adjusted SPI.

Table 13.1

	Supplier A	Supplier B	Supplier C
2nd quarter deliveries	20	18	15
Total value of deliveries			
Value of average delivery	$500	$750	$4,000
Nonconformance charges attributed to each supplier	$3,800	$2,800	$2,900
2nd quarter SPI			
Average shipment from all suppliers	$3,200	$3,200	$3,200
Q adjustment factor			
2nd quarter SPI with Q adjustment			

1. Interpret precisely what the SPI and SPI/Q means for Suppliers A, B, and C.
2. What are some potential challenges when planning to use SPI models?
3. Are there any shortcomings to this type of total cost model? If so, what are they?
4. Why might a company use this type of model instead of a total landed cost model?

TOTAL COST MODELING AT DELPHI

Refer back to the Delphi case in Chapter 12 to answer the following questions.

1. Why was developing a total cost model so important at Delphi?

2. Why do you think Delphi developed its own total cost model?
3. What performance metric does Delphi use to evaluate its business? Why is this measure important?
4. How advanced is your company in terms of making purchase decisions based on total cost? If your company is not advanced, what steps should be taken to enhance your company's total cost capabilities?
5. What kind(s) of total cost model would most benefit your company?
6. What groups would you involve at your company if you were responsible for developing a total cost model? What can each group contribute?
7. What factors do you think are important when developing a total cost model? What do you think might be the greatest barriers to developing a total cost of ownership measurement system?
8. Develop a list of characteristics or attributes that would define an effective total cost model.

CALCULATING INVENTORY CARRYING CHARGES— PROBLEM 1

Using the following data, calculate (1) the total inventory carrying charge and (2) the *per pound* inventory carrying charge for inventory that is *used during normal production*:

- 144,000 pounds of a raw material used each year
- Raw material costs $1.75 per pound
- Demand occurs at a steady rate throughout the year
- Inventory is received at the start of each month and used throughout the month until it reaches zero at the end of the month
- Inventory carrying charge is 24% annually
- The average inventory method is used: ((BI + EI)/2) = Average inventory for a period

Total carrying charges for this item:

Per pound carrying charge for this item:

CALCULATING INVENTORY CARRYING CHARGES— PROBLEM 2

Using the following data, calculate (1) the total inventory carrying charge and (2) the *per unit* inventory carrying charge for inventory that is *used during normal production*:

- 264,000 units are used each year
- The per unit cost is $5.75
- Assume demand occurs at a steady rate throughout the year
- Inventory is received at the start of each month and used throughout the month until it reaches zero at the end of the month
- Inventory carrying charge is 21% annually
- The average inventory method is used: ((BI + EI)/2) = Average inventory for a period

Total carrying charges for this item:

Per unit carrying charge for this item:

CALCULATING INVENTORY CARRYING CHARGES— PROBLEM 3

Using the following data, calculate (1) the total inventory carrying charge and (2) the *per pound* inventory carrying charge for inventory that is *used as safety stock*:

- Item: chemical raw material
- 480,000 pounds of this raw material used each year
- Cost: $11.50 per pound
- Two months' worth of annual demand to be held as safety stock
- Inventory carrying charge is 21% annually

Total carrying charges for this safety stock:

Per pound carrying charge for this safety stock:

CALCULATING INVENTORY CARRYING CHARGES— PROBLEM 4

Using the following data, calculate (1) the total inventory carrying charge and (2) the *per unit* inventory carrying charge for inventory that is *used as safety stock*:

- Item: chemical raw material
- 150,000 pounds of this raw material used each year
- Cost: $14.50 per pound
- One months' worth of annual demand to be held as safety stock
- Inventory carrying charge is 23% annually

Total carrying charges for this safety stock:

Per unit carrying charge for this safety stock:

CALCULATING INVENTORY CARRYING CHARGES AT FLEXCON

FlexCon, a $3 billion maker of industrial engines, has made a decision to out-source engine pistons, a part of the engine that the company has been producing internally. This exercise addresses several kinds of inventory carrying charges associated with buying pistons from an external supplier.

This company has generally been complacent about estimating the various inventory carrying charges that the company incurs across its supply chain. However, a desire by executive management to better manage working capital has resulted in a need to more thoroughly understand supply chain costs.

The aggregated volume for pistons over the next several years is critical to this analysis. A team arrived at the piston forecast by first determining the forecast for FlexCon engines, which is an independent demand item. The team then determined the total number of pistons required to support engine production. Pistons are a dependent demand item (i.e., dependent on the demand for the final product). Forecasted annual volumes for pistons are 300,000 units.

The following information relates to the outsourcing of pistons:

Unit Price: The supplier quoted a unit price of $12.20 per piston, given the expected demand for pistons.

Replenishment Inventory Carrying Charges: FlexCon will receive pistons once a month from its supplier. The company will assume inventory carrying charges for pistons received at the start of each month and then consumed at a steady rate during the month. For purposes of calculating inventory carrying, the team expects to use the average inventory method. The formula for determining the average number of units in inventory each month is:

((Beginning inventory at the start of each month +
$\qquad$ Ending inventory at the end of each month)/2)

The team assumes that ending inventory each month is zero units (excluding safety stock, which requires a separate calculation). The production group is expected to use all the pistons that are received at the beginning of each month. The carrying charge applied to inventory on an annual basis is 14% of the unit value of the inventory.

Your Assignment: Use Table 13.2 to calculate the *total inventory carrying charge* associated with the monthly receipt and use of pistons to support production. Next, calculate the *per unit* inventory carrying charges associated with the monthly receipt and use of pistons to support production.

Table 13.2   Year one inventory carrying charges

	Beginning Inventory	Ending Inventory	Average Inventory	Inventory Carrying Cost
January	30,000	0		$
February	30,000	0		$
March	30,000	0		$
April	27,000	0		$
May	25,000	0		$
June	25,000	0		$
July	23,000	0		$
August	21,000	0		$
September	22,000	0		$
October	23,000	0		$
November	23,000	0		$
December	21,000	0		$
			Total Inventory Carrying Costs	

Total Charge: $\underline{\hspace{4cm}}$

Per Unit Charge: $\underline{\hspace{4cm}}$

Safety Stock Requirements: FlexCon has decided to hold safety stock of pistons equivalent to one month's average demand, at least for the first year of the contract. This results in an inventory carrying charge, which the team must calculate and include in its total cost analysis. While it is likely that FlexCon will rely on, or draw down, safety stock levels at some point in time, for purposes of planning, the team has decided not to estimate when this might occur. Inventory carrying charges include working capital committed to financing the inventory, plus charges for material handling, warehousing, insurance and taxes, and risk of obsolescence and loss. FlexCon's inventory carrying charge for safety stock is 18% annually, a figure that FlexCon's finance group provided.

Your Assignment: Calculate the *total inventory carrying charge* associated with carrying an average of one month's annual demand as safety stock. Next, calculate the *per unit* charge associated with carrying an average of one month's annual demand as safety stock.

Total Charge: _____

Per Unit Charge: _____

TOTAL COST ELEMENTS EXERCISE

Identify the discrete or individual cost elements that you would include in a *total landed cost model.* For each cost category or element (see Table 13.3), identify whether the data for that element will likely be actual data, data based on averages, or data based on external assumptions. Also, indicate the expected source of the data and how often the data will be reviewed.

Table 13.3

Cost Element or Category	Type of Data (actual, average, or assumption)	Source of Data

INSOURCING/OUTSOURCING TOTAL COST ANALYSIS AT RENTEX

Rentex Motor Drives is a division of a large U.S. manufacturer of industrial machinery and equipment. The parent company makes circulating pumps, high-capacity cooling fans, and compressors. Rentex Motor Drives manufactures the electric motors that power much of this machinery and equipment. Rentex has a world-wide customer base and sells motors not only to its parent company, but also to other customers across the globe—some of whom are direct competitors of Rentex's parent company.

Recently the company developed an electric motor assembly that will be a key component in a new circulating pump being manufactured and sold by one of Rentex's sister companies. The circulating pump will be sold to the manufacturers of oil-fired burners used for home heating. Each circulating pump will require a single electric motor assembly.

Rentex must now decide whether or not it should outsource or internally manufacture the motor assembly. To help with the analysis, a cross-functional team has been formed. Members of the team have been assigned the responsibility of analyzing from a total cost perspective whether or not Rentex should outsource or internally manufacture the electric motor assembly.

A European supplier that produces motors for a number of Fortune 500 companies has submitted a detailed proposal to Rentex for building the subassembly. However, confounding this analysis is an internal bias against outsourcing the motor, particularly since there is a strong union presence within Rentex's facilities. Furthermore, management at Rentex believes that the electric motor assembly design might be adapted in the future to enable its use in new applications in the chemical processing industry, thereby representing a future growth opportunity.

As an initial step the cross-functional team has gathered the required information to guide the firm's decision process.

Outsourcing Costs

Rentex's marketing group estimates that volumes for the motor assembly are:

> Year 1   4,500 units
> Year 2   5,250 units
> Year 3   6,000 units

The European supplier of electric motors has quoted a price of $105 per unit, FOB ex works,[2] with 5% price decreases per year for Year 2, and again for Year 3. The team assumes these price decreases are due to productivity improvements from higher volumes, the positive effects of learning at the supplier, and greater operating efficiencies. The prices have not been negotiated and the team believes that negotiation may lead to a lower unit price. If the new line of circulating pumps is successful, it is estimated that the life of the product cycle will be six years, reaching a peak of 7,000 units in Year 4, with a 10% reduction per year in volume as the product reaches the end of its life. It is estimated that the product will be completely phased out at the end of Year 6.

Shipping, handling, and receiving: Shipping, handling, and receiving costs at the buyer are estimated to be $15 per unit and should remain constant.

Tooling: The supplier has stated that it will cost $30,000 to fabricate the tooling and fixtures required to produce the electric motor. Rentex's policy is to assume ownership of tooling, so Rentex is responsible for the tooling costs. It's estimated that the tooling will have a usable life span of at least 6 years, with proper preventive maintenance (which the supplier has agreed to perform at no additional cost). The team plans to allocate tooling costs evenly over the first three years.

Quality-related costs: The team has decided to include quality-related costs in its outsourcing calculations. During the investigation of the supplier, a team member collected data on the process that would likely produce the motors. The team estimates that the supplier's defect level, based on process measurement data, is 1,000 parts per million (ppm). Rentex's quality assurance department estimates that each supplier defect will cost Rentex $1,850 in direct nonconformance costs. Unfortunately, with quality problems there are always hidden costs that are difficult, if not impossible, to model.

Supplier capacity: The team has concluded the supplier has available capacity to satisfy Rentex's current and near-term requirements for the motor. To mitigate supply chain risk, Rentex plans to hold one month's worth of the assembly as safety stock.

Insourcing Costs

Rentex's cost engineering department has provided the following *per unit cost estimates* for internally manufacturing and assembling the motors during Year 1 of a three-year planning cycle:

Direct labor	$18.75	Cost of receiving components	$3.25
Direct materials	$36.25	Supplemental factory supplies	$3.15
Transfer profit[3]	$20.75		

Initial tooling and line modification costs: The start-up costs (including tooling) to modify existing production lines and equipment to accommodate production of the new motor will be $40,000, which will be spread out evenly over three years.

Depreciation expense: Depreciation expense on production equipment and tooling is considered a noncash item and is not included in the insourcing analysis.

Engineering design costs: Engineering costs to design, develop, and improve the production process will be $80,000 and will be spread evenly across the first three years of production.

Factory and corporate overhead: Overhead is allocated at 180% of direct labor.

Cost increases: In Years 2 and 3, management expects a 2% annual increase in material costs and a 3% increase in direct and overhead labor rates.

Quality-related costs: The team estimates that Rentex's finished electric motor quality defects to be 2,750 ppm. Rentex's quality assurance department estimates that each defect costs the company $1,250 in nonconformance costs.

Preventive maintenance costs: Rentex's maintenance manager estimates that preventive maintenance of the production equipment required to produce the motors will cost $15,000 in Year 1, and will increase at the rate of 3% per year thereafter.

Assignment Questions

1. Prepare a three-year insourcing/outsourcing total cost analysis and identify your recommendation based on your analysis. This analysis should include a build-up of the total unit cost by cost element. Be sure to identify any expected savings, if any, from outsourcing.
2. Identify and evaluate any qualitative factors that should be considered during this analysis.
3. A challenge when developing total cost models involves including all relevant cost elements. Identify any costs that might be missing from your model. What are some hidden costs that are often difficult to include in the analysis?
4. Another challenge when developing total cost models for insourcing/outsourcing analysis is the proper allocation of internal overhead. What are your recommendations for properly allocating overhead?
5. Assume that the insourcing overhead costs that were expected to go away with outsourcing do not all go away. How does this affect the mechanics or outcome of the insourcing/outsourcing analysis?

REFERENCES

1. FOB (free on board) vessel means the supplier is responsible for transportation charges to the port in China.
2. Buyer is responsible for the cost and delivery of goods from the seller's location.
3. Transfer profit is the internal profit from selling to another unit in the company. This company views its units as profit centers, so profit must be included. Furthermore, the supplier has included profits in its quoted price.

14

BEST PRACTICES IN
MANAGING INVENTORY

The need to manage a firm's investment in inventory comprises a major part of working capital management, which is an important topic within the finance world. This is somewhat intuitive since inventory usually comprises a major part of the current assets account on a balance sheet. Recall from Chapter 1 that, from a technical perspective, financial managers view working capital as the difference between current assets and current liabilities. And, they tend to emphasize the management of accounts receivable and payable as the primary ways to manage that capital. Conversely, supply chain professionals often take a different view of working capital by focusing on the inventory side of the formula.

This chapter addresses one of the most important topics in supply chain management (SCM) today—the effective management of inventory, and working capital, across the supply chain. As with chapters that begin the other sections of this book, this chapter presents a set of best practices associated with inventory management. This chapter is the longest in the book, reflecting the magnitude of this topic. The next chapter will present a variety of financial tools and techniques for managing inventory and working capital, and Chapter 16 applies these financial techniques through hands-on exercises.

UNDERSTANDING INVENTORY

Before reviewing a set of best practices, let's make sure we understand this thing called inventory. When viewed as something tangible (i.e., a noun), inventory consists of the financial value and the physical quantity of materials and goods held by an organization to support production (raw materials, subassemblies, work in process), support activities (repair, maintenance, consumables), sales (merchandise, finished goods), and customer service (spare parts).[1] Without question, the control and management of inventory is a major part of SCM. We can also talk about inventory as an action, such as *let's take an inventory of your skill set*. In this case, we view inventory as a verb, which is not the focus of this chapter.

Something we must never forget is that wherever inventory resides within a supply chain, someone owns that inventory. The possession of inventory brings with it certain financial obligations. Inventory always has a financial component, including how to value that inventory, as well as how to account for carrying that inventory. This is why it is important to take not only an operational perspective, but also a financial perspective when managing inventory.

Depending on the source, we might conclude that inventory is the greatest thing since sliced bread, or it presents a clear and present danger to the future of the world. The disciples of lean manufacturing look at inventory and swear at it. Others look at the virtues of inventory and swear by it. To some degree, looking at inventory as something good and, at the same time, something not so good, is legitimate. To put it simply, a supply chain cannot operate without inventory. Conversely, excess inventory causes financial hardship. It is important to make correct decisions about what inventory to hold, how much to hold, where to hold it, and the schedule, timing, and frequency of replenishment.

Let's review the right and wrong reasons for holding inventory. Clearly, if we are holding inventory for the wrong reasons, we have opportunities to make improvements. Unfortunately, inventory is often used to cover serious supply chain problems. Instead of addressing the root causes of problems, we hide them with inventory. It is a great pacifier, as it covers many business ills. Some of the supply chain problems that inventory helps disguise include:

- Poor planning, poor forecasting, and high forecasting error
- Supply chain theft
- Unreliable supplier lead times, poor on-time supplier delivery, and poor supplier quality
- Poor production yields that require more inputs to achieve a desired output
- Poor or no inventory control and planning systems, resulting in larger quantities of inventory to ensure we do not run out
- Poor cycle counting systems, which reduce confidence in the accuracy of inventory records
- Inability to place inventory in the right locations across a supply chain
- Poor internal inventory handling and control procedures

- Buying large quantities to receive lower unit prices, the benefit of which may be outweighed by higher carrying charges that are not calculated
- Inability to quantify the true cost of holding inventory, making it less painful to hold excess inventory
- Poor inventory shelf life management, including poor management of excess and obsolete inventory

This list contains some real bad habits. What, then, are some of the right reasons to make an investment in inventory? Obviously, a manufacturing company requires inventory to meet its production schedules and to satisfy customer orders. Many companies also need spare parts inventory to support their aftermarket. And, let's not forget that a retailer could not even operate without finished goods. Without inventory we would be looking at empty shelves.

Other not-so-obvious reasons exist for holding inventory. Purchasing a larger quantity of inventory could be a smart decision if a lower price outweighs additional carrying costs. And, as supply chains become riskier, planners are showing a willingness to use inventory as a risk buffer. Forward buying of inventory (i.e., buying in anticipation of some event) can also be a reason for holding inventory if a buyer believes there is a pending shortage in the marketplace, such as a workforce strike or a supplier shutdown, or an expected price increase. The point here is that an investment is made in inventory because it is the result of a logical analysis rather than as a means to hide supply chain problems.

INVENTORY MANAGEMENT BEST PRACTICES

As with previous sections of this book, we will start with a presentation of best practices. Without question inventory control and management is a dynamic and ongoing process. The good news is there are many practices and ways to better manage inventory. The bad news is there are many practices and ways to better manage inventory. Narrowing down to a concise set is a challenge, to say the least.

Manage Working Capital the Right Way

Let's take a step back and present inventory management within the context of working capital management. We are doing this because that is how financial professionals view this topic. The most common approach taken by finance professionals when managing working capital is to pay less attention to inventory and focus instead on accelerating receivables and delaying payables. Unfortunately, this approach often damages buyer-seller relationships. A number of research studies have concluded that getting paid in a reasonable time is one of the most important outcomes that suppliers seek from their relationship with a buyer. Far too many finance professionals disregard this important point, as they unilaterally extend payment terms with suppliers.

Dave McClure, a columnist for the accounting website *cpapracticeadvisor.com* says that in any economic downturn, or in their quest to quickly show financial improvements, companies often consider improving cash flow by extending their payment cycle to suppliers. He maintains that larger companies, in particular, will use this strategy since they are not worried about being cut off by suppliers.[2] Typically, this strategy involves stretching payments from net 30 days to 45, 60, or even 90 days. Suppliers usually see this as a coercive exercise of power.

McClure argues there are negative effects that should make extending payables a strategy of last resort, and not the common practice it is today. First, an extension of 30 to 45 days in the payment of invoices can lead to economic harm for small or entrepreneurial companies that do not have financial depth. Second, even when suppliers absorb the loss of revenue, there may be consequences. Some suppliers will seek out more reliable customers to avoid the pain of inadequate cash flow. Third, the only tool that suppliers have to counter a payables-extension strategy is to raise their price or to add a fee to each invoice that goes past a reasonable period. Suppliers may also consider raising their price to cover any cash shortfall. Even if payables return to a reasonable period, the supplier will likely continue with the higher prices as a hedge against future shortfalls. The next chapter shows how to calculate the cost to a supplier when a buyer lengthens payment terms. A smart supplier will try to embed this cost into its selling price.

Best practice firms understand that working cooperatively with suppliers offers better ways to improve working capital than arbitrarily extending payment terms. These firms know that not all working capital management techniques are equal in their effectiveness, or how they affect buyer-seller relationships. Why emphasize the one approach that we know is going to anger suppliers?

View Inventory Control and Inventory Management Separately

A logical sequence of events takes place as we manage inventory. It is imperative to first achieve a high level of record integrity. Record integrity is the result of activities and procedures designed to ensure that physical material on hand (POH) equals the electronic record of material on hand (ROH). Record integrity exists when the physical inventory on hand and the electronic record on hand are equal (POH = ROH).

Any difference between POH and ROH represents error, just as the difference between actual demand and forecasted demand is an error. This error can be the result of operationally mismanaging inventory, which affects the physical (POH) side of record integrity. Error can also result from systems-related sources, which affect the computerized side (ROH) of record integrity. Concern over managing inventory should arise only after we have confidence in the integrity of inventory records. Inventory control precedes inventory management.

Why is record integrity so important? First, it is difficult to manage what we cannot control. A logical place to start when thinking about inventory management is to make sure there is agreement between physical and electronic inventory. Second, error and variability in supply chains is often compensated for with excess inventory, usually in the form of safety stock, safety lead-times, and higher minimum stocking levels. Each of these affects the financial investment in working capital. Third, controlling inventory instills operational discipline, something that is crucial for effective SCM.

The effects of poor record integrity on supply chain operations are often severe. When physical inventory exceeds the amount the system believes is available (POH > ROH), the physical inventory cannot be sold or used to satisfy customer demand since supply chain systems operate off the ROH. Congratulations—you have made an investment in a nonproducing asset. When the record on hand is larger than what is physically available (ROH > POH), the very real risk exists that an item will be scheduled for production, or even sold to a customer, when in fact, it is not available. This usually leads to backorder situations and dissatisfied customers.

In many ways, the pursuit of perfect record integrity is similar to the pursuit of perfect quality. In this case, we are trying to achieve zero defects regarding the quality of inventory handling, records, and information. When record integrity falls short, steps must be taken to identify the sources of error—with corrective action taken. This will require asking some important questions:

- Are record errors exhibiting a random or systematic pattern across stock keeping units (SKUs)?
- How severe are the differences between physical stock and electronic records?
- Are proper receiving, stock keeping, and withdrawal procedures and systems in place?
- Is theft a problem?
- Are computerized systems updating inventory records in real time, or is there a lag?
- Are the suppliers shipping quantities that match their documentation?
- Are effective cycle-counting procedures used?
- Is inventory scrap and obsolescence accounted for correctly?
- Are employees trained to properly move, handle, and disburse material?

Best practice companies hold specific individuals or groups accountable for record integrity. And, they routinely investigate and report the reasons for less than perfect record integrity. Record integrity indicators should be part of any supply chain measurement portfolio.

After a firm has its inventory under control, it can begin to think about inventory management. Inventory management consists of the activities employed to maintain the right amount of inventory items, whether they are raw materials or finished goods. The objective of inventory management is to provide uninterrupted production, sales, and/or customer-service levels at a minimum total cost. Since inventory is such a large component of current assets, inventory problems can, and do, contribute to losses or even business failure.

Practice Perpetual Rather than Periodic Cycle Counting

Cycle counting is vastly different under a perpetual versus periodic inventory control system. A perpetual system involves continually validating the accuracy of inventory by regularly counting a portion or sample of total SKUs on a daily or weekly basis so that every item in inventory is counted at least several times a year.[3] It almost always relies on sampling to determine the items to count. The counterpart to a perpetual system is a periodic cycle counting system. Periodic cycle counting usually happens once or twice a year and consists of a *wall-to-wall* counting of all inventory.

Organizations whose inventory items have a large unit cost or larger total value generally keep a day-to-day record of changes in inventory to ensure accurate and ongoing control, which aligns well with a perpetual counting system. These records also provide audit trails. Organizations with inventory items with small unit costs generally update their inventory records at the end of an accounting period or when financial statements are prepared.[4] This is more indicative of a periodic cycle counting system.

Why are perpetual systems recommended over periodic systems? An item with an inventory issue or problem can be counted in a timely fashion with a perpetual system. Periodic systems do not offer such timeliness or flexibility. Next, taking several days to do nothing but count parts is a tough way to make a living. Employees often become careless in their counts after only several hours, leading to counting errors. A perpetual system is also less disruptive to day-to-day operations. Finally, these systems provide an ongoing measure of inventory accuracy and can be tailored to focus on items that have a higher value, higher volume, or are critical to supply chain operations. The use of perpetual systems practically screams *best practice*.

Understand How to Handle Physical Inventory and Inventory Records

Inventory control requires operational discipline. While receiving and stock keeping systems are increasingly automated, the human element is always present to some degree. Employees must understand proper procedures for physically handling inbound stock, fulfilling production schedules, and satisfying customer orders. A disciplined inventory control system will feature a range of desirable practices, including:

- A receiving process that is understood and followed by all employees
- Employee background checks
- Inbound receipts that are checked to verify that quantities match documentation
- Quality sampling to verify the condition of inbound inventory, particularly for suppliers with performance issues
- Proper cycle counting procedures with inventory accuracy regularly reported and reviewed by management and employees
- Stock movements with proper documentation
- Inline weight checking to ensure the inventory accuracy of outbound customer orders
- A clean, well-lighted, and organized workplace
- Automated systems and technology, such as barcodes and radio frequency identification (RFID), to ensure consistency and minimal errors
- No unaccounted stock residing physically within a facility
- Proper disposition of scrap and obsolete inventory

Use Demand and Supply Chain Planning Systems and Processes

Perhaps the most important information that flows across a value chain is estimates of product and service demand. Best-practice companies understand well, the need to have a demand planning system and process that provides insight into any future claims on their output. And these companies know they must seamlessly link their demand planning capabilities with their supply planning capabilities.

Demand planning includes the steps and the process to arrive at estimates of anticipated demand. A demand estimate includes all the claims on a company's output for a particular period, including forecasted demand, actual orders for which commitments are made, spare parts requirements to support aftermarket needs, and adjustments resulting from changes in inventory policies. Many supply chain systems use demand estimates as a primary data input. An argument can easily be made that demand planning is a company's most important business process. Good things happen once we have a solid understanding of demand. Conversely, a poor understanding of demand makes life less enjoyable.

The counterpart to demand planning is supply planning, which involves the steps taken to ensure that materials, components, and services are available to support the demand plan. Unfortunately, the coordination and hand-off of information between the demand and supply sides of the value chain have often been less than stellar. While most companies engage in some form of demand planning, the link to the supply side is often incomplete.

Best practice companies demonstrate certain characteristics as they relate to effective demand and supply planning. These include (1) the use of systems and practices that help balance demand and supply across a supply chain, (2) an emphasis on organizational design features that support demand and supply chain planning, (3) the ability to practice demand management, and (4) constantly pursuing better demand estimates and forecasts.

Systems and Practices

The first characteristic involves the use of systems and practices that help balance demand and supply across a supply chain. Two of the more advanced systems to align supply and demand are sales and operations planning (S&OP) and collaborative planning, forecasting, and replenishment (CPFR) systems.

S&OP is an internal, cross-functional process that creates a six-to-18-month production schedule for product categories and families. The objective of S&OP is to develop an output plan that minimizes total costs, given a specific demand plan. Given that cost minimization is a major objective of S&OP, finance plays a major role in any planning exercise. The S&OP process, which is conceptually similar to aggregate planning, routinely reviews customer demand and supply resources, and updates plans quantitatively across a rolling time horizon.

Consider the case of an East Coast company that forecasts monthly in a make-to-stock environment. The supply chain group at this company analyzed the forecasting error of its finished products to better manage its inventory investment.[5] The company found that its SKUs had an average error of 50% when comparing actual and predicted monthly demand using the mean absolute deviation technique of error assessment. A closer investigation revealed some disturbing findings. Material planners believed that a four-week safety stock for all items would alleviate the impact of poor forecasting, thereby reducing the need to be concerned with forecast accuracy (remember that inventory is a wonderful pacifier). Furthermore, no single manager or group was accountable for forecast accuracy. And, while the company relied on a sophisticated software product to generate forecasts, no one really understood the system, including many of its untapped features. Marketing, which technically had responsibility for generating forecasts, admitted that forecasting was a nuisance and not the best use of time. Finally, an analysis across the company's 1,000 SKUs found that products were all forecasted the same way, which sometimes resulted in unusually poor forecasts, misallocated inventory across geographic locations and product lines, and problems meeting delivery schedules for key customer orders. As a result this company created a cross-functional S&OP group to coordinate its product forecasting and finished-goods distribution.

Another demand and supply planning process is CPFR. CPFR follows a defined framework that combines the intelligence of multiple trading partners in the planning and fulfillment of customer demand. It has the stated objective of increasing product availability to customers while reducing inventory, transportation, and logistics costs.[6] CPFR involves collaborative forecasting, which involves collecting and reconciling information within and outside the organization to come up with a single projection of demand. Demand and supply plan leaders routinely practice these more advanced planning techniques.

Organizational Design Features

The second characteristic of effective demand and supply planning is an emphasis on organizational design features. A central supply chain planning group at a leading chemical company has responsibility for all the activities associated with demand and supply planning and execution, except production. Using sophisticated algorithms, individual planners have responsibility for managing the flow of a product's material and information from suppliers all the way through to customers. No hand-offs of information take place between demand and supply, creating a clear accountability for demand planning, supply planning, and customer service.

Another innovative feature is to make a single executive responsible for demand and supply planning activities rather than relying on separate executive leaders. An example involves creating the position of vice president of SCM with responsibility for worldwide supply chain planning and replenishment, demand and finished good forecasting, inventory planning, primary customer order fulfillment and logistics, and integrating supply chain activities with operational positions. While other design features promote cooperation between demand and supply planners, these two are leading edge.

Demand Management

The third characteristic of demand and supply chain planning leaders is that they do not simply react to changes in demand patterns—they try to influence these changes. Demand management attempts to influence customer orders while trying to reduce the uncertainty of when those orders will occur. Even though a forecast is a projection into the future, most techniques rely on history as the basis of that projection. Demand management moves beyond demand estimation or planning, which at times, is a reaction to demand changes.

Demand management can be a powerful way to promote a balanced flow of goods across a supply chain. An example here involves the aftermarket (i.e., spare parts) division of a major automotive company. This company's distribution centers process orders each evening for replacement parts ordered by the company's vast dealer network. Not surprisingly, the demand for replacement parts processed throughout the week is not consistent. Monday evening's orders are usually heavier because they include orders from Saturday, sometimes Sunday, and Monday (these facilities do not ship over the weekend). Conversely, orders received at the end of the week are usually lower than those received earlier in the week. This imbalance, if left unattended, often affects labor, equipment, transportation requirements, and customer service.

These short-term demand fluctuations are addressed by creating different types of orders and pricing structures. Daily orders, the primary type of order processed by these facilities, are picked, packed, and shipped the day they are received. Dealers use this type of order when they have an immediate need and cannot satisfy that demand from their internal inventory.

Stock orders, a second order type, receive a 15 percent discount and are submitted once a week by dealers to replenish their internal inventory. These orders help the distribution centers balance their daily workload from two perspectives. First, dealers are assigned the day when they can submit their order. Historical demand data helps these facilities determine when best to schedule each dealer's stock-order day. Second, each center has up to two days to ship the order from the submit date. On nights with lower daily demand a facility can pick some or all of any outstanding stock orders on their first day. On other nights, the facility might defer some orders until the second day if that helps balance the workload. While not completely leveling day-to-day demand, segmenting orders goes a long way toward making volume fluctuations less erratic. This supports more efficient workforce management as well as the assignment of delivery vehicles.

A fourth characteristic of demand and supply planning leaders—pursuing better demand estimates and forecasts—is so important, it warrants its own section.

Pursue Better Demand Estimates and Forecasts

Recall that, at a broad level, demand estimates include all the claims on expected output for a given period. This includes forecasts of anticipated demand; actual orders for which commitments have been made but not yet delivered; service and spare-part requirements to support the aftermarket; inventory level adjustments, including adjustments to safety stock levels; and promotional items. Best practice companies relentlessly pursue better demand estimates and forecasts.

The largest component of a demand estimate is a product forecast. Many companies fail to recognize the impact that inaccurate forecasting has on supply chain performance. The downside of poor forecasting includes higher inventory volumes and carrying charges, poor customer service as inventory is misallocated across locations and products, and excessive safety stock levels. For companies that are serious about better inventory management, improving the quality of product forecasts and improving record integrity are the two best places to start. While many practices are associated with companies that excel at forecasting, the following are usually part of their portfolio.

Best practice companies assign clear accountability for forecasting accuracy to an executive or supply chain group. This includes accountability for accuracy, as well as for continuously improving the forecasts and forecasting system. It is difficult to overstate the linkage between accountability and forecasting effectiveness. What does it mean when no one is accountable? It means no one is accountable. The inevitable outcome is a lack of ownership and organization drift. Lesson number one is to demand that someone assumes accountability for the integrity of forecasts.

Supply chain leaders also regularly measure forecast accuracy. One survey revealed that fully two-thirds of respondents reported their typical forecast accuracy was between 50 and 80 percent, which is not overly impressive. Forecast accuracy should be computed regularly and compared against preestablished benchmarks. The following list provides some thought-starters when evaluating forecast error:

- Are forecasts consistently over- or under-forecasted?
- Are forecasting errors randomly distributed?
- Is someone accountable for the integrity of the forecast?
- Do we understand the forecasting methodologies we are using?
- Do we understand why actual demand varies from forecasted demand?
- Are better forecasting tools or refinements available?
- Is a diverse set of error assessment techniques used?
- Are forecasts being manually overridden by planners?
- Is the time between forecast intervals adequate?
- Is the system sensitive enough to realize actual demand pattern changes?
- Is the system too sensitive to seemingly minor demand changes?

Best practice companies apply Six Sigma and other quality improvement techniques when studying forecast error. Instead of improving the quality of a tangible product, they improve the quality of information.

Best practice companies also recognize that different forecasting models fit different scenarios. A *one-size-fits-all* approach is usually not the best way to forecast demand. One of the companies mentioned earlier forecasted its 1,000 SKUs essentially the same way. It should come as no surprise, the result was a higher level of forecast inaccuracy. A detailed analysis revealed that each product could be placed into one of four categories—existing products with relatively stable demand, promotional items, export-only items, and new products with no historical demand. Each segment presents its own set of forecasting challenges that requires unique forecasting models. Leading companies understand this well.

Best practice companies also rely on quantitative systems to identify the forecasting algorithm and model that best fits their demand pattern. Furthermore, these forecasts are updated frequently as new information becomes available. The bottom line is that research evidence suggests that quantitative models are generally more accurate than qualitative or managerial forecasting techniques. This does not mean we should ignore managerial inputs when managers have contextual knowledge that is difficult to quantify or when managers are domain experts. On the other hand, best practice companies are careful to avoid using salesperson estimates of demand to drive their forecasting efforts, given the games that sometimes surround the setting of sales quotas. Knowing when and how to apply rigorous analytical techniques is a forecasting best practice.

Demand estimation is critical, and forecasts are a key part of the demand estimate. Better forecast accuracy should be on the wish list of every supply chain manager. The financial waste and costs that result from ineffective demand planning, while rarely calculated, is surely impressive.

A Classic Example of Better Forecasting

A powerful example of the benefits of better forecasting and product placement can be found at Longs Drug Stores.[7] The company worked with a third party to identify the best possible combination of when to order prescription drugs, how to ship them, and how much to carry in retail outlets on any given day. A system pulls data each day from point-of-sale terminals at hundreds of stores. Then, using two years of historical data and a forecasting algorithm that includes 150 variables per product that predicts consumer demand out to 91 days, the company determines finished goods requirements daily for its retail outlets. The system also determines the amount to order from suppliers.

Pharmacists at the retail level and buyers at the distribution center have always had a general knowledge about demand peaks and valleys for their drugs. Unfortunately, it was impossible to manually consider all the variables that affect demand. To compensate, stores routinely ordered higher than necessary quantities of expensive drugs, many of which sat on the shelf for months at a time.

What effect has improved forecasting had on the company's financial performance? The new system reduced system-wide inventory by 26%, leading to $30 million in savings. This system also freed up $60 million in working capital, which the company used to acquire a 20-store drug store chain. The results are so encouraging that Longs signed an extension with its third-party forecaster with the expectation of extending the system to include nonprescription products.

Minimize Manual Overrides to Programmatic Forecasts

It is a rare company that focuses on the number of times supply chain personnel override programmatic forecasts. Perhaps this should not be the case. Better companies routinely investigate and report the reasons for manual changes or overrides to programmatic forecasts. And, the truth is there will always be some legitimate reasons for manually overriding programmatic forecasts. Overrides, however, should be the exception, not the rule. At some level, management must ask why they invested in a system if they do not plan to follow it.

Most software-driven forecasting systems offer a great deal of functionality. Something that most systems can do is track which forecast was more accurate—the system-generated forecast or manual override. Unfortunately, some companies fail to utilize this option. One company found that its supply chain planners manually changed over 50% of programmatic forecasts each month. After some investigation, it found that the programmatic forecasts were clearly more accurate than the manually changed forecasts. So why do we have these overrides?

Several reasons help explain why employees might not follow the output of a programmatic system. Employees may simply not understand the logic that creates a product forecast, or they do not understand the system itself. This lack of understanding leads to skepticism, which leads to a greater likelihood of manual changes. One forecasting software package includes 24 proprietary algorithms that magically find the best fit for a set of historical data. Unfortunately, the algorithms are proprietary, which means users of the system have no idea what transpires inside the so-called *black box*. Employees may also feel threatened by the system (perhaps for good reason). In the employee's mind, if a system can seamlessly generate forecasts, why does the company need that employee anymore? It often comes down to how well a company manages its change process.

Best practice companies know that programmatic forecasting systems should produce more accurate outcomes than *rule of thumb* or less sophisticated forecasting techniques. These companies measure how many overrides occur each forecasting period, and they work to minimize the number that occur. Manual overrides are like making an investment in inventory. There are right reasons for holding inventory, and there are wrong reasons. Similarly, legitimate reasons may exist for manually overriding a programmatic forecast, and there are less legitimate reasons for overriding the forecast. The objective should be to minimize the less legitimate reasons.

Simplify and Reuse Components during Product Development

The benefits derived from simplified and reused components during product design are extensive. Simplified designs almost always require fewer part numbers, resulting in fewer suppliers, reduced transactions to support the inventory, higher product quality, and lower inventory management costs. The elimination of unnecessary components also reduces a product's cost, which reduces the value of the inventory required to support customer demand and service requirements. A primary objective at the beginning of any product development project should be to reduce, standardize, and reuse components wherever possible.

Many companies apply value-engineering techniques during product design to reduce part count and costs by asking the following questions:

- Can any part of the design be eliminated (i.e., simplified) without impairing performance and functionality?
- Can the design be changed to permit the use of simplified and less costly production methods?
- Can less expensive, but equally effective materials be used?
- Are standardized or existing items available that can replace customized parts and components?
- Can the production process be streamlined or simplified?

A thorough review of product complexity and customized versus standardized requirements during product development should reduce the working capital required to support product requirements.

Financially Model the Impact of Inventory Initiatives

Recall from Chapter 1 that most executive committees and boards of directors include people who are usually not from the supply chain world. Talking about faster inventory turns or reduced inventory probably does not mean much to a group that is obsessed with strategy, corporate-level indicators, and financial results. While it is sad to say, you have not been speaking their language.

A best practice is to model the corporate impact of inventory changes. To do this we will employ something called the Strategic Profit Model, also known as the DuPont Model. Virtually anyone who studies finance knows this model. The Strategic Profit Model allows the user to input data from an income statement and balance sheet to arrive at a corporate return on assets (ROA). (Some sources present the model in terms of return on equity, while others say it calculates return on investment.) When modeled using Excel, the user can manipulate the values in various cells to evaluate the potential effect on ROA.

Modeling the corporate impact of inventory changes is a best practice, which is explained more thoroughly in Chapter 15. Chapter 16 provides exercises that will allow the reader to perform *what-if* scenario analysis using the Strategic Profit Model.

Manage Inventory Flow Seamlessly from Suppliers to Customers

An organizational best practice is to manage supply chain inventory from a holistic or big picture perspective rather than from a narrower or functional perspective. As a response, some organizations have created new positions and developed systems to support a balanced and continuous flow of inventory from supplier to end customer. Perhaps no company has taken a more holistic view of the supply chain than Eastman Chemical. In its efforts to better manage its investment in inventory, the company has created a process it calls *stream inventory management*.

The supply chain planning group at Eastman Chemical includes all the activities involved with supply chain planning and execution but not production. The planning group reports to an executive with responsibility for managing inventory investment. Incoming customer orders and outgoing purchase orders pass through this group, which maintains targets for all major inventory categories. This group manages inventory as a company-wide number rather than as separate amounts spread across the business.

To support its efforts Eastman Chemical developed an information technology (IT) system that, along with improved forecasting, analyzes all customer orders and then applies algorithms to translate finished goods requirements into material requirements. Raw material inventory enters the system to replenish the inventory that exited the system to satisfy customer orders. Stream inventory management balances inventory inflows with finished goods outflows. It acts as a pull system.

Does this system really help manage the company's inventory investment? After introducing stream inventory management, total inventories declined from 12% of sales to 7% of sales. At one point, Eastman maintained 20 million pounds of a raw material called paraxylene to support annual production of 520 million pounds of a material used to produce soda bottles. The company now maintains 14 million pounds to support 1.5 billion pounds of annual production. Comparable results have been achieved for other inventory items. Combining new organizational positions with IT systems to better manage the flow of inventory across a supply chain is a best practice worth emulating.

Search for Innovative Ways to Manage the Volume, Velocity, and Value of Inventory

How managers view inventory often differs, depending on where they reside in the value chain. While financial planners view inventory in terms of funds, which is expected, since balance sheets are always presented in terms of money, supply chain planners typically view inventory in terms of units. What is the right viewpoint? Actually, best practice companies know that taking multiple perspectives about inventory is a healthy way to manage this unique asset.

Companies that are serious about managing inventory must visualize inventory in terms of the three Vs—the volume, velocity, and value of inventory. Figure 14.1 presents the *Three V Model of Inventory Management*, including the key objectives, measures, and examples of activities that relate to each dimension.[8] As this figure reveals, inventory is multidimensional.

Volume relates to the amount of inventory at any given time and at any given point within a supply chain. As firms pursue more frequent deliveries from suppliers, the average inventory within a system decreases. This will lead to lower volumes, and if this reduction is performed properly, will lead to a variety of benefits, including better space utilization and lower inventory carrying charges.

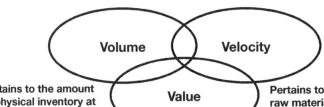

Pertains to the amount of physical inventory at any given time across the supply chain

Key Question: How much and what types of inventory do we own?

Key Measures: Total units, total pounds

Examples of Activities Affecting Volume: Better forecasting; supplier consignment

Pertains to the unit cost and total dollar value of inventory

Key Question: What is the unit cost and total value of the different types of inventory we own?

Key Measures: Total dollars, period-by-period unit value changes, ratio of sales to working capital, cash conversion cycle

Examples of Activities Affecting Value: Product simplification and standardization; leverage purchase agreements

Pertains to how quickly raw material and WIP become finished goods that are accepted and paid for by the customer

Key Question: How fast do we move inventory toward the customer?

Key Measures: Inventory turns, material throughput rates, order-to-cash cycle time

Examples of Activities Affecting Velocity: Lean purchasing, logistics, and operations; make-to-order

Figure 14.1   Three V model of inventory management

Velocity refers to how quickly raw material and work-in-process inventory can be transformed into finished goods that are accepted and paid for by the customer. Velocity refers to speed. As the rate at which inventory moves from suppliers, through operations, and to customers accelerates, this will also reduce the average amount of inventory on hand at any given time. Faster velocity leads to a lower commitment of working capital and improved cash flow. It is also an ideal way to increase capacity without any significant capital investment. Supply chain managers who are serious about improving the velocity of inventory across a supply chain will practice the Theory of Constraints, which is the systematic study of the bottlenecks that constrict flow.

Value pertains to the cost of inventory. This is the perspective that financial planners take, since this is the way inventory appears on the balance sheet. A procurement group that negotiates a lower unit price with a supplier will see a lower value of inventory. This will result in a lower cost of goods sold, which directly affects gross profit and eventually, net income.

While certain actions can predominantly affect a specific variable (velocity, volume, or value), there is often interdependence among these variables. The point here is that organizations must pursue activities and approaches that positively affect the volume, value, and velocity of inventory, wherever it resides in a supply chain. Taking a multidimensional view of inventory is what makes this such an interesting topic.

Pursue Lean Supply Chain Initiatives

Any discussion of inventory management must include a reference to lean, which seeks to shorten the time between a customer order and shipment by eliminating waste, including the waste that results from unnecessary inventory. One study concluded that over 80% of small manufacturers and 90% of large manufacturers improved their material throughput rates and lowered their average inventory levels after implementing lean supply chain practices.[9]

Most organizations should pursue at least some of the practices that underlie a lean supply chain by focusing on three major elements—lean purchasing, lean logistics, and lean operations. Some key features of lean purchasing include a drastically reduced supply base, frequent shipments of small lot sizes (according to strict quality and delivery standards), and close buyer-seller relationships that feature longer term agreements. Lean purchasing also requires stable production schedules that are matched to final product requirements (rather than economic lot sizes), extensive sharing of demand information, and electronic data interchange systems.

On the inbound logistics side of the supply chain, lean requires a reduced number of transportation carriers, longer-term contracts to secure dedicated services, and electronic linkages with carriers. Lean logistics also demands the use of specialized vehicles and handling equipment to accommodate frequent deliveries of smaller quantities within a closed-loop pick-up and delivery system.

Figure 14.2 illustrates a traditional and redesigned inbound supply chain. A traditional inbound supply chain features suppliers producing to their own build schedule, storing that inventory until needed by the customer, and then shipping usually less-than-truckload shipments to the customer. The customer then receives and stores the goods until it requires them. Besides extending the time that inventory resides in a system, this approach also involves many non-value-added steps. A process mapping study revealed over 30 steps or activities to move an item from the end of a supplier's production process to the start of the buyer's production process. A redesigned supply chain requires only six steps or activities.

We can conclude that most of the steps in a traditional supply chain contain waste, including waste due to the slower movement of inventory through the upstream portion of the chain. This example considers only a single link between a

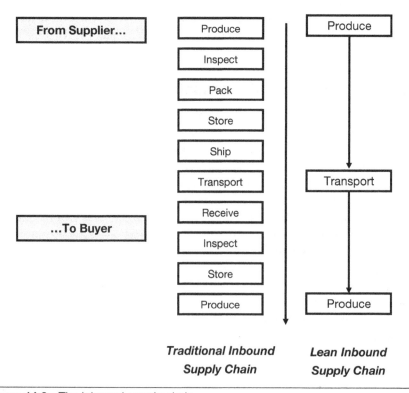

Figure 14.2   The inbound supply chain

first-tier supplier and buyer. Imagine how much inventory and waste takes place for complex items with hundreds of first-tier suppliers and thousands of sub-tier suppliers, all operating within a traditional production and logistics network. Best practice companies pursue lean supply chain practices as a way to achieve dramatic inventory improvements.

Consider the case of Boeing. As the company implements lean principles it is asking suppliers to produce and deliver components using just-in-time techniques. Integrated Defense Systems, for example, has adopted an enterprise-wide online supply chain tool it calls consumption-based ordering. This tool allows Boeing to share its inventory levels with suppliers. Using this tool, suppliers aggregate demand and order at their own discretion—building and shipping only when Boeing inventory levels fall below a certain threshold.

This shift in responsibility permits Boeing and its suppliers to set inventory levels based on consumption rates, which enabled Boeing to reduce its storage facilities at production sites. It also enhances Boeing's ability to forecast and improve cash flow. "If you visited a Boeing facility a few years ago, you would have seen warehouses filled with raw materials and inventory," commented a senior Boeing executive. "We now receive parts just-in-time at a given assembly area."[10]

Five major areas characterize lean operations, although some sources will have a somewhat expanded list. These areas include setup reduction, physical layout changes, pull systems, uniform facility loading, and level scheduling. Table 14.1 summarizes the key features of each area and their relationship to better inventory

Table 14.1   Elements of lean operations and their impact on inventory management

Setup Time Reduction	• Setup reduction is the systematic process of minimizing equipment downtime between job changeovers • Less downtime allows smaller lots to be run, resulting in lower average inventory levels
Facility Layout Changes	• The objective of layout changes is to overcome the inherent disadvantages of traditional layouts, including excessive movement, complex tracking, bottlenecks that impede flow, and higher work-in-process inventory
Uniform Loading	• Uniform loading involves synchronizing interdependent work centers across the supply chain to a single demand signal so there is a balanced and steady flow of inventory
Pull Systems	• Only required material is pulled from upstream entities based on requests from downstream entities • Pull systems result in no unnecessary inventory
Level Scheduling	• Involves building the same product mix or performing similar work every day during a given period • The predictability of a level schedule results in better inventory flow across the supply chain

management. It is hard to conceptualize best practice firms not emphasizing lean initiatives and inventory reduction.

CONCLUDING THOUGHTS

A need to maximize investment returns, including investments in inventory, will be an ongoing challenge. As organizations search for ways to reduce costs and maximize returns, innovative or improved ways to manage inventory present enticing opportunities. The best practices highlighted here, each of which supports better inventory control or management, will go a long way toward ensuring SCM is an important part of a firm's financial success. The next chapter presents financial techniques for understanding and managing inventory.

REFERENCES

1. From http://www.businessdictionary.com/definition/inventory.html.
2. http://www.cpapracticeadvisor.com/blog/10628023/why-extending -payables-is-a-really-bad-idea.
3. Ted Hurlbut, Cycle Counting, *Inc. Magazine*, June 1, 2005, from http://www.inc.com/resources/retail/articles/200506/counting.html.
4. From http://www.businessdictionary.com/definition/inventory.html.
5. This example is based on interviews with company managers.
6. Source:www.scm.ncsu.edu/public/cpfr/index.html.
7. Adapted from Amy Doan, "Vitamin Efficiency," *Forbes*, November 1, 1999, 179-186.
8. This model first appeared in Robert J. Trent, "Managing Inventory Investment Effectively," *Supply Chain Management Review*, March/April 2002, 31.
9. Robert E. White, John N. Pearson, and Jeffrey Wilson, "JIT Manufacturing: A Survey of Implementations in Small and Large U.S. Manufacturers," *Management Science*, vol. 45 no. 1, January 1999, 1-15.
10. From http://www.boeing.com/news/frontiers/archive/2005/march/mainfeature1.html.

15

MANAGING INVENTORY— THE FINANCIAL PERSPECTIVE

The world of supply chain management benefits directly from using the creative and the critical side of your brain. Nowhere is this more evident than in the management of inventory. It should come as no surprise that many creative ways exist to address the value, velocity, and volume of inventory across a supply chain. But, at some point creative thinking must give way to critical thinking as these ideas undergo a thorough analysis.

This chapter presents various financial and financially related ways to manage your company's investment in inventory. The truth is there are dozens of ways to improve inventory management. This chapter provides insight into a smaller, yet hopefully interesting set of ways to manage inventory.

MANAGING COST ADDERS

You may not realize it, but suppliers often add fees or inflate their selling price to compensate for poor customer behavior. These additional fees and costs are what we call *cost adders*. The most common examples of customer behaviors that create additional costs include changing order quantities just before delivery dates; changing due dates; extending payment terms; and asking suppliers to perform ancillary services, such as testing or design, with no additional compensation.

Let's consider some examples. A major U.S. industrial company is known for paying invoices in 90 days even though suppliers ask for payment within 30 days. Not only does this company pay late, it still takes the discount offered by the supplier for early payment! To say this company demonstrates a disregard and arrogance toward its suppliers would be an understatement. Suppliers would be remiss if they did not try to recoup these expenses through cost adders.

Another example involves a U.S. customer who uses foreign suppliers, and insists that any financial transactions involve only U.S. dollars. This essentially transfers 100% of the currency fluctuation risk to the foreign supplier. What looks like a good deal for the U.S. customer may not be all that good. Suppliers surely understand they have taken on the currency risk and will take costly steps to manage that risk. They will try and recoup these costs through a cost adder.

In still another example, a supplier told a major customer it could take 5% off its invoice if it did not make quantity or date changes within 10 days of the scheduled delivery date. While this company was celebrating the opportunity to realize a 5% price reduction (high-fives were said to be exchanged among the procurement group), the reality is that the supplier had been adding a 5% cost adder to its price to compensate for the customer's frequent quantity and delivery date changes. The irony is that a measurement system will likely view this as a cost savings if the customer is able to change its behavior rather than as a penalty that has been assessed over many years.

Why are added costs part of a discussion on inventory from a financial per-spective? Cost adders have a clear financial effect because they inflate the value of inventory. As mentioned, inventory is considered as current assets on the balance sheet. And, current assets are a major portion of a firm's working capital com-mitment. Inflated inventory values also affect corporate performance indicators, particularly return on assets (ROA) and return on invested capital.

Perhaps the most visible behavior that creates costs for a supplier is unilaterally extending payment terms. Typically, finance professionals want to accelerate the collection of receivables and extend their payables. But—and this is an important point—suppliers are not stupid. They know that when a customer extends pay-ment terms from the standard 30 days to 60 or even 90 days that it costs them money and affects their profitability. At some point these suppliers will want to recover any cost penalties. Unfortunately, the trend today is for large customers to use their power to extend payments to 120 days.

There are two ways to think about the effect of extended payment terms on suppliers. The first is the effect on the supplier's profit margin after a customer extends the payment term length. The second is the extra cost to carry a customer financially when the payment term is unilaterally extended. The following illus-trates both scenarios.

Assume a supplier sells an item to a customer for $5,000 on 30-day credit terms. The supplier expects an 8% operating profit margin on this sale (which assumes the customer pays in 30 days) with a 10% cost of capital. What is the cost to the supplier, or the *cost to carry* the receivable for 30 additional days? In other words, what is the cost to the supplier of the extended payment term, and what is the effect on the supplier's operating margin if the customer takes an additional 30 days to pay its invoice?

The supplier's expected operating profit from this sale is $5,000 × .08 = $400. Let's assume the $5,000 includes the cost to finance the sale for 30 days, until payment is received (this 30-day finance charge is a cost that was included in the price). What is the effect of the *additional* 30 days on the supplier's profit margin?

The financial cost to the supplier of the extended 30-day payment term is the $5,000 selling price × 10% cost of capital × 30/365, or $41.09. The new expected operating profit is $400 − $41.09 = $358.91. The effect of the extended payment term reduces the operating profit margin on this sale from 8% ($400/$5,000) to 7.2% ($358.91/$5,000). This may not be acceptable to the supplier. The CEO of Federal Mogul, a major supplier to the automotive industry, commented, "I'm willing to concede business if we cannot continue to operate on the margins or terms that are reasonable for our organization."[1]

This example illustrates that extending payment terms directly affects a seller's profit and profit margin. Extended payment terms transfer margin from the seller to the buyer as the seller acts as a source of credit to the buyer. A customer that consistently refuses to pay on time is delusional if he thinks the seller has not performed the calculations that we just performed. The finance charge for an extended payment term is a cost that smart suppliers will try and recoup through cost adders. After Kellogg's extended its payment terms to suppliers to 120 days, a company spokeswoman said, "It gives Kellogg's and our suppliers more flexibility to manage our businesses more effectively through better cash flow management."[2] One has to really stretch their imagination to see how this new-found source of flexibility helps suppliers.

COST OF FORGOING A TRADE DISCOUNT

Most suppliers offer incentives in the form of a trade discount for early invoice payment. For example, a supplier may offer 2/10 net 30. This means the customer can take 2% off the invoice amount if paid in full within 10 days. If the discount is not taken, full payment is expected within 30 days. Interestingly, while many companies think about how to extend their payments to suppliers, which often damages the buyer-seller relationship, it might be better to analyze the benefit of paying early. This involves calculating the cost of forgoing a trade discount. Calculating the cost of forgoing a trade discount is relatively straightforward and involves the following formula:

Cost of not taking a discount =

(stated rate per period) × (number of periods per year)

where:

stated rate per period = (discount %)/(1 − discount %) and number of periods
per year = 365 days/(due date − discount period)

Let's illustrate this with an example. Assume a supplier offers payment terms to customers of 2/10 net 45. This means the customer can take 2% off the invoice amount if paid within 10 days. Otherwise, full payment is expected within 45 days.

What is the cost of forgoing the trade discount? First, calculate the stated rate per period, which is (.02)/(1 − .02) = .0204, or 2.04%. Next, calculate the number of periods per year, which is 365/(45 − 10) = 10.4. Finally, calculate the cost of not taking a discount, which is (.0204 × 10.4) = .21, or 21%.

How do we interpret this number? Unless a customer can earn better than a 21% return on the money it is withholding from the supplier, it makes financial sense to take the 2% discount and pay on the tenth day. It is highly unlikely any firm can achieve that rate of return. So, why do firms not take the discount? Unfortunately, not everyone knows the formula for calculating the cost of not taking a trade discount. And, some firms are simply more accustomed to extending their payment terms to suppliers. What they do not do well is think through the effects this has on the buyer-seller relationship.

CALCULATING WORK-IN-PROCESS TURNS

Inventory turnover is an important measure when evaluating the efficiency of a company's supply chain operations. The higher the inventory turn ratio, the faster a firm is turning over (or using) its inventory. Since inventory is an asset, we want to use that asset as efficiently as possible. Recall from an earlier chapter the discussion of inventory carrying or holding costs. It costs money to hold inventory—keep it moving toward its final destination.

Finance professionals look at inventory turns at a high level since they calculate turns as sales/inventory. So, if sales for a year are $50,000,000 and inventory is $25,000,000, there would be two inventory turns per year. While this approach has some merit, it is usually not complete or granular enough to truly understand a company's inventory management.

Some individuals will refine this formula by taking the average amount of inventory for a period rather than the snapshot figure provided on a balance sheet. Remember from Chapter 1 that sales figures cover a period of time, while balance sheet data, which is where inventory data reside, reflects a point in time. To address this, some firms calculate the average inventory over a given period.

Average inventory equals a beginning inventory level added to an ending inventory level with the sum divided by two. For example, if inventory at the beginning of a financial period is $100,000 and inventory at the end of the financial period is $90,000, average inventory equals $95,000: ($100,000 + $90,000)/2. This same logic works for units. If the beginning inventory for an item is 45,000 units and the ending inventory is 50,000 units, the average inventory is (45,000 + 50,000)/2 = 47,500 units. Still others will modify the inventory turns formula by calculating turns as the result of sales/cost of goods sold for a given period. As with virtually every financial indicator, more than one way exists to present the data.

Let's illustrate a method for calculating an inventory turn measure that is not used too often—work-in-process (WIP) inventory turns. Not calculating this measure is a mistake, since it helps us understand if work is flowing faster through a work center or if it is slowing—perhaps due to bottlenecks or other inefficiencies. It is possible that WIP within a work center is increasing, yet the center is actually operating more efficiently compared with a previous period when there was less work-in-process. How can that be?

Let's say your manager believes your work center is having some problems managing its WIP. In fact, he goes so far as to say that he is *tripping over the stuff out there*. To address his concern, you have collected the following data to get a more objective view of the situation. The following are guidelines for calculating a WIP turns measure:[3]

1. Determine the output for a specific period
2. Annualize that period's output to simulate a full year's worth of output (for example, monthly output × 12)
3. Divide the yearly output by the period's average WIP level to determine the WIP turns. Average WIP inventory = (Beginning WIP + Ending WIP)/2

1. November output: 80,000 units	1. December output: 88,000 units
2. Annualized output: (80,000 × 12) = 960,000 units	2. Annualized output: (88,000 × 12) = 1,056,000 units
3. Beginning of month WIP: 30,000 units Ending WIP: 38,000 units Average WIP: (30,000 + 38,000)/2 = 34,000 units	3. Beginning of month WIP: 38,000 units Ending WIP: 34,000 units Average WIP: (38,000 + 34,000)/2 = 36,000 units
Monthly WIP Turns: (960,000/34,000) = 28.2	Monthly WIP Turns: (1,056,000/36,000) = 29.3

What can we conclude? Since WIP turns increased, which is good, your work center is actually operating more efficiently compared with the previous month. In fact, instead of being criticized, you should tell your manager (1) you believe this improved performance warrants a raise and (2) to quit hanging around your work area and causing trouble. Of course, after telling your manager, in no uncertain terms, that you do not appreciate him hanging around, it might also be a good idea to have your resume up to date.

STRATEGIC PROFIT MODEL SCENARIO ANALYSIS

The Strategic Profit Model, also popularly known as the DuPont Model, is a technique that allows the user to take data from financial statements to calculate a company's ROA. From Chapter 1, we know that ROA is an important financial indicator. In fact, some would argue it is one of the most important corporate indicators. How a firm utilizes its assets to generate sales is a primary area of interest. The DuPont Model uses the following formula to arrive at a firm's ROA:

ROA = Net profit margin × Total assets turnover

Where and how did this model originate? According to one source.

"The DuPont Model of financial analysis was created by F. Donaldson Brown, an electrical engineer who joined the giant chemical company's Treasury Department in 1914. A few years later, DuPont bought 23 percent of the stock of General Motors Corporation, and gave Brown the task of cleaning up the car maker's tangled finances. This was perhaps the first large-scale reengineering effort in the U.S. Much of the credit for GM's ascension afterward belongs to the planning and control systems of Brown, according to Alfred Sloan, GM's former chairman. Ensuing success launched the DuPont Model towards prominence in all major U.S. corporations."[4]

Figure 15.1 illustrates the mechanics of the Strategic Profit Model calculation. The data in this figure are from an actual company that previously operated in Pennsylvania. As the reader can see, the company's ROA of 1.33% is surely below the company's required hurdle rate, which explains why this company no longer exists. (The company's return on invested capital is also similarly low.) Recall from Chapter 1 that when a company's return rate is consistently lower than its required rate of return (i.e., its hurdle rate or cost of capital), then the company is moving toward insolvency. Note that this company had a tax credit from a previous fiscal year loss, which is why a minus sign appears in front of the income tax figure.

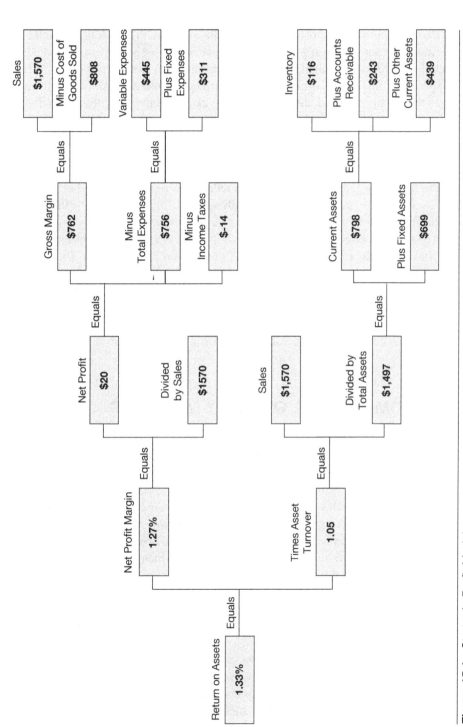

Figure 15.1 Strategic Profit Model

Perhaps the most important feature of the Strategic Profit Model is the opportunity for supply chain professionals to perform *what if* scenario analysis. In fact, the words *what if* might be the two most important words when engaging in supply chain financial planning. With the Strategic Profit Model, once a current financial state is modeled, different scenarios can be analyzed to determine their effect on ROA. What would be the effect on ROA, for example, if a firm is able to reduce its inventory and turn it twice as fast as it currently does? Doubling inventory turns is mathematically the same as reducing the amount of inventory on a balance sheet by half, while holding sales constant. After making an adjustment to the inventory cell in a spreadsheet to reflect this reduction, hit a button and then watch as the projected ROA magically appears. Or, what would be the effect if the procurement group enters into a series of contracts that lowered a company's overall cost of goods by 4%? The *what if* scenario analysis is a powerful tool for forecasting the effects of supply chain initiatives on a key indicator. The model is used to analyze scenarios that do not only include inventory values.

Developing your capability to engage in scenario analysis by using the Strategic Profit Model will separate you from the mere mortals that populate your organization. You will possess a skill that few others in your organization possess. Chapter 16 provides the opportunity to perform *what if* analysis for two companies.

ECONOMIC ORDER QUANTITY MODELING

A well-established approach for managing inventory is the economic order quantity (EOQ). The EOQ finds the optimal quantity that reflects the lowest total cost between ordering and inventory carrying (i.e., holding) costs for a specific level of annual demand. Finance will play a central role when identifying these costs.

Figure 15.2 illustrates the EOQ cost trade-offs. As the EOQ increases, so does inventory carrying charges, since a larger amount of inventory enters the system with each delivery. Fewer orders means higher average inventory levels. However, larger order quantities mean fewer orders per year, which reduces ordering cost. Conversely, as order size decreases, inventory carrying costs go down as average inventory levels decrease, but more orders take place given an annual demand, which increases order costs. Keep in mind the EOQ tells us how much to order but not when to order. The next section on reorder point systems addresses the issue of when to trigger an order.

The EOQ approach is often used for items that are not managed on a lot-for-lot (LFL) basis. With LFL a company only orders the amount needed without consideration to a lot size (the EOQ is essentially a lot size). The challenge with using the EOQ model is not mathematical, although the EOQ model has other

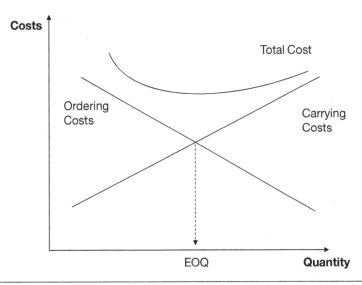

Figure 15.2   EOQ cost trade-offs

versions that are more complex, including economic production models and quantity discount models. The challenge has always been in obtaining reliable demand estimates and determining accurate ordering and carrying costs. The following is the basic EOQ formula:

$$Q = \sqrt{\frac{(2DS)}{H}}$$

Q = Economic order quantity
D = Annual demand
S = Ordering costs per order in $
H = Annual inventory holding cost per year in $

EOQ Example

A company is managing an item using an EOQ model. The item has a demand (D) of 15,000 units annually and the cost to carry one unit in inventory (H) is $7.25 per year. (Refer to Chapter 12 for a discussion of the components that comprise inventory carrying charges.) The ordering cost (S) for this item is $22 per order. The EOQ calculation will be:

$$Q = \sqrt{2(15,000)(\$22)/7.25} = 301.7 \text{ or } 302 \text{ units}$$

Each time this company orders this item, it will order 300 or so at a time. That is the quantity that represents the lowest total cost point given a level of demand,

and associated carrying and ordering costs. Although the EOQ model has been in existence for quite some time, it is still considered one of the best ways to manage traditional inventory items.

REORDER POINT SYSTEMS

The need to forecast the right amount of stock to satisfy customer demand is a primary objective of any inventory control and management system. At a macro level, a primary objective of inventory management is to have a reserve of products to meet demand, while minimizing the amount of cash tied up in inventory.[5]

A review of any operations management textbook will reveal that a popular method for managing inventory is a Min/Max reorder point system. This technique triggers a replenishment request when inventory hits a preestablished reorder point. The system places a replenishment order that is calculated to arrive before a stockout occurs. Inventory is replenished up to a predetermined maximum level. For lean purists, the reorder point is a type of pull signal. No stock replenishment occurs unless a reorder point triggers an order.

The reorder point allows for optimization and automation by creating a purchasing cycle that keeps an inventory system stocked to meet consumer demand. It is designed to determine the standard deviation of unit demand and lead time for consecutive product replenishment. Longer lead times result in greater variability around demand and delivery times. As a result, longer lead time, coupled with greater uncertainty, often results in more safety stock.

Does a reorder point system actually help manage inventory more effectively? Anecdotally, a Boeing unit in Wichita, Kansas reveals the value and discipline that a Min/Max ordering system provides. The introduction of a new Min/Max reorder point system allowed the company to reduce inventory by more than $300 million in a single year.[6]

Other topics may come into play with reorder point systems. Because demand is not always predictable, and doesn't behave in a normal fashion, most companies are willing to accept some level of safety stock as a means to mitigate supply chain risk. Safety stock is a minimum level of stock maintained to prevent stockouts or shortfalls due to unforeseen circumstances. Safety stock provides coverage, for example, if a supplier delivery takes longer than a projected lead time. The downside to safety stock is that it adds to the amount of inventory maintained within a supply chain. And, that inventory has an associated carrying charge.

It is possible to find supply chain professionals who do not agree that Min/Max reorder point systems are effective. Their argument is that demand is often not known with any confidence or degree of certainty. This uncertainty makes the use of a reorder point system problematic since the calculations rely on demand as a primary input. But, is this really a problem with the reorder point system, or is it indicative of a much larger problem pertaining to a company's inability to estimate its demand? Poor demand estimation is a problem that will affect many supply chain systems, not just a lowly reorder point system.

Another argument against Min/Max systems is that supplier lead times are often too unreliable to be factored into the reorder point formula. This is something that would also make the use of a material requirements planning (MRP) system problematic. Again, is this a problem with the reorder point system or is it part of a larger problem? An argument that does have merit occurs when a demand pattern is so uncertain or volatile that any system that requires predictability becomes ineffective. And, reorder point systems, like any pull systems, operate best with predictability. The reality is that a reorder point system offers an important way to manage certain inventory items, particularly lower value components or items stocked for sale in a distribution center.

Calculating the Reorder Point

Establishing the maximum level for an item is analogous to establishing a Kanban quantity in a just-in-time system. This is a decision that supply chain planners make. Referring to the previous section, it is not unusual to use the calculated EOQ as the amount to set as the maximum level for an item. While a maximum level is customized to your business needs and can be arrived at in different ways, the formula for establishing the reorder point is the same:

Reorder level = Safety stock + (Average daily usage × Lead time)

This straightforward formula is a virtue of a reorder point system. Daily usage is the quantity of each item required or sold during a typical day. Obviously, it's always a good idea to review the daily usage figure as demand patterns change—perhaps due to a true change in demand or because of fluctuations during holidays or other seasonal periods. This number is almost always an average daily usage. Ideally, the range in the daily demand is limited rather than wide. A wide range means there is more uncertainty (i.e., volatility) in the demand pattern. And, as any supply chain management professional understands, excessive variability is not a friend. Stability, on the other hand, is always welcome. Variability in demand patterns is one reason supply chains utilize safety stock. Demand variability can be modeled by using more complex formulas, which are beyond the scope of what we are trying to do here. Readers should reference just about any operations management textbook for a more thorough coverage of reorder point formulas.

The lead time in the reorder point formula is simply the time between the point of reordering an item (in days or weeks) and when it is delivered. Lead times should not be a mystery, since lead time data are required for a variety of supply chain planning and execution systems, including MRP and scheduling systems. The challenge comes when lead times are unreliable. A direct correlation exists between the unreliability of lead times and the amount of safety stock present within a supply chain.

Reorder Point Example

Assume a company has an average demand for 400 units of a component each day and that the supplier takes five days to deliver replenishment orders. The company has decided to maintain three days of demand on hand in the form of safety stock. What is the reorder point (i.e., the min level) for this item?

Based on the reorder formula (Reorder point = $S + (D \times L)$), the reorder point will include safety stock of 1,200 units (400 units per day $\times$ three days demand held as safety stock) plus 2,000 units (400 units required per day $\times$ 5 days lead time), or 3,200 units. Thus, once the inventory level for this item reaches 3,200, a reorder request is triggered. Because safety stock costs money to hold, supply chain planners must weigh the cost of safety stock against the cost of a potential stock out.

What the reorder point does not tell us is how much to order. That is based on an EOQ formula or some other algorithm that determines order quantities. A reorder point tells us when to order; an EOQ tells us how many to order.

CASH CONVERSION CYCLE

The big dog when thinking about working capital management from a financial perspective is the cash conversion cycle (CCC). The conversion cycle is a metric that calculates the number of days it takes a company to convert its resource inputs into cash.[7] The CCC measures the time each net input dollar is tied up in the production and sales process before it is converted into cash through sales to customers. The conversion cycle considers the time needed to sell inventory, the time needed to collect receivables, and the time a company is afforded to pay its bills without incurring penalties. The CCC is also known as the cash cycle. It is calculated as:

CCC = Days inventory outstanding (DIO) + Days sales (receivable) outstanding (DSO) – Days payable outstanding (DPO)

The CCC is extremely important for retailers and similar businesses that have significant inventory, receivables, and payables. It shows how quickly a company can convert its products into cash. The shorter the CCC, the less time capital is committed to working capital, and thus the better off a company is from a cash flow and profitability perspective. The reader will have the opportunity in Chapter 16 to calculate the CCC for two actual companies. Table 15.1 explains how each of the formulas used in the CCC are calculated as well as how to interpret the results.

Table 15.1   Cash conversion and working capital formulas

Measure	Interpretation
Days Sales Outstanding (DSO): Accounts receivable/(total revenue/365)	A decrease in DSO from one period to another represents an improvement, an increase a deterioration. When comparing companies from the same industry, a lower DSO is better.
Days Inventory Outstanding (DIO): Inventory/(total revenue/365)	A decrease in DIO from one period to another represents an improvement, an increase a deterioration. When comparing companies from the same industry, a lower DIO is better.
Days Payables Outstanding (DPO): Accounts payable/(total revenue/365)	An increase in DPO is an improvement, a decrease a deterioration (although keep in mind the potential negative effect of extending payment terms with suppliers). When comparing companies from the same industry, a higher DPO is better.
Days Working Capital: (Accounts receivable + inventory − accounts payable)/(total revenue/365)	The lower the number of days, the better. When comparing companies from the same industry, a lower days working capital is better.

Source: CFO Magazine.

Cash Conversion Cycle Illustrated

Let's go back to Chapter 2 and reexamine Orbital Sciences to illustrate how to calculate a company's CCC. From the income and balance sheet, we need four pieces of information to calculate the conversion cycle—accounts payable, accounts receivable, inventory, and sales. We will also calculate the company's *days working capital*. Table 15.2 provides that information.

The following shows the calculations for arriving at the CCC for a three-year period:

DIO: Inventory/(total revenue/365)
Current year: ($61,675)/($1,365,271/365) = 16.5 days
Previous year: ($61,251)/($1,436,769/365) = 15.6 days
Two years ago: ($64,335)/($1,345,923/365) = 17.4 days

DSO: Accounts receivable/(total revenue/365)
Current year: ($613,672)/($1,365,271/365) = 164.1 days
Previous year: ($537,438)/($1,436,769/365) = 136.5 days
Two years ago: ($384,880)/($1,345,923/365) = 104.4 days

DPO: Accounts payable/(total revenue/365)
Current year: ($281,631)/($1,365,271/365) = 75.3 days
Previous year: ($257,113)/($1,436,769/365) = 65.3 days
Two years ago: ($234,379)/($1,345,923/365) = 63.6 days

Table 15.2   Data to calculate the CCC—Orbital Sciences

Period Ending	Dec 31, Current Year	Dec 31, Previous Year	Dec 31, Two Years Ago
Net Receivables	613,672	537,438	384,880
Inventory	61,675	61,251	64,335
Accounts Payable	281,631	257,113	234,379
Total Revenue	1,365,271	1,436,769	1,345,923

All figures are in thousands of $.

Now, let's calculate the cash conversion cycle for the three periods using the formula:

$$CCC = DIO + DSO - DPO$$

	Current year	Previous year	Two years ago
DIO	16.5	15.6	17.4
+ DSO	164.1	136.5	104.4
− DPO	75.3	65.3	63.6
= CCC	105.3 days	86.8 days	58.2 days

While this company is relatively consistent in its *DIO*, it shows a significant increase in its *DSO*. This is slightly offset in an increase in *DPO*. At some level a major change in the amount of sales outstanding in terms of receivables could affect the company's cash flow.

If all we are interested in is the CCC without knowing the specifics of DIO, DSO, or DPO, we could calculate the *working capital in days of sales*. The working capital in days will also equal the CCC:

Days Working Capital =
(Accounts receivable + inventory − accounts payable)/(total revenue/365)

	Current year	Previous year	Two years ago
Accounts receivable	$613,672	$537,438	$384,880
+ Inventory	$61,675	$61,251	$64,335
− Accounts payable	$281,631	$257,113	$234,379
=	**$393,716**	**$341,879**	**$214,836**

For the current year, the days working capital = $393,716/($1,365,271/365) = 105.3 days

For the previous year, the days working capital = $341,879/($1,436,769/365) = 86.8 days

For two years ago, the days working capital = \$214,836/(\$1,345,923/365) = 58.2 days

This analysis reveals that the number of days it takes this company to convert its resource inputs into cash is lengthening over a three-year period, which is not a positive sign. The company is becoming less efficient at managing the money it has tied up in working capital. Supply chain professionals, through their inventory management efforts, play a major role in what is one of the most important concepts in finance.

CONCLUDING THOUGHTS

For too many years, and for a logical reason, the need to manage inventory effectively has largely been ignored. Inventory resides on the balance sheet as a current asset, right next to money and marketable securities. Who doesn't feel good about assets—especially current assets? In general, assets are good and liabilities are bad. What could be simpler than that?

A relentless need to reduce costs has created a sense of urgency to search in every nook and cranny for cost savings. The need to manage inventory effectively will never go away, as long as firms appreciate the need to manage costs and the importance of managing working capital. And each day, more and more firms appreciate this importance. After all, inventory comprises one of the largest components of current assets. It also brings with it some serious carrying costs. As this chapter showed, inventory is also a key component of the CCC—a cycle that is ingrained in the heads of corporate executives. Inventory is also a major factor affecting a firm's ROA, cash flow, and net income. Your firm's inventory footprint is all over your financial statements. The need to manage that footprint has never been greater.

REFERENCES

1. Serena NG, "Firms Pinch Payments to Suppliers," *The Wall Street Journal*, April 17, 2013, page A1.
2. Stephanie Storm, "Big Companies Pay Later, Squeezing Their Suppliers," *The New York Times*, April 7, 2015, p. B1.
3. Traditional WIP reporting systems generally focus on the amount of dollars or volume currently on the shop floor. An improved approach measures WIP turns, which is an indicator of asset utilization over time because it relates WIP levels to system output.

4. From http://www.sjrbiz.info/Current%20Classes/Financial%20 Accounting%20Class/Dupont%20Model%20in%20a%20Nutshell.pdf.
5. Lisa Poulsen, http://www.businessbee.com/resources/operations/how-to -optimize-your-inventory-system-with-the-reorder-point-formula/.
6. From http://www.boeing.com/news/frontiers/archive/2005/march/ mainfeature1.html.
7. Adapted from http://www.investopedia.com/terms/c/cashconversioncycle .asp.

MANAGING INVENTORY— APPLYING FINANCIAL TECHNIQUES

This chapter provides the opportunity to apply the concepts presented in Chapter 15. This includes estimating cost adders that might result from extended payment terms to suppliers; calculating economic order quantities (EOQ) and reorder points; calculating work-in-process (WIP) turns; calculating the cost of forgoing a trade discount; performing *what if* scenario analysis using the Strategic Profit Model; identifying cash conversion cycles (CCC) using data from actual companies; and identifying ways to better manage inventory using the Three V Model of Inventory Management.

ESTIMATING COST ADDERS—PROBLEM 1

Your company has unilaterally decided to extend its payment terms to suppliers. While you know, in the short term, this will likely lower your company's working capital requirements at the expense of the supplier, you also know that at some point, suppliers will likely try to recoup any additional costs through cost adders in the form of higher prices.

Use the following information to (1) calculate the extra cost to the supplier when a customer extends payment length and (2) calculate the effect on a supplier's profit margin after a customer extends the payment term length.

A supplier sells an item to a customer for $15,000 with payment expected in full within 30 days (assume the $15,000 includes the cost to finance the sale for 30 days until payment is received). The supplier has a 10% operating profit margin on this sale and has a cost of capital of 12%. The customer plans to extend unilaterally the payment term to 50 days.

What is the cost to the supplier, or the *cost to carry* the receivable for 20 additional days?

What is the effect on the supplier's expected profit margin on this sale when the supplier extends the payment period from 30 to 50 days?

ESTIMATING COST ADDERS—PROBLEM 2

A supplier sells an item to a customer for $125 on 45-day credit terms (assume the $125 includes the cost to finance the sale for 45 days until payment is received). The supplier expects a 15% operating profit margin on this sale and has a cost of capital of 12%. The customer plans to extend unilaterally the payment term to 90 days.

What is the cost to the supplier, or the *cost to carry* the receivable for 45 additional days?

What is the effect on the supplier's expected profit margin when the supplier extends the payment period from 45 to 90 days?

EOQ MODELING—PROBLEM 1

A company is interested in calculating a lot size to use whenever it has a need to reorder a particular item. You have been asked to help determine the EOQ. Using the EOQ formula presented in Chapter 15, calculate the EOQ for this item, given the following information:

Annual demand = 12,325 units
Annual holding cost (H) = $4.50 per unit
Ordering cost (S) = $25 per order

What is the EOQ?

If the inventory carrying charge percent used to arrive at the annual holding cost decreased while all other factors remained the same, what would be the effect on the EOQ?

If the annual demand for this item increased while all other factors remained the same, what would be the effect on the EOQ?

If this company put in place an electronic ordering system that reduces ordering costs while all other factors remained the same, what would be the effect on the EOQ?

EOQ MODELING—PROBLEM 2

Since you performed so well helping this company calculate its EOQ for the previous item, this company now wants you to help again. Using the EOQ formula presented in Chapter 15, calculate the EOQ for this item, given the following information:

> Annual demand = 100,000 units
> Annual holding cost (H) = $17.50 per unit
> Ordering cost (S) = $200 per order

What is the EOQ?

MIN/MAX REORDER POINT SYSTEMS—PROBLEM 1

A company is interested in establishing a reorder point for an item using a Min/Max reorder point system. If the company wants to maintain 200 units of safety stock, what is the reorder point if the item has an average daily usage of 30 units and a lead time of four days?

If this company wants to increase the safety stock that it plans to hold from 200 to 365 units, what would be (a) the annual carrying charge per unit when holding 200 units of safety stock and (b) the annual carrying charge per unit cost when holding 365 units of safety stock when:

> Annual demand = 11,000 units
> Unit price = $12.50
> Inventory carrying charge = 20%

Inventory carrying charge per unit when holding 200 units of safety stock:

Inventory carrying charge per unit when holding 365 units of safety stock:

MIN/MAX REORDER POINT SYSTEMS—PROBLEM 2

Another company is interested in establishing a reorder point for an item using a Min/Max reorder point system. If the company wants to maintain 1,000 units of safety stock, what is the reorder point if the item has an average daily usage of 80 units and a lead time of ten days?

Reorder point:

If this company wants to increase the safety stock that it plans to hold from 1,000 to 1,200 units, what would be (a) the annual carrying cost per unit when holding 1,000 units of safety stock and (b) the annual carrying cost per unit cost when holding 1,200 units of safety stock when:

> Annual demand = 28,000 units
> Unit price = $16.50
> Inventory carrying charge = 22%

Inventory carrying charge per unit when holding 1,000 units of safety stock:

Inventory carrying charge per unit when holding 1,200 units of safety stock:

WORK-IN-PROCESS TURNS EXERCISE—PROBLEM 1

Your manager has been reviewing a recent production report and has decided to have a talk with you about an increase in the amount of WIP that seems to be populating your work area. Even though you explain that overall volumes have increased recently and that an increase in WIP is expected, your manager insists that the increase in WIP will adversely affect working capital and cash flow. You are not convinced the issue is as severe as your manager seems to believe.

To support your point you have collected some data to back up your case that the increase in WIP is not an issue. Using the following steps and Table 16.1, calculate and interpret a WIP turns measure:

1. Determine the output for a specific period
2. Annualize that period's output to simulate a full year's worth of output
3. Divide the year's output by the period's average WIP level to determine the WIP turns. Average WIP inventory = (Beginning WIP + Ending WIP)/2

Table 16.1

1. November output: 20,000 units	1. December output: 25,000 units
2. Annualized output: _____	2. Annualized output: _____
3. Beginning of month WIP: 10,000 units Ending WIP: 12,000 units Average WIP: _____	3. Beginning: 12,000 units Ending WIP: 14,000 units Average WIP: _____
Monthly WIP Turns: _____	Monthly WIP Turns: _____

What do you conclude?

WORK-IN-PROCESS TURNS EXERCISE—PROBLEM 2

Use the data in Table 16.2 to calculate the WIP turns for May and June.

Table 16.2

1. May output: 50,000 units	1. June output: 48,000 units
2. Annualized output: _____	2. Annualized output: _____
3. Beginning of month WIP: 20,000 units Ending WIP: 26,000 units Average WIP: _____	3. Beginning: 26,000 units Ending WIP: 24,000 units Average WIP: _____
Monthly WIP Turns: _____	Monthly WIP Turns: _____

What do you conclude?

COST OF FORGOING A TRADE DISCOUNT

Given the following information, what is the cost of not taking the trade discount offered by a supplier?

1. Terms: 3% discount if paid in full by 7 days, otherwise net payment is due in 45 days.

    Cost of not taking the discount as a percentage rate: _____

2. Terms: 2% discount if paid in full by 10 days, otherwise net payment is due in 30 days.

    Cost of not taking the discount as a percentage rate: _____

3. Terms: 2% discount if paid in full by 12 days, otherwise net payment is due in 60 days.

   Cost of not taking the discount as a percentage rate: _____

4. Terms: 1% discount if paid in full by 10 days, otherwise net payment is due in 45 days.

   Cost of not taking the discount as a percentage rate: _____

STRATEGIC PROFIT MODEL SCENARIO ANALYSIS— PART A

This exercise requires you to evaluate Flextronics, a contract manufacturer servicing the electronics industry, under various scenarios using the Strategic Profit Model.

Using the financial data in Tables 16.3 and 16.4 and the template in Figure 16.1, answer the following questions. When populating the model with data, be sure to work from right to left.

Table 16.3 Income statement: Flextronics

Period Ending	Mar 31, 20XX	Mar 31, Previous Year
Total Revenue	26,108,607	23,569,475
Cost of Revenue	24,668,386	22,403,227
Gross Profit	1,440,221	1,166,248
Selling General and Administrative	874,796	805,235
Nonrecurring	16,663	11,600
Others	28,892	29,529
Operating Income or Loss	519,870	319,884
Total Other Income/Expenses Net	(57,512)	65,190
Earnings before Interest and Taxes	400,454	328,815
Interest Expense	—	—
Income before Tax	400,454	328,815
Income Tax Expense	34,860	26,313
Net Income from Continuing Ops	365,594	302,502
Discontinued Operations	—	(25,451)
Net Income	365,594	277,051

Table 16.4   Balance sheet: Flextronics

		All numbers are in thousands
Period Ending	**Mar 31, 20XX**	**Mar 31, Previous Year**
Cash and Cash Equivalents	1,593,728	1,587,087
Short-term Investments	—	—
Net Receivables	2,697,985	2,111,996
Inventory	3,599,008	2,722,500
Other Current Assets	1,509,605	1,349,818
Total Current Assets	**9,400,326**	**7,771,401**
Long-term Investments	—	—
Property, Plant, and Equipment	2,288,656	2,174,588
Intangible Assets	377,218	343,552
Other Assets	433,950	302,014
Total Assets	**12,500,150**	**10,591,555**
Accounts Payable	5,102,668	4,056,980
Short/Current Long-term Debt	32,575	416,654
Other Current Liabilities	2,521,444	1,699,151
Total Current Liabilities	**7,656,687**	**6,172,785**
Long-term Debt	2,070,020	1,650,973
Other Liabilities	571,764	521,039
Minority Interest	38,629	—
Total Liabilities	**10,337,100**	**8,344,797**
Common Stock	7,614,515	8,015,142
Retained Earnings	(4,937,094)	(5,302,688)
Treasury Stock	(388,215)	(388,215)
Other Stockholder Equity	(126,156)	(77,481)
Total Stockholder Equity	**2,163,050**	**2,246,758**

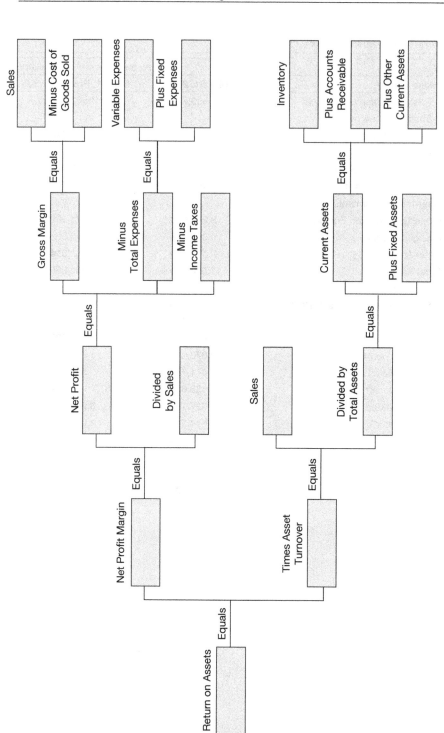

Figure 16.1

1. Place the company's current financial numbers in the Strategic Profit Model spreadsheet and calculate the company's *return on assets (ROA)*. The current scenario is the *base model.*

Base model ROA:

Next, place the company's previous year's financial numbers in the Strategic Profit Model spreadsheet and calculate the company's return on assets base model:

If there is a difference between the current and previous year's ROA, what caused the change?

Calculate and discuss the effect on ROA using the base model for the following scenarios. Evaluate the effect of each scenario individually against the base model. Treat each scenario separately:

- **Scenario 1:** The supply management group negotiates a series of longer term contracts with suppliers that lower the company's cost of goods sold by 4%.

  Effect on base ROA:

- **Scenario 2:** An inventory management team puts in place a new planning system that increases inventory turns by 35%.

  Effect on base ROA:

- **Scenario 3:** Flextronics negotiates agreements with third-party logistics providers that transfer 12% of the company's total fixed assets to the supplier and increases costs of goods sold by 4%.

  Effect on base ROA:

- **Scenario 4:** An inventory management team develops a new forecasting system that, along with lean improvements, reduces the total inventory requirements in terms of dollar value by 11%.

Effect on base ROA:

Looking at the scenarios independent of each other, which has the greatest expected impact on ROA? Which has the least effect?

STRATEGIC PROFIT MODEL SCENARIO ANALYSIS— PART B

This exercise requires you to evaluate Micron Technology, a producer of semiconductor chips and other electronic devices, under various scenarios using the Strategic Profit Model.

Using the financial data in Tables 16.5 and 16.6 and the template in Figure 16.2, answer the following questions. When populating the model with data, be sure to work from right to left.

Table 16.5 Income statement: Micron Technology

	All numbers are in thousands	
Period Ending	Aug 28, 20xx	Aug 29, Previous Year
Total Revenue	**16,358,000**	**9,073,000**
Cost of Revenue	10,921,000	7,226,000
Gross Profit	**5,437,000**	**1,847,000**
Research Development	1,371,000	931,000
Selling General and Administrative	939,000	554,000
Nonrecurring	40,000	126,000
Operating Income or Loss	**3,087,000**	**236,000**
Total Other Income/Expenses Net	(2,000)	1,280,000
Earnings before Interest and Taxes	3,085,000	1,516,000
Interest Expense	352,000	231,000
Income before Tax	2,733,000	1,285,000
Income Tax Expense	128,000	8,000
Minority Interest	(34,000)	(4,000)
Net Income from Continuing Ops	3,045,000	1,190,000
Net Income	**3,045,000**	**1,190,000**

Table 16.6 Balance sheet: Micron Technology

Period Ending	Aug 28, 20xx	Aug 29, Previous Year
		All numbers are in thousands
Cash and Cash Equivalents	4,150,000	3,436,000
Short-term Investments	384,000	221,000
Net Receivables	2,906,000	2,329,000
Inventory	2,455,000	2,649,000
Other Current Assets	350,000	276,000
Total Current Assets	**10,245,000**	**8,911,000**
Long-term Investments	1,790,000	895,000
Property, Plant, and Equipment	8,682,000	7,626,000
Intangible Assets	468,000	386,000
Other Assets	497,000	439,000
Deferred Long-term Asset Charges	816,000	861,000
Total Assets	**22,498,000**	**19,118,000**
Accounts Payable	2,698,000	2,115,000
Short/Current Long-term Debt	1,638,000	1,585,000
Other Current Liabilities	475,000	425,000
Total Current Liabilities	**4,811,000**	**4,125,000**
Long-term Debt	4,955,000	4,452,000
Other Liabilities	1,102,000	535,000
Minority Interest	802,000	864,000
Total Liabilities	**11,670,000**	**9,976,000**
Misc. Stocks Options Warrants	57,000	—
Common Stock	107,000	104,000
Retained Earnings	2,729,000	(212,000)
Capital Surplus	7,879,000	9,187,000
Other Stockholder Equity	56,000	63,000
Total Stockholder Equity	**10,771,000**	**9,142,000**

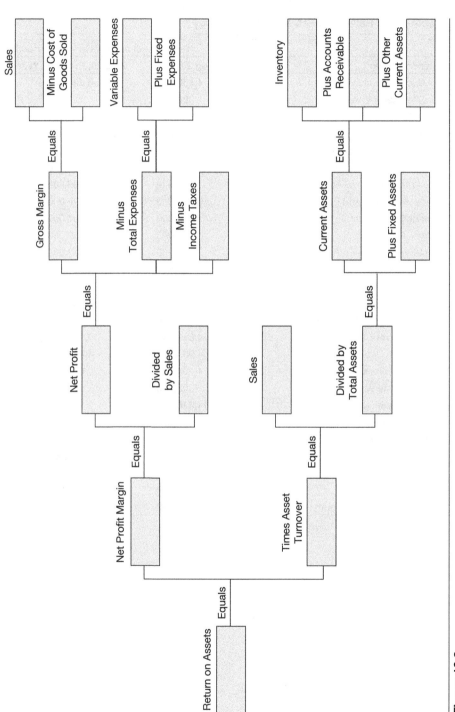

Figure 16.2

2. Place the company's current financial numbers in the Strategic Profit Model spreadsheet and calculate the company's ROA. The current scenario is the *base model*.

Base model ROA current year:

Next, place the company's previous year's financial numbers in the Strategic Profit Model spreadsheet and calculate the company's ROA base model:

If there is a difference between the current and previous year's ROA, what do you think caused the change?

Calculate and discuss the effect on the current year's ROA using the base model for the following scenarios. Evaluate the effect of each scenario individually against the base model. Treat each scenario separately:

- **Scenario 1:** The supply management group negotiates a series of longer term contracts that lower the company's cost of goods sold by 5%.

  Effect on base ROA:

- **Scenario 2:** An inventory management team puts in place a new planning system that increases inventory turns by 30%.

  Effect on base ROA:

- **Scenario 3:** Micron Technology negotiates agreements with third-party logistics providers that transfer 12% of the company's total fixed assets to the supplier and increases costs of goods sold by 4%.

  Effect on base ROA:

- **Scenario 4:** An inventory management team develops a new forecasting system that, along with some lean improvements, reduces the total inventory requirements in terms of dollar value by 19%.

Effect on base ROA:

Looking at the scenarios independent of each other, which one would have the greatest expected impact on ROA?

CALCULATING THE CASH CONVERSION CYCLE— FLEXTRONICS

Using the financial statements presented for Flextronics and Tables 16.7 and 16.8, calculate the company's current and previous year's days sales outstanding (DSO), days inventory outstanding (DIO), days payable outstanding (DPO), and the CCC.

$$DSO + DIO - DPO = CCC \text{ where:}$$

Table 16.7

Days Sales Outstanding (DSO): Accounts receivable/(total revenue/365)
Days Inventory Outstanding (DIO): Inventory/(total revenue/365)
Days Payables Outstanding (DPO): Accounts payable/(total revenue/365)

Table 16.8

	Current Year	Previous Year
Days Sales Outstanding (DSO)		
Days Inventory Outstanding (DIO)		
Days Payable Outstanding (DPO)		
Cash Conversion Cycle (CCC)		

What do you conclude about Flextronic's CCC over the two-year period?

CALCULATING THE CASH CONVERSION CYCLE— MICRON TECHNOLOGY

Using the financial statements presented earlier for Micron Technology and Tables 16.9 and 16.10, calculate the company's current and previous year DSO, DIO, DPO, and the CCC.

$$DSO + DIO - DPO = CCC \text{ where:}$$

Table 16.9

Days Sales Outstanding (DSO): Accounts receivable/(total revenue/365)
Days Inventory Outstanding (DIO): Inventory/(total revenue/365)
Days Payables Outstanding (DPO): Accounts payable/(total revenue/365)

Table 16.10

	Current Year	Previous Year
Days Sales Outstanding (DSO)		
Days Inventory Outstanding (DIO)		
Days Payable Outstanding (DPO)		
Cash Conversion Cycle (CCC)		

What do you conclude about Micron Technology's CCC over the two-year period?

THREE V APPROACH TO INVENTORY MANAGEMENT EXERCISE

Using the Three V Model of Inventory Management (see Figure 16.3) presented in Chapter 14 as a guide, identify creative ways to improve the control and management of inventory.

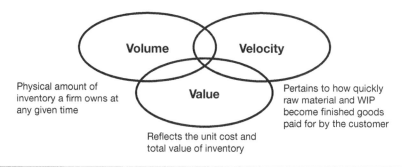

Figure 16.3

1. Ways to reduce the average *volume* of inventory:

2. Ways to reduce the average *value* of inventory:

3. Ways to increase the *velocity* of inventory through your company's supply chain:

INDEX

Note: Page numbers followed by "*f*" indicate figures; and those followed by "*t*" indicate tables.